Armed State Building

A Volume in the Series

CORNELL STUDIES IN SECURITY AFFAIRS

edited by Robert J. Art, Robert Jervis, and Stephen M. Walt

A list of titles in this series is available at www.cornellpress.cornell.edu.

Armed State Building

CONFRONTING
STATE FAILURE,
1898–2012

PAUL D. MILLER

Cornell University Press

ITHACA AND LONDON

First published 2013 by Cornell University Press

Printed in the United States of America

Library of Congress Cataloging-in-Publication Data

Miller, Paul D., author.
    Armed state building : confronting state failure, 1898–2012 / Paul D. Miller.
        pages cm. — (Cornell studies in security affairs)
    Includes bibliographical references and index.
    ISBN 978-0-8014-5149-2 (cloth : alk. paper)
    1. Nation-building. 2. Failed states. 3. Postwar reconstruction. 4. Intervention (International law) I. Title.
    JZ6300.M55   2013
    327.1'1—dc23   2013008335

Cornell University Press strives to use environmentally responsible suppliers and materials to the fullest extent possible in the publishing of its books. Such materials include vegetable-based, low-VOC inks and acid-free papers that are recycled, totally chlorine-free, or partly composed of nonwood fibers. For further information, visit our website at www.cornellpress.cornell.edu.

Cloth printing   10 9 8 7 6 5 4 3 2 1

Contents

[v]

Preface

I served in Afghanistan with the United States Army in 2002. I also served in the White House on the National Security Council staff as Director for Afghanistan from 2007 to 2009, during the last sixteen months of the Bush administration and first eight months of the Obama administration, on the staff of the Deputy National Security Advisor for Iraq and Afghanistan. I assisted with the presidential transition and supported the Afghanistan-Pakistan strategy reviews in 2008 and 2009. These experiences demonstrated to me the tremendous resources and capabilities of the United States and our partners and allies around the world for delivering international assistance, yet also the equally tremendous challenge of bringing our resources to bear in a concerted, coherent way to achieve goals halfway around the world in a broken state in the midst of war, extreme poverty, and a foreign culture. None of my colleagues doubted that we should do everything possible to succeed, but many began to wonder as the years went by if we *could* succeed. I heard many soldiers, officers, bureaucrats, aid workers, and analysts ask, "Can this be done? Can we succeed? What does it take to succeed in an environment like this? Have we ever done anything like this before?"

This book is an effort to help them answer these questions, and it is dedicated to them and to the people of Afghanistan.

The views and errors in this book are my own. All statements of fact, opinion, or analysis expressed are mine and do not reflect the official positions of the US Army, the Department of Defense, the White House, the Central Intelligence Agency, either presidential administration for which I worked, or any other organization or agency. Nothing in the contents should be construed as asserting or implying US government authentication of information or endorsement of the author's views. This

[vii]

material has been reviewed by the CIA and the National Defense University to prevent the disclosure of classified information.

In the long journey of this book, and the longer journey of life and work, I have incurred many debts. I would like to thank Robert Baldwin, high school English teacher, for inspiring me to learn; Josh Mitchell, college philosophy professor, for teaching me that ideas matter; Alan J. Young, Army drill sergeant, for showing me that I am capable of more than I thought possible; Harold E. Brown Jr., friend and fellow soldier who gave the last, full measure in Afghanistan; my wife Jennilee for her patience, support, and love; my son Liam and daughter Lily, for giving Daddy much needed laughter and study breaks; and my parents, whose love and sacrifice I am only now beginning to understand.

[1]

Introduction

> The American Army therefore began its duties in occupied territory with only the scantest information. . . . From the beginning therefore there was a crying need for personnel trained in civil administration. . . . The conclusion from these facts is incontestable; the American army of occupation lacked both training and organization to guide the destinies of the nearly 1,000,000 civilians whom the fortunes of war had placed under it temporary sovereignty.
>
> —Col. Irwin L. Hunt, March 4, 1920

THE QUESTION AND ITS IMPORTANCE

The United States deployed an army of 45,000 soldiers to Cuba in 1898 to help insurgents rebel against the Spanish Empire. The war was short and the Cubans victorious, but Cuba was in ruins and appeared in need of American help. Faced with similar situations in Guam, Puerto Rico, and the Philippines, the McKinley administration freely annexed territory and imposed imperial rule, but Cuba was different. The war was fought to liberate Cuba; denying Cuba sovereignty would be a betrayal of the war's purpose, and Congress duly forbade the island's annexation with the Teller Amendment. McKinley improvised a solution: "As soon as we are in possession of Cuba and have pacified the Island it will be necessary to give aid and direction to its people to form a government for themselves." McKinley told Congress, "It should be our duty to assist in every proper way to build up the waste places of the island, encourage the industry of the people, and assist them to form a government which

Colonel Hunt's comment on the aftermath of World War I is found in Coles and Weinberg, Civil Affairs: Soldiers Become Governors, 6.

shall be free and independent, thus realizing the best aspirations of the Cuban people."[1] The United States would govern Cuba *temporarily* to help Cubans learn how to govern Cuba *permanently*. It denied Cuban *de jure* sovereignty to build its *de facto* sovereignty, and imposed military rule in the name of protecting Cuban sovereignty. To give effect to its liberal mandate, the military government rebuilt roads, cleaned streets, oversaw four elections—and left.

The US administration of the island was thus the first instance of armed liberal state building, a century before the superpower entered Iraq or Afghanistan. The brief intervention in Cuba from 1898 to 1902 opened up a new option in foreign policy, one that would grow in prominence over the coming century. Since 1898 the United States and, later, the United Nations have undertaken forty military deployments whose purpose was to foster effective and liberal governance in weak states. The United States successfully rebuilt the West German and Japanese states after World War II but failed to build a functioning state in South Vietnam, despite spending more money, deploying more troops per person, and devoting more years to the effort. After the Cold War the United Nations oversaw relatively successful campaigns to restore order, hold elections, and organization postconflict reconstruction in Mozambique, Namibia, Nicaragua, and elsewhere, but those successes were overshadowed by catastrophes in Angola, Liberia, and Somalia. The effort in Iraq from 2003 to 2011 and the ongoing one in Afghanistan (2001 to 2012) are yielding mixed results, again despite the high levels of resources dedicated to the project and the relatively long duration of the missions there. Together, the United States and United Nations have achieved even a minimal degree of success in only 48 percent of completed cases since 1898.[2] Policymakers have yet to discover reliable policy options that lead to success in armed state building operations.

The policymakers' dilemma is rooted in a deeper, theoretical quandary. Scholars openly admit that they do not understand what causes state building to succeed or fail: "Not only is there no clear blueprint for successful statebuilding, but we have not come far in developing theories or models" to help explain outcomes.[3] "There are no good theories

---

1. President McKinley, "Message to the Congress," 66–67.
2. That is, 48% of cases (12 of 25) in which the intervention ended no later than 2001, giving us at least ten years of postintervention developments by which to judge the ultimate outcome. The figure rises to 57% of cases (20 of 35) if we include cases whose ultimate outcome is highly probable, despite either being still ongoing or having ended more recently than ten years ago. See table 1.3 for a tabulation of cases and their outcomes, and appendix B for a description of how I measured success and failure.
3. McMahon and Western, "Introduction: The Supply Side of Statebuilding," 2.

that explain how to succeed at" state building.[4] "Policy perspectives framing armed statebuilding lack conceptual or strategic clarity."[5] Scholars and policymakers display an "insufficient understanding of state-building's complexities" and their "ongoing efforts to build effective, legitimate government institutions in war torn countries rely on a limited foundation of knowledge" because state building is "poorly understood."[6] State builders "lack any viable theory about how to build a functioning state apparatus" under the conditions that prevail in failed states.[7] State builders' "lack of knowledge about how to engineer a successful postconflict operation . . . poses a real problem."[8] We have no existing, comprehensive theories that explain the outcomes in armed state building operations. This book is a response to that problem. Under what conditions, if any, can outside powers or international institutions strengthen and liberalize weak states? What strategies of state building are most appropriate to the different conditions of state failure? *What causes the success or failure of armed state building campaigns by liberal powers?*

Understanding armed state building is important for both scholarship and policymaking. Understanding state building is a building block for scholars' efforts to understand state behavior generally. But understanding state building also helps policymakers who undertake state-building efforts to be more effective. That is, on balance, a good thing: while even successful state-building efforts sometimes have mixed results, they appear to achieve more good than harm. When done right, state-building operations help weak states recover from war, recover from human rights atrocities, reestablish public order, and foster democracy and prosperity. In short, they can facilitate human flourishing.[9]

WHAT IS ARMED STATE BUILDING?

Part of the lack of clarity over the causes of success and failure in armed state building stems from a prior ambiguity about what it is. Most recent definitions emphasize the importance of building institutions: State building is "a broad international undertaking to construct a set of accountable and transparent governing political and economic

---

4. Mearsheimer, "Hans Morgenthau and the Iraq War," 238.
5. Chandler, introduction to *Statebuilding and Intervention*, 13.
6. Paris and Sisk, "Introduction: Understanding the Contradictions," 13, 15.
7. Fearon and Laitin, "Neotrusteeship and the Problem of Weak States," 37.
8. Barnett, "Building a Republican Peace," 109.
9. Paris, "Does Liberal Peacebuilding Have a Future?," 97–111.

institutions."[10] It is "the creation of new government institutions and the strengthening of existing ones."[11] It is "the creation or buttressing of institutions of government."[12] It is the "(re-)building of public institutions that enable weak, failing, or failed states to (re-)gain the capacities to perform the core functions of modern states."[13] State building is "constructing or reconstructing institutions of governance capable of providing citizens with physical and economic security."[14]

These definitions are accurate but incomplete. They give a sense for what international state builders do in a state-building campaign, but they do not sufficiently distinguish state building from other activities that also involve building institutions, such as aid, development, imperialism, and democratization. Additionally, these definitions emphasize the role of institution building to the exclusion of two other essential elements of armed state building: the role of power and of norms.

Armed state building is an exercise of military power by great powers to compel failed or collapsed states to govern more effectively. In this respect, armed state building is the latest chapter in the history of interaction between the developed world and the developing world.[15] It is not simply an extension or variant of international aid and development. Scholars who treat it as such miss a fundamentally important variable—the presence of international military forces—that changes the dynamic between international and local actors. Aid and development assistance involve technical training and transfers of funds; armed state building is, partly, a military operation. International military forces alter the local balance of power and partly override or supplant a weak state's de facto sovereignty in a way that international aid does not, even aid with conditionality. Aid and development can take place over decades with little to no media attention or public scrutiny. Armed state building typically occurs in concentrated pockets of time with high levels of attention and scrutiny. Armed state building is not only a technical exercise in institutional capacity development: it is also an exercise of political, military, and economic power by one state (or a collection of states) over another.

Stressing the role of power in armed state building raises an uncomfortable question: Is it simply another form of imperialism? Imperialism and armed state building bear similarities to each other. Both involve strong states wielding power over weak ones, in large part through

10. McMahon and Western, "Introduction: The Supply Side of Statebuilding, " 2.
11. Fukuyama, *State-Building: Governance and World Order*, ix.
12. Chappuis and Hänggi, "Interplay between Security and Legitimacy," 33.
13. Heupel, "State-Building and the Transformation of Warfare," 59.
14. Chandler, *Empire in Denial*, 1.
15. Paris, "International Peacebuilding," 637–56.

military deployments. Both involve great powers trying to change the military, political, economic, and sometimes cultural traits of weaker states. In both cases states attempt to impose domestic institutions on other states in part because they believe it will extend their own influence and alter the balance of power in their favor.[16] State building and imperialism are ways of extending international influence to polities and regions that do not or cannot perform Westphalian sovereignty.[17] State building is not entirely selfless.[18]

Armed state building differs from imperialism in a crucial respect, however: the norms invoked to justify intervention, and the way those norms are reflected in international actors' behavior. Put another way, defining state building only as an attempt to build institutions of government begs the questions: Which institutions? What kind of government? State building involves decisions about the design of the state, and "robust approaches to state design cannot sidestep decisions and debate about regime type."[19] Much of the literature implicitly assumes that state builders can simply build institutions without answering these questions. They cannot: any effort to build a state involves norms, articulated or not, about what a state is and ought to be. Armed state building is thus an attempt to spread norms about what states are, what they should be, and how states govern; it is the attempt by great powers to compel weak states to abide by *norms of statehood*.

The first and most basic norm of statehood that distinguishes state building from imperialism is *sovereignty*. State building spreads the norms of the Westphalian system of individual, mutually exclusive, coequal sovereign units; imperialism rests on the norm of imperial supremacy and colonial dependence. Imperial powers did not recognize the sovereignty or independence of their colonies. State builders tend to go out of their way to stress the sovereignty of the state being rebuilt. Imperial powers governed other states for the benefit of the imperium first and the colony second, if at all. By contrast, today's international state builders claim—plausibly—to be at least attempting to work for the benefit of the target state. The difference in norms is reflected in a clear difference in behavior. Imperialists used colonies for imperial glory, riches, or a competitive edge against other empires. State builders aim to end wars, consolidate peace, spread development, increase regional stability, or eliminate threats. Imperialists extracted resources; state builders expend tremendous resources and

16. Owen, "Foreign Imposition of Domestic Institutions," 375–409.
17. Chandler, *Empire in Denial*.
18. Rubin, "Politics of Security," 25–47.
19. Call, "Ending Wars, Building States," 9.

[5]

rarely receive an economic benefit for their efforts. Imperial rule was intended to last indefinitely, and did last for far longer than armed state building missions typically do; state builders are, if anything, too hasty to look for an exit and do not contemplate indefinite rule. Imperial rule was unilateral; armed state-building operations tend to be multilateral, consistent with international law, and usually blessed by an international body. Armed state building is thus a means by which the norms of sovereign statehood are diffused to the areas of the world in which those norms are least observed.[20] It is a conveyer belt by which conventions about sovereignty are transmitted from strong states to weak ones—a tool used by strong states to construct the meaning of sovereignty and statehood and socialize weak states to abide by them.[21]

The second key difference between armed state building and imperialism is *liberalism*. Over the last century, and especially since the end of the Cold War, armed state building has been defined by liberal norms. These interventions "were more than merely technical (or ideologically neutral) exercises in conflict management . . . they all promoted a particular model of political and economic organization: liberal market democracy."[22] Building up weak states has involved an explicit effort to build liberal democratic states. Imperialism, by contrast, was guided by a norm that the European powers had an imperial mission to "civilize" the rest of the world.[23] State builders stress the rights and privileges of the individual citizens of the weak state, reflected in state builders' commitment to economic development, political liberalization, and frequent elections. Imperialists tended to resist local self-government, elections, citizens' participation, and the public articulation of grievances against the imperial power. Imperialists and state builders employ a different rhetoric and different symbolic actions, which are important tools in international relations: state builders emphasize partnership instead of paternalism. Crucially, these differences create a fundamentally different bargaining dynamic between outside powers and local actors—a key factor in the outcome of such operations.

By looking at the combination of the role of power and of norms in state building, we can distinguish between several subtypes of

---

20. Fearon and Laitin, "Neotrusteeship and the Problem of Weak States," 5–43; Paris, "International Peacebuilding."
21. Ruggie, *Constructing the World Polity*; Wendt, "Anarchy Is What States Make of It," 391–425; Wendt, *Social Theory of International Politics*.
22. Paris, *At War's End*, 13.
23. Paris, "International Peacebuilding."

international interventions in weak states as to which norms are being promoted and what tools of power are employed. For the sake of parsimony, I propose two basic norms: liberal and imperial.

Table 1.1 situates armed state building in relation to other related phenomena and helps us define it with greater precision. *Armed international liberal state building is the attempt by liberal states to use military, political, and economic power to compel weak, failed, or collapsed states to govern more effectively and accountably, as understood by Westphalian and liberal norms.* State building thus differs in essential ways from, for example, European or Soviet imperialism. In this book, I use "state building" in this sense, and I focus on efforts led by the United States or the United Nations during the last century.

Table 1.1, however, also illustrates a difficulty in isolating state building as a topic of study. State building is closely related to a number of widely different international actions: not only imperialism, but also development, democratization, peacekeeping, and postconflict reconstruction. It is also related to or involved in political development, counterinsurgency, and military occupation. These fields of study have insights relevant to state building, although they are not the focus of this book. Given the close relationship between state building and other interventions, it is important to describe how state building is different.

First, state building is related to, but distinct from, democratization. All armed state building missions, as I have defined them here, include democratization as a goal, but not all democratization interventions involve the deployment of armed force. Some international interventions to promote democracy take the form of technical and financial assistance.

Second, state building is distinct from domestic political development because of the involvement of outside powers. Polities have their own

TABLE 1.1. Subtypes of International Interventions

		Tools Used	
		Military, Political, and Economic	Political and Economic
Norms Promoted	Liberal	Armed state building, peace building	Aid, development, and democratization
	Imperial	Conquest and colonization	Creation of satellites, dependencies, and clients

internal processes of development and change, with or without international intervention. These dynamics have been studied for decades in comparative political science as the problem of "political development." The interaction between state-building efforts and domestic political-development dynamics is understudied and likely to yield valuable insights: "Modern state building could benefit greatly from a reading of the earlier 'development' debates."[24] I attempt to provide such a reading in this book.

Third, state building is distinct from economic development, although the latter seems to succeed best when joined with the former. The United Nations Millennium Declaration outlining development goals declared that "success in meeting these [development] objectives depends, *inter alia*, on good governance within each country."[25] As with democratization, state-building missions include development as a goal, but not all development efforts qualify as state building.

Fourth, and more complex, state building is narrowly different from peace building and postconflict reconstruction. According to the United Nations, "Peacebuilding measures address core issues that effect [*sic*] the functioning of society and the State, and seek to enhance the capacity of the State to effectively and legitimately carry out its core functions."[26] However, the relationship between state building and peace building is complex. Some scholars classify state building as a subtask supporting peace building.[27] Others have pointed out that state building can undermine peace when it threatens the interests of local elites,[28] and stressed the tradeoffs necessary in choosing between building peace and building states.[29] State building is best seen as a contributor to long-term peace building by addressing the conditions that give rise to conflict, but also as a potentially destabilizing activity that can hurt short-term prospects for peace. I draw on the literature about peace building and postconflict reconstruction throughout this book.

Finally, state building is an essential part of counterinsurgency and successful military occupation. Some state-building interventions take place during a civil war or insurgency, in which case rebuilding the state is part of a war effort. Counterinsurgency is a combined political and military campaign to defeat insurgents, but unlike conventional military operations "the primary objective of any COIN [counterinsurgency]

24. Roberts, "Hybrid Polities," 172.
25. UN General Assembly Resolution 55/2, "Millennium Declaration."
26. UN, *United Nations Peacekeeping Operations: Principles and Guidelines*, 18.
27. Paris and Sisk, "Introduction: Understanding the Contradictions."
28. Cramer, "Trajectories of Accumulation."
29. Jarstad, "Dilemmas of War-to-Democracy Transitions," 17–36.

operation is to foster development of effective governance by a legitimate government."[30] State building can be seen as the civilian side of a counterinsurgency campaign. Similarly, David Edelstein argues that building effective state institutions is a military occupier's best exit strategy.[31] I draw on this literature briefly in my discussion of the military aspect of armed state building.

THE ARGUMENT OF THIS BOOK

The argument of this book is that there are different types of state failure and, therefore, different strategies of state building will be appropriate in different circumstances. I draw the types of state failure from five different dimensions of statehood: security, legitimacy, capacity, prosperity, and humanity (outlined in chapter 3). States can fail along any dimension, suggesting five types of state failure: anarchic, illegitimate, incapable, unproductive, and barbaric. *Anarchic* states are void of physical security. *Illegitimate* states are perceived by their inhabitants as being fundamentally unjust. Institutions of government have ceased functioning and are unable to deliver goods and services in *incapable* states. Economic production and exchange has ceased in *unproductive* states. And *barbaric* states are defined by their efforts to deliberately undermine human flourishing as a matter of state policy, for example through genocide or ethnic cleansing.[32] I develop this typology in chapter 4.

In response to these challenges, state builders can employ different strategies. The literature to date has typically defined state-building strategies in terms of the right sequence or priority of effort—for example, "liberalization first," "institutionalization first," or "security first." This is an unhelpful way of framing strategies of state building for two reasons. First, it is unlikely that any sequence would be appropriate for all types failed states. I address this in further detail in chapter 2. Second, focusing on sequencing overlooks another crucial choice state builders have to make: the degree of control or authority they will exercise within the failed state. For example, the Allied occupation of West Germany

---

30. US Department of the Army and US Marine Corps, *U.S. Army/Marine Corps Counterinsurgency Field Manual*, chap. 1, paragraph 113.
31. Edelstein, "Occupational Hazards," 49–91.
32. I have described these five types of failure in their most extreme form for illustrative purposes. States may not fail to such a severe degree. A failure of security, for example, may take the form of full-blown civil war or of looting, sporadic terrorism, widespread criminal violence, or simply the credible threat of war.

involved direct administration of the German government, while the UN mission in Namibia simply observed, reported on, and encouraged ongoing reform.

In practice, state builders have two basic choices to make. First, they must choose a basic emphasis for their efforts by either: (1) enforcing order, (2) building institutions, (3) spreading liberty, or (4) winning converts. Second, state builders must choose what degree of control they will assume within the failed state. They can (1) monitor and encourage ongoing reform efforts, hoping that increased transparency and the presence of a neutral third-party will decisively change the dynamic within the failed state; (2) take an active role in training and equipping local civilians and security forces; or (3) assume sovereign authority and directly administer the government and armed forces of the weak state. I call these, respectively, the Observer, Trainer, and Administrator strategies. Thus, strategies of state building can be defined by their emphasis and by their invasiveness. I develop this typology of state building strategies in chapters 5 and 6.

Much of the literature argues for the priority of a single overall strategy, or the importance of building a particular institution (for example, the treasury or the justice sector). It is unlikely that anything so specific can be applicable across all state-building cases, considering the diversity of conditions within them. At the same time, it is also unrealistic to assume that conditions within the states are wholly determinative of state-building operations. That is to argue that the international community has no impact on failed states' trajectories at all, when it has had demonstrable and positive impact in some countries. The question is: What conditions and policies made success possible in those cases?

Armed state building is more likely to succeed when state builders match their strategy to the *type and degree of state failure* in the target state. State builders have to apply efforts and resources to the dimensions of statehood in which the state has failed, and must apply them in greater degrees the more broken the state is. Different strategies and resource levels will be appropriate depending on how failed that state is, and in which sectors it has failed. The greater the degree of failure in any dimension, the more important it is for state builders to address it: the area of greatest failure is likely to be the main driver of ultimate success or failure of the effort.

For example, a state in the midst of civil war may require the imposition of a military government, while a postconflict state with only sporadic violence may require only a peacekeeping or peace-enforcement force. Similarly, a postconflict state that retains a strong base of infrastructure and human capital might only need the infusion of reconstruction assistance, while a state that has suffered widespread physical damage and seen the flight of its educated citizens may require an international transitional authority to get its institutions of governance functioning again. State builders have some flexibility in selecting their approach to different sectors because, while the typology offered here presents hard categories into which we can classify failed states, in practice each type of state failure occurs along a spectrum. Adaptation is a key virtue for state-building efforts.

My hypothesis has the virtue of common sense. However, it is remarkable how rarely it has been applied in practice. Foreign policy process (not the focus of this book) does not always arrive at the most obvious or commonsensical solution to problems. Rationality is only one of many factors that shape international behavior. Bureaucratic rivalry and domestic opinion, for example, often shape international behavior in ways that do not maximize the chances of success. And, though my hypothesis may appear simple in this summary, it is considerably more complex as I develop it in chapters 3 and 4. Defining and measuring statehood, state failure, and strategy are difficult issues; they are vastly more so in combination.

If my theory correctly predicts the outcome of more cases of state building than other theories, two causal mechanisms are likely at work: first, a strategy tailored to a failed state's circumstances is likely to change material conditions within the state most effectively and rapidly; and second, changes in the material conditions will change the bargaining dynamic between international and local actors, making cooperative state building easier to achieve and thus creating a virtuous circle.

A Brief History

There is a curious historical myopia in much of the literature on state building because it grew largely out of reflections on the UN experience after the Cold War. The emphasis of the literature seems to imply that the United Nations was the first agent to attempt to foster liberal change in other societies, that international support for democratization started in 1989, or that military interventions outside the UN system are necessarily imperialistic.[33] None of these assumptions stand up to scrutiny; and scholars reflect a general awareness of that fact when they

---

33. For example, Paris, *At War's End*, Chandler, *Statebuilding and Intervention*, Chappuis and Hänggi, *Facets and Practices of State-Building*, and Howard, *UN Peacekeeping in Civil Wars* all emphasize UN post–Cold War operations.

(inconsistently) include non-UN cases, post–World War II cases, or cases of mixed state building and war. It seems at least possible that part of the difficulty in developing a good theory to explain state building is that scholars have wrongly narrowed the focus of their research, failed to consult the full range of historical evidence, and thereby have cut themselves off from potential insights available from a wider data set. A brief history should help clarify the discussion.

State-building operations almost always occur in the wake of war. Defeated states, weak states caught in the crossfire, or states emerging from civil war are broken by violence and destruction. Victorious (or uninvolved) outsiders emerge with relatively greater power. Rebuilding states can seem to great powers an attractive and plausible way to reorder the postwar political environment to better serve their interests. The United States first attempted to use military force to build capable governments in the conquered Southern states of the Confederacy and in the ungoverned Western territories in the nineteenth century (a case of domestic, as opposed to international, state building). America's acquisition of overseas territory following its victory in the War of 1898 presented policymakers with a new problem: what to do with the new foreign territories, how to govern them, and to what purpose. The brief US state-building operation in Cuba from 1898 to 1902 seemed to offer a middle way between imperialism and nonintervention. Policymakers troubled by instability in poor, weak states could contemplate an intervention that was shorter and less expensive than imperialism, provoked less trouble than annexation, could be cast as humanitarian and selfless, promised more lasting effects than the brief Marine landings that had become the norm in the nineteenth century, and demonstrated the country's great power status to the world. For the next thirty years, US policymakers exercised this option several times in the Caribbean and Central America to protect US hegemony in the Western Hemisphere, including the approach to the Panama Canal. While some scholars treat this as an expression of US imperialism, it differed decisively from European imperialism: the Americans typically worked (albeit rarely with lasting success) to hold elections, rebuild institutions, and leave.

Shortly after it wound down its Caribbean involvements, the United States emerged victorious from World War II, while much of the rest of the industrialized world lay in ruins. Allies needed help, and conquered enemies could not be trusted to rebuild their own governments. The United States—largely on its own, though some Allies contributed to the missions in West Germany and Austria—embarked on five simultaneous large-scale state-building operations. Several of the missions still stand as the largest and most ambitious (and most successful) ever attempted. Collectively, they involved well over a million Allied soldiers; the United States gave in excess of $130 billion in economic and military assistance.[34]

There were relatively few state-building operations during the Cold War. There are three reasons. First, decolonization created scores of new states, all of which jealously guarded their newfound sovereignty. Their growing clout in the United Nations—which was founded to protect sovereignty, not to fix failed states—hardened the general norm against outside interventions. It was also not yet evident that many of the new states would fail in coming decades. The global reaction against imperialism made any kind of intervention suspect, and a naïveté took hold about political development and nation building in the Third World. Second, the United States and the United Nations both attempted one large operation apiece—in South Vietnam and the Democratic Republic of the Congo, respectively. Both failed spectacularly, lessening the appeal of state building as a policy option. Third, the political standoff between the superpowers made international agreement on state-building operations infeasible. State building inevitably involves norms of governance. The Soviets recognized this and objected to the Congolese operation on the grounds that state building was not a technical, apolitical task fit for the neutral United Nations. Decolonization, the Cold War deadlock, and the failures in the Congo and South Vietnam ensured a pause in armed state-building operations for several decades.

Dozens of weak states were left broken by the superpowers' proxy wars in the late Cold War period and by the ethnic wars that flared up in the aftermath of the fall of the Soviet Union. The victory of the liberal states in the Cold War left them with unmatched power, and they faced no imminent geopolitical threats. They, through the agency of the United Nations, sought to remake the world safe for liberalism. The resulting proliferation of state building resulted in over half of all cases of state building since 1898, as liberal powers deployed military forces in every region of the world, from Haiti to Angola to Cambodia, in the pursuit of the democratic peace.

After the terrorist attacks of September 11, 2001, the United States overthrew two governments and engaged in protracted state-building and counterinsurgency campaigns in Iraq and Afghanistan. US policymakers claimed at various points that the campaigns were intended to

---

34. In 2009 constant dollars. The figure does *not* include the cost of ongoing military operations.

destroy terrorist groups, deny them safe haven in failed states, deny them access to weapons of mass destruction; spread democracy; and eliminate the root causes of terrorism. The expansive vision of building liberal states around the world to protect US security would seem to imply an active agenda of armed state building, especially if it dovetailed with the post–Cold War role of the United Nations in state building. But it is unclear if the interventions represent a new trend in US foreign policy or aberrations unlikely to be repeated. Which of the two it turns out to be likely depends in large part on the long-term political and economic trajectories in Iraq and Afghanistan.

Measuring Success and Failure

I count forty cases of US- or UN-led state building initiated since 1898, the broadest set of cases studied in the literature to date. (See appendix A for details on case selection.) How many succeeded? The question is important: before we can understand what causes success, we have to establish what success looks like. Measuring success in state building is notoriously difficult. Is success the mere absence of violence? Or does it also necessarily involve the removal of the roots of conflict through political reconstruction and economic growth? How effective and—crucially—how democratic must a state be to be counted a success? When do we measure success: Immediately on the withdrawal of international troops? At the first postintervention election? A generation afterward?

Instead of characterizing interventions simply as a "success" or "failure," it is more helpful to distinguish between degrees of success and failure (see table 1.2). Few state-building missions result in an unqualified and comprehensive success, but that does not mean they all fall short to the same degree. For example, there is an important difference between an outcome in which a state is at peace although still grappling with the economic and political legacy of state failure, and one in which violence continues or even grows worse. Therefore I distinguish between success, shallow success, mitigated failure, and failure. A success is a case in which a state is at peace, its economy is growing, and its institutions of governance are maturing. A shallow success is one in which a state is at peace but does not show signs of economic or political progress. A mitigated failure is typically a case in which security eroded during or soon after the international operation ended, or in which economic and political conditions regressed. A failure is a case in which no goals were met. (See appendix B for a detailed

[14]

TABLE 1.2. Measuring Success and Failure

Achieved all goals for >10 years.	Success
Achieved stability, continuous liberal governance, and no atrocities for >10 years; failed to show economic and political progress.	Shallow Success
Did not sustain stability, continuous liberal governance, and no atrocities for >10 years. Showed economic and political progress.	Mitigated failure
Did not achieve goals.	Failure

discussion of the variables I used to measure success and failure and the threshold criteria I used for each category along the success/failure spectrum.)

In determining success or failure, I compared a state's trajectory for a decade after the intervention to its condition at the start of the intervention. I did not compare it to a global or objective standard of good governance and prosperity. Many of the cases I consider successes or shallow successes, such as Mozambique, El Salvador, and Nicaragua, are states that remain poor and ill-governed compared to rich, peaceful states. However, they are better governed and more prosperous than they were after years of war, and they exhibit trend lines of improvement. Critics may argue that this is too generous: states naturally improve politically and economically after a war, and my methodology thus artificially inflates the number of successful state-building operations. But some states do not improve after war; rather, they return to war or struggle economically for years afterward. State builders and local actors never know beforehand if they are truly at the end of a war, or simply in a hiatus. The goal is to help ensure it is the former, not the latter. An international intervention can do just that; it can change the trajectory of a society's development, break vicious cycles, and create an environment of security in which trust can regrow. Such achievements should surely be counted a success, even if they leave a society still grappling with the physical and psychological devastation of war. Second, measuring success or failure by reference to a global or objective standard of peace and prosperity is simply unrealistic for policymakers and unhelpful for scholars. By that standard, the only successful state-building operations in history were the Allied

TABLE 1.3. Cases of Armed State Building, 1898–2012

State	Years	Outcome
Cuba	1898–1902	Failure
Cuba	1906–1909	Failure
Haiti	1915–1934	Shallow Success
Dominican Republic	1916–1924	Failure
Nicaragua	1927–1933	Mitigated Failure
Italy	1943–1946	Success
Austria	1945–1955	Success
West Germany	1945–1955	Success
Japan	1945–1952	Success
South Korea	1945–1948	Mitigated Failure
Congo	1960–1964	Mitigated Failure
South Vietnam	1962–1973	Failure
Namibia	1989–1990	Shallow Success
Nicaragua	1989–1992	Shallow Success
Angola	1991–1997	Failure
El Salvador	1991–1995	Success
Cambodia	1992–1993	Shallow success
Mozambique	1993–1995	Shallow Success
Somalia	1993–1995	Failure
Haiti	1993–1997	Failure
Liberia	1993–1997	Failure
Rwanda	1993–1996	Failure
Bosnia	1995–present	Likely success
Croatia	1996–1998	Success
Guatemala	1997	Shallow success
Central African Republic	1998–2000	Failure
Timor-Leste	1999–2005	Likely shallow success
Sierra Leone	1999–2006	Likely success
Congo	1999–present	Likely mitigated failure
Kosovo	1999–present	Likely success
Afghanistan	2001–present	Uncertain
Côte d'Ivoire	2003–present	Likely shallow success
Iraq	2003–2010	Likely mitigated failure
Liberia	2003–present	Likely success
Burundi	2004–2007	Likely success
Haiti	2004–present	Likely shallow success
Sudan	2005–present	Uncertain
Lebanon	2006–present	Uncertain
Chad	2007–2010	Uncertain
South Sudan	2011–present	Uncertain

occupations after World War II. That standard does not capture the many contributions international actors can make to a postwar society short of such comprehensive success, and it ignores the nuance or the degrees of success that can be achieved short of a complete societal transformation.

Table 1.3 summarizes the forty cases of armed state building between 1898 and 2012.[35]

EXISTING THEORIES

Scholars and policymakers have been seeking for decades to understand how poor societies grow rich and how traditional societies become free. The study of international state building draws from that longer research program. State builders are trying, in effect, to force a presumed historical processes of change and growth forward—which means they at least implicitly operate on a theory of political development. Work from the 1950s and 1960s on "modernization theory" fed into a discussion in the 1970s and 1980s about democratic transitions, which contributed to work in the 1990s about complex peacekeeping operations and ethnic conflict. These in turn evolved into the current research on armed peace building and state building. In chapters 3 and 4 I draw on some of these deeper sources in my discussion about how polities change and grow.

Scholars began to examine the phenomenon of state building in the 1990s, although the terminology did not settle on "state building" until early in the new millennium. Much of the initial work continued to view the new activity of the United Nations through the conceptual lens of traditional peacekeeping. Traditional peacekeeping operations—roughly those that took place between 1945 and 1988—involved UN-mandated forces monitoring cease-fires or separating belligerents. After the Cold War the United Nations began to assume more functions of civilian administration in postconflict societies, including facilitating elections, disarming fighters, and helping write new constitutions. By the end of the decade, the United Nations had assumed the functions of sovereignty in Timor-Leste and Kosovo by way of comprehensively rebuilding their institutions of governance and shepherding them toward self-government. As D. W. Roberts put it, "Whilst not initially known as 'state building,' peacekeeping operations rapidly expanded [after the Cold War]. . . . The nomenclature of multi-dimensional, second generation operations appeared before the statebuilding concept started to crystallize in the literature."[36]

---

35. In measuring success and failure, I do not measure cases that began in 2005 or later because there is not a long-enough track record by which to evaluate their progress. I comment briefly on these missions in my concluding chapter.
36. Roberts, "Hybrid Polities," 171–72.

Explanations for state-building outcomes in this literature fall into roughly three categories. First, some stress the role of state builders' inputs. In this view, success or failure is largely a function of what outside powers put into the effort. Advocates of this view differ as to which input is most important. Some argue that raw material power matters most—for example, the number of troops deployed, the amount of money spent on reconstruction, or the duration of the operation.[37] Others focus less on sheer quantity of troops, money, or time and more on the specific constellation of programs and policies—for example, the relative attention paid to rebuilding ministries, the central bank, or the budgetary process.[38] Especially prominent in recent years is the argument that what really matters is the *sequence* of programs. In this view, state builders simply need to discover the correct order of reconstruction and stabilization programs and prioritize them accordingly. Some argue that the sequence is "security first,"[39] others that it is "institutionalization first,"[40] or "liberalization first."[41]

Second, in opposition to the first view, some stress the role of local conditions on the ground in the failed state. In this view, little of what outside powers do makes much of a difference. State-building operations are determined from the outset by how rich or poor, violent or peaceful, oppressive or free the state is in the first place. Poor countries are likely to stay poor. Ongoing violence prevents outside powers from implementing reconstruction and stabilization, while peace enables citizens to get on with rebuilding their country with or without outside help. And trying to foster democracy in societies with no prior experience or heritage of it is profoundly risky.[42]

Third, there is a small but growing body of research on the interaction between international and local actors. In this view, state building succeeds or fails not because of any one factor, like the number of troops or the average GDP growth rate, but because of the relational dynamic forged between the great power and the local actors who have to live with it. Internationals and local actors establish a bargaining dynamic that can be seen as a type of strategic game. If internationals and locals face

---

37. Dobbins, *America's Role in Nation-Building*; Dobbins, *UN's Role in Nation-Building*.
38. Ghani and Lockhart, *Fixing Failed States*.
39. Etzioni, *Security First*.
40. Paris, *At War's End*.
41. Though he does not use the label, that is the argument put forward by Roderick K. Von Lipsey in *Breaking the Cycle*.
42. This view is reflected, often implicitly, in work on state failure and by critics of the state-building enterprise. See, for example, the essays in Zartman, *Collapsed States* or Rotberg, *When States Fail*, for the first, and Chandler, *Empire in Denial*.

[18]

incentives to reach an amenable bargain in which both gain, state building is likely to succeed.[43] My argument falls broadly in this category.

In this book I examine the outcomes of state-building operations. I explain the outcomes as a function of the match, partial match, or mismatch between the international state builders' strategy of state building and the type and degree of state failure present in the target state. I review historical evidence from several cases of state building over the last century, organizing the case studies as structured-focused comparisons and using process tracing methodology.[44] In chapter 2 I review and critique the "sequencing" theory of state building. I argue that there is no master sequence that is correct for all failed states because different states fail in different ways. I also argue that sequencing is impractical for policymaking because of the complexity of interagency multinational operations, the uncertainties of budget processes, and the vagaries of policy implementation.

In chapter 3 I draw on insights from political theory to develop a definition of the state that is broad and flexible enough to encompass the diversity of actually existing states, yet robust enough to make useful judgments about when and how states fail. I argue that "the state" has five aspects or dimensions to it: the state is a coercive force, a legitimating theory of justice, a provider of benefits and services, an economic actor, and an institution to protect human well-being.

In chapter 4 I engage with the literature on failed states to develop a definition of a failed state. I argue states can fail along any of the five aspects of statehood, resulting in five types of state failure: anarchic, illegitimate, incapable, unproductive, and barbaric states—failures of, respectively, security, justice, capacity, economy, or humanity. Failures in each dimension can occur to greater or lesser degrees, and they can happen independently or, more often, in combination.

In chapter 5 I develop a typology of state-building strategies based on the degree of control or influence the international community exercises, and the sectors or areas of statehood in which it exercises such control. I synthesize the conventional theories about state-building outcomes in a new framework.

---

43. Doyle, Johnstone, and Orr, *Keeping the Peace*; Barnett and Zurcher, "Peacebuilder's Contract," 23–52.
44. George and Bennett, Case Studies and Theory Development in the Social Sciences, chaps. 3–6 and 10.

In chapter 6 I describe different strategies of state building in each aspect of statehood, drawing on the historical record to illustrate the strengths and weaknesses of different approaches.

In chapter 7 I test my theory on cases of state building. I study five cases of state building: West Germany (1945–55), Nicaragua (1989–92), Liberia (1993–97), Sierra Leone (1999–2006), and Afghanistan (2001–10). The five cases reflect a diversity of geographic regions (Europe, Latin America, Africa, and South Asia), time periods (post–World War II, post–Cold War, and post–9/11), international actors (unilateral, multilateral, and blended), and scale (large, long, and costly interventions versus smaller, shorter, less costly ones). More important, the cases show a wide variance of my independent variable. West Germany illustrates a full match between the strategy of state building and the degrees and types of state failure that led to a comprehensive success. Nicaragua illustrates a partial match that led to a shallow success. Liberia illustrates a full mismatch and a corresponding total failure. (I also briefly contrast the 1993 Liberian intervention with the 2003 Liberian intervention because they present a close approximation to a controlled comparison between two cases that are similar in most respects but vary significantly on my independent variable.) Sierra Leone and Afghanistan are useful cases because the independent variable varies *within* each case: the state building strategy changed significantly partway through the intervention in a way that improved the long-term outcome. I use the five dimensions of statehood to structure and focus each case. First, I describe the general background to the case. Second, I describe the failure in each dimension of statehood. Third, I describe the state-building strategy employed (if any) in each dimension of statehood, and assess whether or not it addressed the dynamics of state failure in that dimension of statehood. Fourth, I employ a process-tracing methodology to illustrate how the strategic match, partial match, or mismatch caused the outcome observed in the case.

In the final chapter I summarize my findings, establish conclusions, consider alternative explanations, describe the scope conditions under which my conclusions hold, develop policy recommendations, and suggest avenues for further research.

[2]

The Myth of Sequencing

The dominant view in the theory and practice of state building is that there is a set sequence of efforts that state builders should follow to achieve success. According to this view, there is one reliable sequence of programs, policies, and efforts that, if followed, will successfully rebuild failed states. Advocates of sequencing have never agreed about which sequence is correct, but they agree that there is one. Three prominent versions of this view have appeared over the past two decades: "liberalization first," "institutionalization first," and "stabilization first."[1] Each has its own strengths and drawbacks. But they all share crucial weaknesses. This chapter reviews the theories and concludes by evaluating the strengths and weaknesses of each separately and as a whole.

LIBERALIZATION

The "liberalization first" strategy rests on the notion that states derive their legitimacy from the free consent of the governed, as reflected in elections, majority rule, and representative institutions. Variants of this argument include economic liberalization as an essential component of the strategy, arguing that economic liberalization brings prosperity and thus legitimacy. International state builders should, in this view, engineer liberal political and economic arrangements and shepherd postconflict societies to elections and economic opportunity as a first priority.

---

1. Lake, "Practice and Theory of US Statebuilding"; Schneckener, "Addressing Fragile Statehood,"193–220.

Roland Paris, who reviewed fourteen UN peace-building missions between 1989 and 1999, judged that liberalization was the de facto strategy in every case, and that the 1996 document *Agenda for Democratization* made it the official ideology of UN interventions.[2]

Practitioners and advocates of the "liberalization first" state-building strategy tend to rely, at least implicitly, on insights and arguments from the literature on democratization, modernization theory, and political development from the 1950s and 1960s. Those research programs had as their goal the discovery of the means by which poor, unstable, and autocratic states could turn into rich, peaceful democracies. It assumed there were "stages of economic growth"[3] and a predictable sequence of political development that could be discovered, described, explained, planned, and implemented as a matter of policy.

The political development literature was initially optimistic and focused almost exclusively on economic variables: it assumed that economics drives politics. Scholars noted the high correlation between prosperity and democracy in the rich Western states and argued (or, perhaps, hoped) that correlation meant causation. Economic liberalization and rising prosperity would bring urbanization, growing literacy, and eventually expanded political participation.[4] Seymour Martin Lipset summarized the hypothesis as the belief in the "functional interdependence of [the] elements of modernization," including "urbanization, literacy, voting rates, media consumption and production, and education" as well as overall economic growth. Countries on the path of development face a "need for co-ordinated changes in all of these variables."[5] All good things go together, and in the quest for development, a society cannot have too much of any one.

Modernization theory achieved a second life in the Washington Consensus of the 1990s—an informal accord among rich donor nations, the World Bank, and the International Monetary Fund (IMF) that prescribed free trade, fiscal conservatism, and economic liberalization for poor states seeking modernization and development—as well as in the "liberalization first" paradigm of armed state building. The end of the Cold War, the terrorist attacks of 2001, and the renewed international interventionism that happened in the wake of both events has pressed the questions home again and given new life to half-century-old academic

---

2. Paris, *At War's End*, 36.
3. Rostow, "Stages of Economic Growth," 1–16.
4. Deutsch, "Social Mobilization and Political Development," 493–514; Lerner, *Passing of Traditional Society*; Lipset, *Political Man*
5. Lipset, "Some Social Requisites of Democracy," 81–82.

writings.[6] An effort in 2005 to revise modernization theory argues that beliefs and expectations are the missing variable between socioeconomic development and democratic politics. As people are liberated from a subsistence existence and grow prosperous and economically empowered, they are able to care about immaterial values, such as political liberty. Their newfound economic influence allows them to pursue these aspirations. Thus, economic development causes a change in beliefs and expectations, which causes a pursuit of political liberty: a sequence of human development.[7] The enduring popularity of the liberalization theory accounts for why, in Paris's view, the UN turned to it as its "grand strategy" for peace building after the Cold War.

For example, Roderick Von Lipsey, a former director on the National Security Council staff, writing in the 1990s on postconflict reconstruction, argued that political enfranchisement should be the first priority after the resolution of a conflict. Political enfranchisement gives all parties to a conflict a stake in the emerging postconflict political system. Protections for civil liberties—including freedom of speech, political expression, and religious worship—will ease tensions by allaying minorities' fears of repression. Representative institutions give all factions an incentive to cooperate in the peaceful political system by giving a voice and a vehicle through which to advocate their agenda. Liberal politics allows participation; this ability to participate reduces parties' incentives to renew conflict. Political enfranchisement is thus a sufficient condition for political stability. Economic enfranchisement is the second priority because it spreads wealth broadly, easing social tensions and giving individuals a stake in the economic viability of the postconflict society. Economic enfranchisement is achieved by creating a free market for goods and labor; enabling all citizens to participate in the market equally through a social welfare system that provides a basic level of education, housing, and health care; and by providing the state with access to the tools and capital of the liberal international economic order, such as IMF loans.[8]

Donald Rothchild and Philip Roeder give a more nuanced version of the "liberalization first" argument. Their principal argument is that power-sharing agreements are useful for achieving a short-term cessation of hostilities but harmful for long-term peace because power sharing solidifies sectarian cleavages. In response, they recommend "power-dividing" institutions, by which they mean liberalized politics like civil liberties, multiple majority-rule institutions, and checks and balances.

6. Gilman, *Mandarins of the Future.*
7. Inglehart and Welzel, *Modernization, Cultural Change, and Democracy.*
8. Von Lipsey, *Breaking the Cycle.*

They argue that robust protection for civil liberties lowers the stakes of politics by removing the most contentious issues from governmental control. Civil liberties protections also allows for greater competition and debate *within* ethnic or religious groups, thereby diluting their power to act cohesively and dominate a polity. Representative institutions give everyone a stake in politics; the existence of several such majority-rule institutions ensures no single majority can dominate. Overlapping majorities in different institutions diffuses power throughout the society. In this view, international state builders should indeed start with elections, but they should be elections to "hospital administrations, school districts, and village or borough governments and build upwards" to foster multiple majorities. Finally, checks and balances, much like multiple majorities, ensure power is diffused.[9]

INSTITUTIONALIZATION

Scholars have increasingly criticized "liberalization first" because they claim it actually destabilizes societies instead of stabilizing them. States must be first prepared for liberalization by building strong government institutions. In this view, state builders should prioritize the building of effective and capable institutions of government for two reasons. First, strong institutions are a necessary prerequisite for political stability, especially for political liberalization, in postconflict societies.[10] Second, the state's legitimacy is drawn from its effectiveness in performing the functions of statehood, especially delivering services, and effective institutions of government are essential to service delivery. This might be called the "services first" or "functions first" variant of the "institutionalization first" strategy.[11]

First, building institutions helps stabilize societies and hardens them against the destabilizing tendencies of liberalization and postconflict tension. For example, Michael Barnett argues that to meet the challenges of postconflict societies—arbitrary power, factional conflict, and the state's lack of legitimacy—the international community should

9. Roeder, "Power Dividing as an Alternative," 51–82; Roeder and Rothchild, "Dilemmas of State-Building," 1–26.
10. Huntington, *Political Order in Changing Societies.*
11. I argue in chapter 3 that this is an insufficient view about the sources of a state's legitimacy. Legitimacy comes from a locally shared theory of justice to which the state can appeal and which in turn shapes what kind of benefits and services the state is expected to provide. Until state and society share a theory of justice, the provision of public goods will be a stopgap gesture unlikely to restore a state's legitimacy.

undertake what he calls "republican statebuilding." Republican state building emphasizes institutions that foster deliberation and embody constitutionalism and representation. Deliberation tames factional conflict. It compels actors to present their arguments publicly, which subjects arguments to critique and compels actors to make arguments that appeal across factional or sectarian lines. Constitutionalism tames arbitrary power by establishing the rules of the game and diffusing power across institutions. Representation helps establish the state's legitimacy by ensuring citizens' views are consulted.[12]

Paris offers a similar argument for investing in institutions. In his view, state builders should wait for social tensions to ease before planning for elections; design electoral systems that reward moderation; promote civil society elements that support democracy; regulate speech that incites violence; ensure equitable economic growth; and invest in government institutional capacity. Only after these steps are taken can state builders safely hold elections, guarantee a robust set of civil liberties, and allow for a liberal economic order. As he writes, "Promoting democratization and marketization has the potential to stimulate higher levels of societal competition at the very moment (immediately following the conflict) when states are least equipped to contain such tensions within peaceful bounds. Peacebuilders in the 1990s seemed to underestimate the destabilizing effects of the liberalization process in the fragile circumstances of countries just emerging from civil wars."[13]

The second justification for the "institutionalization first" strategy is that states derive their legitimacy from the effectiveness with which they perform basic functions and deliver services. Scholars have proposed different functions as the ones most essential for a state to perform. Kimberly Zisk Marten of Columbia University proposes three functions, mostly security focused. Ashraf Ghani, Afghanistan's former finance minister and the cofounder of the Institute of State Effectiveness, and Claire Lockhart, the institute's director, propose ten functions, many related to bureaucratic control, fiscal policy, and the administration of resources.[14] Jens Meierhenrich of the London School of Economics proposes six, clustered around the idea that successful states are "usable" in that they serve a function for self-interested citizens. Meierhenrich's functions differ from Ghani and Lockhart's because he defines functionality as the effect the state's actions have on citizens' lives rather than the simple performance of duties. Creating legality and bureaucracy—the focus of much of Ghani and Lockhart's ten functions—are only the first tasks

---

12. Barnett, "Building a Republican Peace," 87–112.
13. Paris, *At War's End*, 6.
14. Ghani and Lockhart, *Fixing Failed States*, chap. 7.

in making the state usable. The six functions Meierhenrich proposes are: "(1) encouraging predictability; (2) creating confidence; (3) lending credibility; (4) providing security; (5) displaying resolve; and (6) controlling resources." Citizens living in a usable state have incentives to preserve, rather than "steal" or undermine, it. External actors can facilitate the development of a usable state by recognizing, constructing, and maintaining it, by which he means that state builders should demobilize combatants, restrict the flow of weapons, build roads and railroads, provide financial support, secure borders and roads, and facilitate transitional justice.[15]

The stress on institution building has led to a sizeable body of literature on the importance of specific institutions. For example, Michael Carnahan and Claire Lockhart argue that the public finance system, including managing the treasury, planning and executing a budget, raising revenue, issuing public debt, and managing state assets, is central to the state's legitimacy and to state building. Effective public finance enables the state to perform other functions competently. It develops the state's ability to execute strategic planning. It facilitates economic growth and service delivery. Transparent handling of resources enhances trust. A rules-based system undercuts spoilers and warlords. Carnahan and Lockhart conclude that international aid should be channeled through the target state's public finance system. Issuing aid directly to the people or through donors and contractors replaces and thereby undermines the state's institutions, undercutting the long-term goal of state building.[16]

Finally, in response to, and partly in agreement with, the stress on institution building, Francis Fukuyama has developed an argument about the dynamics at work in international efforts to build domestic institutions in weak or failed states. While he generally agrees that institution building is essential to state building, he argues that there is a limit to what kinds of ideas and institutions can be successfully transferred from one country to another. The international community can transfer relatively easily the knowledge of how to design and manage individual organizations, such as bureaucracies and central banks. It cannot generate the cultural norms that underpin such institutions, and it has a difficult time transferring legitimization mechanisms. Even the transferable art of organizational design and management requires extensive context-specific input because organizations often have ambiguous goals, grapple with the perennial principal-agent difficulty, and

15. Meierhenrich, "Forming States after Failure," 153–69.
16. Carnahan and Lockhart, "Peacebuilding and Public Finance," 73–102.

because "norms, values, shared experiences, and intense social relations" shape how organizations behave. The international community sometimes ends up actively undermining weak states' institutions if it provides services directly rather than by building the capacity of the state to provide the services. Fukuyama argues that the international community can best focus its institutionalization efforts on tasks that are highly specific and low in transaction volume—which are easiest to monitor—to get the biggest impact for its investment. He cites central banking, a highly technical activity often limited to one location, as a prime example.[17]

STABILIZATION

The "security first" argument is straightforward. As Charles Call summarizes it, "Without security, other tasks of state building and postconflict reconstruction are impossible."[18] This is especially true of efforts at political liberalization. "Security drives democracy, while democracy does not beget security," according to Amitai Etzioni.[19] Marten's version of the "security first" argument takes as its premise that the state wins legitimacy by performing three basic security functions: protecting its territory from external attack, protecting citizens from criminal violence, and enforcing stable rules for commerce and civic life. International state builders thus should focus on building a state capable of performing those functions, and, meanwhile, international military forces should fulfill those functions. Providing security and stability will also help enhance the legitimacy of the international presence.[20] Diplomat and former ambassador James Dobbins, who led a team of scholars in an influential multivolume study of international interventions, concluded that "the prime objective of any nation-building operation is to make violent societies peaceful, not to make poor ones prosperous, or authoritarian ones democratic. . . . The first-order priorities for any nation-building mission are public security and humanitarian assistance."[21]

Etzioni has developed the strongest and most thorough version of this argument. Like the advocates of institutionalization, he begins

---

17. Fukuyama, *State-Building Governance and World Order*, 57–58.
18. Call, "Ending Wars, Building States," 14.
19. Etzioni, *Security First*, ix.
20. Marten, "Statebuilding and Force," 122–39.
21. Dobbins, *Beginner's Guide to Nation-Building*, xxiii. Dobbins uses "nation-building" to mean much the same that I mean by "state building" here. He does not mean the creation of a national identity.

with a critique of liberalization. He writes, "Liberal democracy cannot be imposed at gunpoint, most assuredly not on societies with little history that would prepare them for it, nations without the tradition of a free press and civil liberties, and without the institutions of a flourishing civil society." But his recommendation is not to build institutions, which he thinks is equally problematic; it is to provide security: "Before these perquisites to liberal democracy can be established, there must be basic security, a measure of social peace, and a stable government . . . democratization cannot lead; it must follow the establishment of basic security."[22]

Etzioni's argument rests on a deep pessimism about the ability of outsiders to effect lasting change in failed states. "Even superpowers have limited leverage over failing states," he argues, to the point that "foreign powers *cannot* democratize and modernize a nation like Afghanistan in the foreseeable future." "Social engineering," by which he means democratization, economic reconstruction, and nation building, is an "extremely primitive art" that "must expect to encounter resistance by those forced to alter their course and who have had little or no say over the design of the planned changes."[23]

What separates Etzioni from advocates of "institutionalization first" is that he clearly applies his pessimism not just to democratization but also to reconstruction and institution building as well. He writes, "It is impossible to fix [failed states'] oil wells, ports, roads, schools, hospitals, utilities, civil service, police, armed forces, markets, and so on as the United States has attempted. . . . There is *no* level of foreign aid at which all needs, indeed even all the major ones, could be properly covered— surely not in short order . . . there is no way to develop all the elements [of the government and economy] in tandem." He summarizes:

> If democratization, development, and nation-building could be accomplished with relative ease, the strategy of according security top priority would be moot. However, given that the opposite is true, one cannot rush regime change and hope it will lead to domestic law and order and contribute to international peace. Security must lead. . . . Democratization, economic development, and nation-building are likely to take much longer, cost much more, and are much more prone to failure than their advocates presume.[24]

22. Etzioni, *Security First*, x.
23. Ibid., 19, 32, 40.
24. Ibid., 75, 84.

Given outsiders' inability to liberalize or rebuild failed states, they should prioritize the provision of basic security. This is not a cynical or amoral choice: it is, in fact, the only ethical option. He writes, "The main reason that the right to security takes precedence over all others is that all the others are contingent on the protection of life—whereas the right to security is not similarly contingent on any other rights . . . dead people cannot exercise their rights." This is true even if it empowers illiberal leaders. As he puts it, "Occupying forces must make the 'second-worst' decision to leave many elements of the old regime in place, and then slowly work to convert them, while allowing considerable time for new and more liberal forces to grow. . . . The occupying powers must initially tolerate illiberal ideological or religious regimes, as long as the leadership in place helps maintain basic security." The conclusion is obvious: "Interventions are best limited to help provide basic security rather than to bring about regime change, using the occupying forces only to advance this mission. Troops should not be used for nation-building or reconstruction."[25]

Echoing Etzioni's argument that security is the key variable explaining success or failure in armed state building, some scholars have studied the causal mechanisms at work within the security sector. For example, international military forces can effectively reduce the incidence of a relapse into violence because they decrease the incentives for aggression and increase the incentives for cooperation in a postconflict environment, calm fears and create space for trust to regrow, prevent spillover or spiraling from accidents, and persuade ex-combatants to retain an inclusive political process.[26] Marten argues that incentivizing service in statebuilding campaigns within military bureaucracies will enhance their effectiveness by drawing top talent to those missions.[27]

The most detailed look at the dynamics of international military forces engaged in state building is in the work of David Edelstein. While his work focuses on military occupation, he notes that state building is often a necessary task to successfully conclude an occupation. Edelstein argues that international military forces engaged in state building face two dilemmas: the duration dilemma and the footprint dilemma. First, the longer international military forces stay, the greater the likelihood that they will overstay their welcome. The local population may come to resent their presence, cease cooperating with them, and even begin to oppose them. However, the shorter they stay, the less the likelihood of a successful outcome of the state building effort. Repeated cases show that

25. Ibid., 6, 29, 31.
26. Fortna, *Does Peacekeeping Work?*
27. Marten, *Enforcing the Peace*, 113–14.

premature withdrawal is one of the principle causes of failure in armed state building. Making credible progress toward concluding the military presence helps alleviate the duration dilemma. Second, the larger and more intrusive the international military forces are, the greater chance they have of transforming the weak state but the greater resentment they may provoke. The smaller or less intrusive the forces are, the more they will be welcomed by the local population—but they will not be capable of achieving as much.[28]

PROBLEMS WITH THEORIES OF SEQUENCING

In this section I highlight problems with each of the three theories of sequencing individually, followed by a discussion of the problems they face in common.

Liberalization

Liberalization was first critiqued by scholars responding to modernization theory in the 1960s and 1970s. Scholars noted that the data did not support the contention that economic liberalization caused stability and democracy. Instead, economic liberalization actually seemed to be a source of instability and political danger because it unleashed new social forces and empowered new elites while threatening established structures.[29] Different goals of development are incompatible: for example, rising prosperity also increases inequality and social unrest. These conflicts might be overcome, some scholars argued, if development goals were pursued in the correct sequence, for example by strengthening political institutions before liberalizing the economy.[30] But others began to question the assumption that economics caused political outcomes in a linear and unidirectional relationship. Some began to look at cultural variables, such as the ethnic composition of a society[31] or at the role of institutions.[32] Still others cast doubt on the idea that there was a set path of progression from poor to rich and autocracy to democracy by describing enduring regimes types—such as

28. Edelstein, "Occupational Hazards," 49–91; Edelstein, "Foreign Militaries, Sustainable Institutions," 81–103.
29. Huntington, *Political Order in Changing Societies*; Olson, "Rapid Growth as a Destabilizing Force," 529–52.
30. Binder, *Crises and Sequences*.
31. Geertz, *Interpretation of Cultures*; Lijphart, *Democracy in Plural Societies*, chap. 10.
32. Huntington, *Political Order in Changing Societies*, 734–49.

"bureaucratic authoritarianism"—that did not fit into the modernization schematic.[33] Professor emeritus Robert Packenham of Stanford
University argued that, contrary to the assumptions of modernization
theory, change and development are not necessarily easy: social, economic, and political development may be at odds with each other; radi-
calism and revolution may contribute to development and democracy,
not harm them; and states often need to concentrate on increasing their
power, not diffusing it.[34] Others argued that the key variable was not
the political or economic situation within poor, weak states at all, but
their dependency on a global economic system outside of their
control.[35]

Advocates of the "institutionalization first" approach have rightly
taken up the critique of modernization theory in their attack on "liberalization first." The "liberalization first" approach "tends to take the existence of functioning states as a given."[36] But the existence of the state is
precisely what is in question under conditions of state failure. Absent
strong institutions, liberalization can be destabilizing: "States emerging
from war do not have the necessary institutional framework or civic culture to absorb the potential pressures associated with political and market competition . . . liberalization prior to institutionalization can unleash
societal demands before the state has developed the institutional capacity to channel, organize, and respond to those demands."[37] Democracy
and capitalism actually encourage and depend on conflict and competition to work; indeed, peaceful conflict is usually seen as a healthy sign in
a democracy. The danger is that such conflict can too easily turn violent
in the immediate aftermath of war and in the absence of strong institutions. Premature liberalization can destabilize fragile polities by unleashing immoderate social forces too soon after the cessation of hostilities.
While mature democracies tend to be stable, the process of becoming one
tends to be unstable.[38]

Institutionalization

"Institutionalization first" has problems of its own. There is no generic
"institution" that outsiders can build. There are only scores of particular
institutions that constitute a government: the "institutionalization first"
strategy begs the question "which institutions?" Candidates abound,

33. O'Donnell, *Modernization and Bureaucratic-Authoritarianism*.
34. Packenham, *Liberal America and the Third World*.
35. Cardoso and Faletto, *Dependency and Development*.
36. Paris, *At War's End*, 46.
37. Barnett, "Building a Republican Peace," 89.
38. Mansfield and Snyder, *Electing To Fight*.

from ministries to legislatures to the justice sector to the treasury. Second, and more seriously, this "institutionalization first" strategy rests on assumptions that institutions foster deliberation, and deliberation calms extremism. It tends to view state building as a technical exercise that will deliver political stability through the correct application of procedural rationality. But the process of building institutions is itself more than a technical exercise. Fukuyama is right to point out that even building effective institutions involves norms and culture, which is problematic when it is outside powers trying to do the building. Institutions involve power, both in their creation and their operation, which few advocates of this approach appear to appreciate. Meierhenrich is atypical among scholars in this literature for recognizing that "realistically, state formation after state failure will bear fruit only if powerful agents, individuals, and groups, support it."[39] Other scholars of this strategy treat institution building and technical assistance as an entirely cooperative endeavor between outside powers and local actors. As any teacher in a classroom knows, transferring knowledge and skills from one person to another necessarily involves a relationship of authority and power. In the context of armed state building, that means a political relationship. An unwillingness to acknowledge political realities can lead to naïve assumptions about local citizens' willingness and ability to accept and make use of institutional capacity programs, and ultimately to ineffective efforts.[40]

Additionally, "institutionalization first" relies heavily on a critique of the inadequacy of "liberalization first," but the critique has been overgeneralized. The critique originated in reaction to the hasty elections in Angola, Bosnia, and Liberia, but critics have gone on to apply the criticism more broadly, with less persuasiveness. For example, Paris believes that the interventions in Guatemala, El Salvador, and Nicaragua succeeded insofar as none of those states reverted to violence during or immediately after the intervention, but then claims that economic liberalization is "undermining the prospects of a stable and lasting peace in all three countries," and thus counts these cases as evidence in support of his theory that liberalization has failed Central America. Paris's assessment is methodologically flawed: as an open-ended judgment about Central America's hypothetical future relapse into violence, it is not falsifiable unless he commits to a specific time frame. But any reasonable time frame has already elapsed: fourteen years after the mission in Guatemala and more than twenty years after the interventions in El Salvador

---

39. Meierhenrich, "Forming States after Failure," 154.
40. Fukuyama, *State-Building Governance and World Order*; Meierhenrich, "Forming States after Failure."

and Nicaragua, all three remain at peace. The Central American cases do not sustain Paris's criticisms of liberalization.

Stabilization

The "security first" argument, the most plausible of all the sequencing theories, still faces several problems. First, Etzioni defends the primacy of security by invoking the outmoded and discredited political development literature: "We need to return to a sort of stages of development theory," echoing Rostow's 1959 theory, in which security is first and "elections are a lagging not a leading element."[41] In this view, there is something inherent or natural about security that precedes other aspects of statehood. The notion of stages implies that there is a starting point and a destination common to all states, and that states could be mapped along a scale according to what stage they are in. As discussed, there is no evidence that states follow a regular or natural progression of development. Etzioni acknowledges that the earlier "stages of development" theory has been "thoroughly debunked," but he does not respond to its critics or explain why it should now be taken seriously other than by saying that we need a more "moderate" and flexible version of it. A theory that has failed to describe, explain, or predict observed facts is still wrong, no matter how moderate and flexible it is.

Etzioni might reply that, even if the rest of the state building sequence is not fixed, security should still come first. But Etzioni himself responds to this and highlights a key weakness of "security first." "Security is based largely on values," he rightly points out, which are embodied in a "shared moral culture." Law enforcement depends on the existence of this shared moral culture. He writes, "A society can function well and remain healthy only as long as most people, most of the time, do what they do because they believe that it is right and just, not because they fear the power of the authorities. Hence the pivotal role of the moral culture and the informal social controls that sustain it."[42] In other words, security and legitimacy go together: security that is imposed without regard to norms of legitimacy simply plants seeds for future conflict. That is why, as I point out in the next chapter, security failures are highly correlated with failures of legitimacy. States that are widely perceived to be illegitimate by their people are also those most likely to experience anarchic failure. Applying this insight to Iraq and Afghanistan, Etzioni argues that the United States should change its public diplomacy to

41. Etzioni, *Security First*, 53.
42. Ibid., 152, 158.

"counter the arguments of violent Islamic beliefs," redirect aid to "fund religion" favorable to our goals, "include religious programming" in US-sponsored radio and TV broadcasts, and help draft new constitutions that "explicitly favor one kind of Islam over another." Etzioni turns out to agree wholeheartedly with advocates of "liberalization first" that state building must include strong efforts to restore a state's legitimacy. He simply argues that the basis should be religion rather than liberalism. This is a dramatic departure from what most scholars or policymakers mean when they talk about "security first." Etzioni has, in trying to address a weakness in "security first," simply transformed the theory into something else.

In fact, the biggest danger of the "security first" approach is that it effectively will become a "security only" approach. "Focusing on the state security apparatus may lead to the establishment and strengthening of authoritarian or semi-authoritarian structures, which in turn would prove counterproductive in other areas of state building," according to Ulrich Schneckener, professor at the University of Osnabruck and head of the Global Issues Research Unit at the German Institute for International and Security Affairs.[43] Charles Call rightly faults the "security-centered" state-building efforts by the United States in the early twentieth century for the rise of the Duvalier and Trujillo dictatorships out of the US-trained security forces in Haiti and the Dominican Republic.[44] Outside powers that adopt a "security first" approach might convey, intentionally or not, that they intend to avoid a broader entanglement in the failed state's political and economic situation. The strategy can become the first step toward lowering the aims of the intervention.

Some scholars advocate just such an approach, based on their skepticism about outside powers' ability to export democracy. The most effective type of intervention, in this view, is international aid to security-sector reform.[45] But the depth of pessimism of the "security first" approach is unjustified. Etzioni writes that "foreign powers *cannot* democratize and modernize a nation like Afghanistan," that it is "impossible" to rebuild a failed state's infrastructure, that there is "*no* level of foreign aid" that could meet failed states' needs.[46] It is clear that Etzioni is either holding up state-building operations to an impossible standard of success or he is simply ignorant of the history of successful

43. Schneckener, "Addressing Fragile Statehood," 211–12.
44. Call, "Fallacy of the 'Failed State," 1491–1507.
45. Toft, *Securing the Peace.*
46. Etzioni, *Security First,* 32, 75.

interventions. If "liberalization first" is too naïve, "security first" is too cynical.

A final problem with the "security first" paradigm is that it may be simply irrelevant in practice for failed states that are not anarchic. For example, contemporary Haiti has poorly functioning institutions and a weak economy but no civil war, insurgency, or terrorism. The "security first" approach thus offers little that is meaningful to policymakers intent on sending a US or UN force to help Haiti in the aftermath of its earthquake.

Problems with Sequencing in General

In addition to the problems highlighted in each theory of sequencing individually, there are major problems with the general theory of sequencing. First, it assumes that there is one right approach for all failed states, which is implausible on its face. Considering the greatly differing conditions in different failed states, from West Germany after World War II to contemporary Somalia, there is no immediate reason to believe that all failed states can be fixed with the same basic approach. Again, the older literature on political development and transitions sheds some light. D. A. Rustow, a prominent scholar of democratization and former professor at the City University in New York, eventually argued in 1970 there was no single path or sequence of economic and political development to be discovered: there may be many roads to democracy, prosperity, and stability. Different factors may be important to growing democracy at different times and within different parts of society.[47] Thomas Carothers, the vice-president for studies at the Carnegie Endowment for International Peace, echoing some of Rustow's arguments, cast doubt on the validity of the entire "transition paradigm." The political development and transitions research programs implicitly assumed that as countries moved away from traditional society or autocracy, they must necessarily be moving toward democracy; that political development was a definable process that unfolded in a discoverable, set sequence; and that state building and democracy building are mutually reinforcing activities. Carothers argued that these assumptions are incorrect. There is no set sequence of development or change. It is chaotic and, so far, unpredictable. Political change is not always or inevitably in the direction of more democracy; countries may move toward greater autocracy or toward anarchy. Democratization can hurt state building by unleashing massive social change before institutions are in place to channel and contain it.[48]

47. Rustow, "Transitions to Democracy," 337–63.
48. Carothers, "End of the Transition Paradigm," 5–21.

The critique of sequencing holds valuable lessons for armed state building. No single variable—economics, culture, institutions, elites, elections, beliefs—explains how countries become rich, peaceful, and democratic. Causation is not unidirectional: there is no simple relationship between economic and politics, culture and politics, and so forth. Some variables, such as economic growth, can both help and hurt the goals of democracy and peace at the same time because of the complexity of the system in which they operate. If there is a discoverable set sequence along which societies must travel to become rich, peaceful, and democratic, no scholar or policymaker has yet made a persuasive case for it. More likely, there is no set sequence. There are many roads to democracy, peace, and prosperity, depending on local conditions.

Paris implicitly admits the same insight concerning peace building in his review of post–Cold War peace-building cases. He writes that the intervention in Croatia was a success, but "the circumstances of the Croatian mission may have been exceptional," namely, that one party to the conflict was defeated and left the territory. Namibia and Mozambique were also unqualified successes, but they "are also unlike most other countries that have recently emerged from civil wars" because their wars were sponsored by outside actors whose removal paved the way for relatively easy reconstruction.[49] Setting aside the question of how unique outside influence was in Namibia and Mozambique (the United States and Soviet Union also fought proxy wars in Central America and elsewhere), Paris is again highlighting that different political, military, and economic circumstances in the failed state have a crucial impact on the outcome of a peace-building mission: outcomes are *not* a straightforward function of the sequence of programs used by peace builders. Paris is right to identify these other variables, but wrong to dismiss them as exceptional.

The second major difficulty with the theory of sequencing is that it overlooks other crucial choices state builders have to make in formulating their strategy of intervention. Designing an intervention is highly complex and involves difficult choices about the force structure, mandate, coalition, resource levels, and degree of control the state builder will assume in the failed state. The sequence of programs or relative priority given to holding elections, building institutions, or preventing violence is only one consideration. Advocates have not adequately explained why any sequence supposedly holds more explanatory power than any other variable.

49. Paris, *At War's End*, 111, 148.

The third difficulty with the theory of sequencing, one that is more pragmatic, is that it assumes sequencing is *possible*, which is increasingly doubtful in highly complex, multilateral operations. Effective sequencing requires dozens of coalition partners, international institutions, nongovernmental organizations, and all the departments, agencies, and services within each contributing state to coordinate and execute an agreed-on sequence. Their ability to coordinate, however, is inversely related to how many actors there are: the more actors, the higher the administrative cost and the greater number of possible relationships and lines of communication between them.[50] Coordination among actors in a multilateral operation is a major difficulty, enough that some scholars claim that its lack is itself a key cause of failure. There is nearly universal consensus that international efforts are almost always poorly coordinated, resulting in duplication of effort, gaps, poor communication, wasted resources, and unneeded programs.[51] The literature on sequencing had largely sidestepped the important question of how to overcome the coordination problem to implement a proper sequence.

Fourth, sequencing theories are difficult to test. Because it is unlikely that multilateral operations could actually use sequencing in practice, few state-building operations in history fit cleanly into one or the other category. Scholars researching state building face enormous challenges trying to operationalize a sequencing variable, that is, how would a researcher measure the presence or absence of "security first" versus "institutionalization first"? For example, the intervention in West Germany is usually called an example of a "security first" operation, but simultaneously with the imposition of a military government the United States also rebuilt Germany's government, disbursed massive economic aid through the Marshall Plan, and held democratic elections in 1946. It seems more a case of "everything first" rather than "security first" or "liberalization first." Similarly, Bosnia is often cited as an example of a "liberalization first" operation because elections were held the year after the war ended, but NATO occupied Bosnia with sixty thousand troops and disbursed billions of dollars of aid—again illustrating the difficulty of characterizing the mission as sequencing security before

---

50. The number of actors, x, yields $(x^2-x)/2$ binary relationships and 2^x-x-1 total relationships. A typical mission with fifty major actors generates 1,225 possible binary relationships among them and over 1 quadrillion total combinations of relationships, a mathematical illustration of the difficulty of coordination in a multilateral operation.
51. Gowan, "UN Peace Operations," 109–30.

liberalization, or vice versa. That means a theory of sequencing is difficult to falsify.

Given these difficulties, scholars and policymakers should jettison attempts to identify a master sequence that unlocks the key to success in armed state building. In the next chapter I lay the groundwork for an alternate approach. My approach rests not on a sequence of efforts but on identifying the type and degree of state failure and designing a strategy to fit it. That effort begins by reexamining the concepts of statehood and state failure that, so far, we have taken for granted.

[3]

Statehood

President Obama's National Security Strategy declares that "failing states breed conflict and endanger regional and global security," and that the United States' "diplomacy and development capabilities must help prevent conflict, spur economic growth, strengthen weak and failing states."[1] Former Secretary of Defense Robert Gates wrote in *Foreign Affairs* that "dealing with such fractured or failing states is, in many ways, the main security challenge of our time."[2] The language about "weak and failing states" reflects a consensus among foreign policy analysts that "states" can "fail." The US government-funded State Failure Task Force (now the Political Instability Task Force, or PITF) was established in 1994 to study the causes and consequences of state failure. The Fund for Peace has published an annual Failed State Index since 2005. The Brookings Institution followed suit in 2008.

But what is a "failed state"? There is surprisingly little consensus about the concept, and there have been few attempts to define it with any amount of rigor. The conceptual ambiguity accounts for the poor state of scholarship and policymaking on rebuilding failed states: it is difficult to know how to rebuild a failed state if there is no agreement on what constitutes state failure in the first place. The quandary goes even deeper. Building weak states presupposes a notion of what a "state" is. More so, building states inevitably involves norms about what a state *should* be. In order to build a state, state builders must first answer: *What is the state?* Scholars and practitioners tend to assume an unproblematic and simplistic definition of statehood; they need greater clarity to design research

1. White House, *National Security Strategy: May 2010*, 8, 11.
2. Gates, "Helping Others Defend Themselves," 2–6.

and policy to address state failure. This theoretical ground is necessary because it fills a gap that conventional theories of state building leave unaddressed. Conventional theories are formulated at the level of foreign policy rather than political theory; their main variables tend to be specific levers and tools available to a policymaker, such as troops and money. But those tools are not the only variables that affect the outcome of a state-building operation. We must understand how those tools interact with preexisting dynamics—political, cultural, and economic—at work within failed states.

Max Weber's universally cited (and often misquoted) definition of statehood in his 1919 lecture *Politics as a Vocation* is that "a state is a human community that (successfully) claims the *monopoly of the legitimate use of physical force* within a given territory."[3] The power of Weber's definition is that he includes several aspects of statehood: legitimacy, coercion, and relation to human affairs. The problem with Weber's definition is that, narrowly interpreted, police and military forces could qualify as states. That is plainly not what Weber intended, but it suggests that in Weber's attempt to locate the hard core of statehood in coercion, he unnecessarily omitted other aspects of statehood, such as the delivery of public goods and the mechanism by which states advance a successful claim to legitimacy.

There are in fact several enduring themes about the nature of statehood and political change in the history of political thought that collectively are broader and richer than Weber's definition. Five themes are especially enduring throughout the history of thought and discussion on the nature of statehood. The state is (1) a coercive force, (2) the embodiment of a theory of justice, (3) a provider of benefits and services, (4) a part of economic production and distribution, and (5) a tool for serving human life.

A Coercive Force

The state wields physical force to defend itself and enforce its rule. The state's coercive power is its most distinctive and universally acknowledged role. Christian thinkers, starting with Saint Paul and Saint Augustine, argued that the state is God's secular instrument to restrain the wicked and uphold temporal order. Paul wrote in Romans 13:1–4, "The authorities that exist have been established by God. . . . If you do wrong,

---

3. Max Weber, *Politics as a Vocation*, 1919. The definition occurs in the fourth paragraph. The lecture is widely available—for example, at http://www.sscnet.ucla.edu/polisci/ethos/Weber-vocation.pdf.

be afraid, for [the ruler] does not bear the sword for nothing. He is God's servant, an agent of wrath to bring punishment on the wrongdoer." Augustine developed the idea of the City of God and the City of Man as distinct spheres, both with legitimate claims on human life. Within the City of Man, God provides the state to compel order among sinners by force. The City of Man requires force because it is an external, worldly order. The state "does not seek to make men truly good or virtuous" like the City of God, but "rather it is interested in [man's] outward actions." Because it is concerned with compelling behavior from sinful human beings, the state is a "coercive order, maintained by the use of force and relying on the fear of pain as its major sanction for compliance to its commands."[4]

Thomas Hobbes drew much the same link between the state, coercion, and violence in his 1651 work *Leviathan*, with a different justification. Absent the restraining force of the state and left in an apocryphal state of nature, human life would be a war of all against all: "During the time men live without a common power to keep them all in awe, they are in that condition which is called war, and such a war as is of every man against every man."[5] The state is the sovereign to whom man gives up his rights and empowers to use coercion so it can bring an end to the brutal state of nature. The commonwealth is "one person, of whose acts a great multitude, by mutual covenants one with another, have made themselves every one the author, to the end he may use the strength and means of them all, as he shall think expedient, for their peace and common defense."[6]

The late Charles Tilly, a prominent historian of state formation and a long-time professor at the University of Michigan, expressed this aspect of statehood most powerfully by arguing, in effect, that the state is *nothing but* the exercise of coercion on a mass scale. Tilly argued that the state can be seen simply as a protection racket writ large: "Since governments themselves commonly simulate, stimulate, or even fabricate threats of external war and since the repressive and extractive activities of governments often constitute the largest current threats to the livelihoods of their own citizens, many governments operate in essentially the same ways as racketeers." State making is thus "our largest example of organized crime." Governments are distinguished from criminals, if at all, because they are able to deploy violence "on a larger scale, more effectively, [and] more efficiently."[7] Tilly goes so far as to

4. Deane, *Political and Social Ideas of St. Augustine*, 117.
5. Hobbes, *Leviathan*, 76.
6. Ibid., 109.
7. Tilly, "War Making and State Making as Organized Crime," 171, 169, 173.

distinguish war making from state making simply by the location of the state's enemies: war making is eliminating external enemies while state making is eliminating internal enemies. The two are related: successful war making requires the development of extractive capacities to collect resources for war; those capacities in turn require the elimination of internal rivals to clear the way for successful extraction. Thus, war making has caused state making, or, "Wars made states, and vice versa."[8]

THE EMBODIMENT OF A THEORY OF JUSTICE

Weber did not say, as he is often misquoted as saying, that the state is the institution with the monopoly on the use of force. He said it was the human community that *successfully claimed* the *legitimate* monopoly on the use of force. Claiming legitimacy in the exercise of political, legal, and military authority necessarily involves appealing to norms about right and wrong ways to exercise that authority—in other words, a theory of justice. The state claims legitimacy by invoking a theory of justice (implicitly or otherwise) that validates its actions, coercion, and existence. As the embodiment of that theory, the state is a carrier of public norms about justice and legitimacy. The state and its officers can engage in symbolic action to acknowledge, appeal to, honor, or denigrate norms of justice in ways that are recognizable and significant to its citizens, and such symbolic action is crucial to the state's claim to legitimacy. Theories of justice thus underpin the state's legitimacy: norms legitimize power.

The state makes its claim to legitimacy in the cultural, religious, ideological, and historical context of the population over whom it seeks to exercise sovereignty. The claim is successful if the notion of justice appealed to is shared by people whose support the state requires. The state is thus a historical and cultural actor, and attention to history, culture, and beliefs are central to the state's ability to make a successful claim to legitimacy. In a society in which there is disagreement about these norms, the state's legitimacy is in question. In these cases the state often becomes a target of competition between groups who intend to capture the state to implement their beliefs about justice at the expense of rivals' views.

Edmund Burke gave classical expression to the idea that the state should be the natural outgrowth of a people's religion, beliefs, and traditions, which in turn undergird, legitimize, and give strength to the state.

---

8. Tilly, *Coercion, Capital, and European States*, chap. 3.

He wrote in 1790: "Religion is the basis of civil society . . . man is by his constitution a religious animal," and the church establishment is "the foundation of [the] whole constitution."[9] Burke argued that tradition is the stuff from which government grows. "Convention must limit and modify all the descriptions of constitution which are formed under it. Every sort of legislative, judicial, or executory power are its creatures."[10] Tradition is also the means by which government survives and is transmitted from generation to generation: "By a constitutional policy, working after the pattern of nature, we receive, we hold, we transmit our government and our privileges, in the same manner in which we enjoy and transmit our property and our lives."[11] Government is thus founded on and legitimized by religion and tradition.

George Wilhelm Friedrich Hegel argued in his lectures on the philosophy of history in the early 1820s (compiled and published in 1837), in effect, that the state was *nothing but* a natural outgrowth of people's beliefs, especially their religion. He argued that religion and culture (he seems to have used the two concepts interchangeably) undergird the state, suggesting that states must govern and draw their notion of justice from the wider culture to remain legitimate: "The general principle which manifests itself and becomes an object of consciousness in the State—the form under which all that the State includes is brought— is the whole of that cycle of phenomena which constitutes the *culture* of a nation." He continued, "Religion is the sphere in which a nation gives itself the definition of that which it regards as the True. . . . The conception of God, therefore, constitutes the general basis of a people's character. In this aspect, religion stands in the closest connection with the political principle. . . . On this account it is that the State rests on Religion. . . . The form of Religion, therefore, decides that of the State and its constitution. The latter actually originated in the particular religion adopted by the nation. "[12]

As Hegel said later, "only in connection with this particular religion, can this particular political constitution exist; just as in such or such a State, such or such a Philosophy or order of Art." He argued that the state is part of an integrated whole with its associated people, culture, history, philosophy, and art: "The constitution adopted by a people makes one substance—one spirit—with its religion, its art and philosophy, or, at least, with its conceptions and thoughts—its culture generally." The state, including its claim to legitimacy and its theory of justice, must be

9. Burke, *Political Philosophy of Edmund Burke*.
10. Ibid., 182.
11. Ibid., 172.
12. Hegel, *Philosophy of History*, 50.

drawn from the wider culture. Thus he warns against efforts to "invent and carry out political constitutions independently of religion," because the state, as he argued, rests on religion.[13]

A CONTRACTOR FOR PUBLIC GOODS AND SERVICES

The state does not limit itself to exercising coercion for defense and internal order and making claims about justice. It also performs other functions which it claims are public goods—an aspect of statehood omitted from Weber's definition. The state provides public goods to bolster its claim to legitimacy and respond to its supporters' needs in what amounts to a contractual relationship, an exchange of benefits for support. Under the umbrella of "public goods" states do a dazzling variety of things beyond providing order and defense. States make rules, adjudicate disputes, build public infrastructure, and administer common resources. Richer modern sates also try to improve their citizens' economic opportunities, provide them with access to health and education services, protect and enhance cultural and natural resources, conduct scientific research and development, and promote general welfare.

There is no set or fixed menu of functions a state performs or public goods it provides that characterizes all states. The functions that states perform and the goods that are considered legitimately "public" change over time and vary across cultures. The constant, underlying theme is that the state performs functions and provides benefits to secure and retain support from people, which means the functions performed and services provided have to be the sort that the state's supporters want and believe are rightly provided by the state. Because the state's claim to legitimacy has to be shared by people whose support it needs, the kind of functions it performs and public goods it provides must be responsive to its supporters' expectations and needs. There is a reciprocal exchange between the state and its supporters: it performs functions and provides benefits that it claims are just; in return, people who share its conception of justice and benefit from its services support the state's claim to legitimacy and provide it with manpower and resources. The performance of functions and provision of public goods is how a state enacts its claim to legitimacy and demonstrates its theory of justice. There is a contract, explicit or implicit, between state and citizen, to exchange public goods for support and legitimacy.

In 1689 John Locke gave classic expression to the theory of the state as a social contract in his *Second Treatise on Government*. Locke suggested

13. Ibid., 53, 46, 52.

that the contract can involve the state's provision of other goods to the citizens than simply an end to universal war. He argued that the state originates in a contract among individuals to ensure mutual protection and, importantly, property guarantees and reciprocal rights. He founded the state not merely on its coercive role but on its role in preserving property and adjudicating disputes. He wrote that "the great and chief end, therefore, of men's uniting into common-wealths, and putting themselves under government, *is the preservation of their property*," a category into which Locke subsumed "lives, liberties, and estates."[14] Property was insecure in the state of nature not because of universal war (or not *only* because of it) but because there were no rules for regulating contracts, no judges to adjudicate disputes, and no police power to enforce agreements. The state came into being to provide these goods, including guaranteeing the basis for commercial life, ensuring fair process at trials, and providing legal protection for property rights. The provision of these goods, in turn, is the reason citizens agree to be subordinate to the state and recognize its legitimacy.

In the twentieth century John Rawls advanced the social contract tradition in his 1971 book *A Theory of Justice*. Rawls posited that justice is the principle of fairness that people would choose if ignorant of their own identity and circumstances. In this "original position," behind a "veil of ignorance," rational self-interested actors would agree to grant each person as much liberty as is consistent with an equal degree of liberty for all, and to arrange any inequalities for the benefit of the least-advantaged persons. The role of the state is to protect liberty and provide such "primary goods" as will enable people to use their liberty to pursue their conception of the good life. Primary goods include law and order, education and opportunity, and even self-respect. The provision of these goods, including liberty, is the state's responsibility under the contract agreed to in the original position, which supports the theory of justice chosen by rational actors and legitimizing the state's role.[15]

Over time social contract theory has come more and more explicitly to be identified with democratic, liberal, and majoritarian forms of government. The connection is understandable: elections can be understood as a reenactment or renewal of the original contract and a means for securing actual, not just hypothetical, consent to the state's authority. Democracy is a mechanism for consulting people about which services they want, or what theory of justice they favor. It is a means for continually modifying the terms of the contract.

14. Locke, *Second Treatise on Government*, 66.
15. Rawls, *Theory of Justice*.

[45]

However, it is true that most citizens of most states in history have never been asked to actually agree to a social contract, which might cast doubt on the applicability of contract theory for a general theory of statehood. I argue that the social contract and the public provision of goods are not unique features of democracy; they are a part of any regime type. At a basic level all states, including nondemocratic ones, provide some goods to retain the support of some people, at least, including elites whose influence the state needs to survive. Philosophically, Immanuel Kant attempted to provide a global foundation for the social contract that did not require actual agreements in history. His argument illustrates how all regimes, not just democracies, can claim that they represent the true or right social contract. Kant argued that we are not morally free to be unreasonable. We are morally obligated to choose rational acts: morality compels us to be free. But reason and freedom are possible only in civil society. As he put it, "The first decision the individual is obliged to make, if he does not wish to renounce all concepts of right, will be to adopt the principle that one must abandon the state of nature in which everyone follows his own desires, and unites with everyone else in order to submit to external, public, and lawful coercion."[16] Thus free, rational beings are morally obligated to choose civil order over the state of nature and recognize that government is legitimate. Whether or not there was a historical, literal agreement to create the state, Kant argues that all rational, free, moral men are obligated to agree to its existence and legitimacy, and in fact are coauthors of the state's actions.

Kant's argument is a prototype for how nondemocratic regimes frame their relationship to the social contract. All regimes involve a contract—albeit often an irrevocable, unamendable one about which no consultations were held prior to its imposition. For example, theocratic regimes offer spiritual services and military regimes offer martial and valorous services to justify their rule, with no reference to elections or representation. Critics may argue that such imposed systems cannot be described as a "contract," which requires consensual agreement. But just as Kant argued that the social contract exists and is valid because it would be agreed to by truly free and rational citizens, so nondemocratic regimes could claim that they are partners to a social contract agreed to by the truly "pious" or truly "patriotic" citizens and that those citizens are the ones to whom the state is responsible. Such claims are often circular: the government's rule is legitimate because it is supported by the truly pious citizen; the truly pious citizen is, of course, the one who supports the government's rule. My point is not to evaluate the credibility of such circular claims but to highlight that all states

16. Kant, *Political Writings*, 137.

make such claims, that such claims constitute the contract between the state and (at least a subset of) its citizens, and that such claims define the type of public goods and services the state provides.

An Economic Actor

The state is an economic actor. It requires financial and material resources to exist and function. It extracts resources from its citizens, its territory, and from other states. It taxes and regulates the production of food, goods, and services. The state faces a tension: it must extract resources to survive, but the process of extraction can risk its legitimacy. People and groups may contest the means by which it extracts resources, the amount it extracts, or the distribution of its extractive activity across the population. They may also seek to divert the state's distribution of economic goods for their particular benefit. The state's extractive and economic power, like its cultural power, make it a target for competition among groups who try (often successfully) to capture and use it for their own economic benefit. The nature and scope of the state's economic activity is thus often shaped by the type of economy, the influence of economic groups and elites, and the general level of prosperity in which it operates. With such varying influences, the degree of a state's involvement in production and consumption, its goals in doing so, and the way it goes about economic activity varies considerably across time and cultures.

The state's role as an economic actor is closely tied to its role as a coercive force and as a set of institutions. The more effective the state is as an economic actor, and the more prosperous the society, the more well funded and capable its security forces and civilian institutions will be. In turn, more effective and impartial security forces and civilian institutions will foster a better environment for the production and exchange of goods and services and for investment, innovation, and trade.

The state's economic nature was recognized early, but attention focused almost entirely on how the state reflects the economic interests of some groups in society at the expense of others. Aristotle described how economic groups vying for influence to advance their self-interest shape the state as an economic entity. He famously concludes that regimes based on the middle class are the most stable: "A state aims at being, as far as it can be, a society composed of equals and peers; and the middle class, more than any other, has this sort of composition. It follows that a state which is based on the middle class is bound to be the best constituted." Middle class men are the extreme between the greedy, violent upper class and the mean, uneducated lower class.

[47]

Middle class men "are the most ready to listen to reason [and] suffer the least from ambition." They are secure in themselves, do not covet, are not coveted, and are free from the intrigues of other classes. He argued that a society made up only of the rich and poor will be a society of masters and slaves based on enmity, not a political community based on equality.[17]

The point is not to settle the question of which class, if any, the state should most reflect, but to note the general character of Aristotle's analysis: he explained political behavior by reference to economic conditions. The state is shaped by its relationship to economic activity. The emphasis on how the state reflects the economic interests of some groups within society at the expense of others obscures a simpler point: the state is necessarily an economic actor; it is shaped and influenced by, and shapes and influences in turn, the economic forces of the society over which it is sovereign. The point may appear too obvious to merit much attention, but it is an important counterbalance to Burke, Hegel, and their present-day counterparts who underplay or entirely overlook the economic dimension of the state in their effort to highlight the state's role as a cultural and historical actor.

The point may be best highlighted by looking at this dimension of statehood in isolation, as if no other dimension mattered. That was precisely the contribution of Karl Marx, who took the insight that the state is an economic actor to (or perhaps beyond) its logical extreme: he argued that it was nothing but an economic actor, an extension of those class interests that underlie the movement of history. Marx's co-author, Friedrich Engels, distilled the message of the *Communist Manifesto* in an 1883 preface: "Economic production and the structure of society of every historical epoch necessarily arising therefrom constitute the foundation for the political and intellectual history of that epoch."[18] In an 1846 letter Marx wrote that a "particular state of development in the productive faculties of man" yields "a particular form of commerce and consumption"; in turn, these result in "a corresponding civil society," along with "particular political conditions." Political conditions, the terminus of a long chain of cause and effect, are "only the official expression of civil society."[19] More famously, in his *Contribution to the Critique of Political Economy* comes the oft-quoted passage that summarizes Marx's view on the relationship between politics and economics.

17. Aristotle, *Politics of Aristotle*, 181.
18. Tucker, *Marx-Engels Reader*, 472.
19. Ibid., 136–37.

Legal relations as well as forms of state are to be grasped neither from themselves nor from the so-called general development of the human mind, but rather have their roots in the material conditions of life. . . . The sum total of [the] relations of production constitutes the economic structure of society, the real foundation, on which rises a legal and political superstructure and to which correspond definite forms of social consciousness. The mode of production of material life conditions the social, political, and intellectual life process in general. . . . With the change of the economic foundation the entire immense superstructure is more or less rapidly transformed.[20]

Marx's formulation of the state as an economic actor is simple, clear, and powerful and has been tremendously influential. Contemporary political science has sometimes followed Marx's tendency to reduce the state to an expression of underlying economic realities. Exponents of "modernization theory" in the 1950s and 1960s focused almost exclusively on economic variables. Seymour Martin Lipset, a denizen of the movement, noted the irony in 1960: "The association between economic development and democracy has led many Western statesmen and political commentators to conclude that the basic political problem of our day is produced by the pressure for rapid industrialization." Fix the economy, and democracy will follow. He concludes, "This view marks the victory of economic determinism or vulgar Marxism within democratic political thought."[21]

Lipset rightly frowned on the "vulgarity" of economic determinism. It is reductionist and underemphasizes other aspects of statehood. If Tilly reduced the state to brute force and Hegel to mere religion, Marx reduced it to economic forces. None are a helpful way of looking at statehood in isolation. But just as it would be wrong to overreact to Hegel by turning to Marx, so it would be wrong to overreact against Marx by denying the state's economic dimension altogether. Marx was neither the first nor the last to highlight the state's relationship to the economy. Even the thinkers of classical economic liberalism acknowledge a role for the state. The state must at least raise revenue to pay for the army, police, and courts to guarantee peace, maintain order, and adjudicate disputes. State regulation that mandates disclosure of information is also consistent with classical economic liberalism because free, full, and perfect information is a precondition for a fully competitive and efficient market.

20. Ibid., 3–6.
21. Lipset, *Political Man*, 68.

A Tool for Serving Human Life

Finally, the state is a tool for serving human life. The state is a *human* institution, concerned with *human* affairs, and claims to be dedicated to *human* good. The state is a collection of human beings acting in ways that relate to other human beings. This is not an obvious tautology. This dimension of statehood is underappreciated, with real results for how we think of states and their behavior. Because the state is fundamentally a human-regarding institution, its quality can be assessed in part according to how it treats human beings and what effect it has on human life.

Including this dimension of statehood is an important counterbalance to the earlier discussion of the cultural dimension of statehood. In our earlier discussion about the state as a carrier of public norms about justice, I refrained from adjudicating between competing theories of justice, implying that any theory of justice was valid for defining statehood and that we cannot condemn some states as failed or illegitimate states on the grounds that we disagree with how they claim legitimacy; it is enough *that* they claim legitimacy, and do so successfully within their realms. With this dimension of statehood—the state as a servant and tool of humanity—I am reestablishing a small place from which to make claims about the validity of states, claims with limited criteria (how states treat humans) but universal scope. The ability to make these kinds of claims has important implications for our understanding of what causes state failure, our definition of a failed state, and the insight that there are different kinds of failed states.

Aristotle articulated the classic case for the state as a tool for human good. He defined the state as the association whose aim is the good of human flourishing. The good of its citizens—of all human beings—is to act "in conformity with excellence or virtue." Politics is the science of this good. He said, "The end of politics is the best of ends; and the main concern of politics is to engender a certain character in the citizens and to make them good and disposed to perform noble actions." The statesman is to "devote special attention to excellence, since it is his aim to make the citizens good and law-abiding." The good is defined as happiness, which is found in the contemplative life.[22]

Aristotle's conception of the state's fundamental character as human regarding was tied to his teleological conception of human life and the good. Later thinkers and statesmen, unable to agree on what was the purpose and good of human life, jettisoned teleology as a legitimate basis for public philosophy. In the twentieth and twenty-first centuries,

22. Aristotle, *Nicomachean Ethics*, Book I: 7, 9, 13. See also Book I: 2, 4, and Book X: 7–8.

University of Chicago professor Martha Nussbaum has attempted to re-cast an Aristotelian conception of human flourishing, and to use that as a better criterion by which to assess development efforts in poor states, without teleological commitments. Nussbaum composed a list of central functions that all human beings perform, capabilities without the posses-sion of which one is not fully human. These capabilities are the most basic and fundamental outlines or boundaries of human life, some of which are "ground floor" capabilities beneath which we are more akin to mere beasts, others of which are outer limits beyond which we would be more akin to gods. She included mortality, health, sensations of plea-sure and pain (minimizing nonuseful amounts of the latter), use of the five senses, imagination, cognition, commitment to things and people outside of us, love, the ability to show concern, the ability to form a rela-tion to nature, laughter, the singleness of being human, and the ability to 'form a conception of the good' and to plan one's life. Broadly speaking, Nussbaum drew the contours of human life around the physical body, social interaction, and certain intellectual and emotional operations. Nussbaum's intention is explicitly political. She intends to use the list to measure development progress, social justice, and the "quality of life" in poor countries. She writes, "We cannot tell how a country is doing unless we know how the people in it are able to function in the central human ways." Implicit in her political intention is an understanding of what states are: states are tools for facilitating basic human functioning. Devel-opment is not a matter of increasing GDP per capita, which can mask gross inequalities and the effect of money on human functioning, but of facilitating better human lives, as defined by the core, universal human functions.[23]

The state as a tool for human life is tied to its role as a provider of pub-lic goods, and in turn to the state's theory of justice. The goods it pro-vides often contribute to human flourishing, and the promotion of human flourishing is also often (but not always) a part of a state's claim to legitimacy. The two aspects of statehood are distinguishable, however: what counts as a public good varies across time and cultures; but human needs and human functioning are universal.

SUMMARY

There are five enduring themes in political thought about the nature of statehood. The five dimensions of statehood are interrelated. The provision of public goods constitutes, in part, the state's claim to

---

23. Nussbaum, "Human Functioning and Social Justice," 202–46.

legitimacy and makes up part of its theory of justice. The provision of security and protection of human functioning can be seen as the paramount goods it provides. The state's economic management is part of its contract with the population. Because these five enduring themes of political thought are interrelated, we can synthesize them to reformulate a definition of the state, building on Weber's but incorporating other aspects of statehood:*The state is a human institution that successfully invokes a theory of justice: (1) to claim the monopoly of the legitimate use of physical force, the right to expropriate resources and perform other functions at its discretion, and sovereign authority to make and enforce rules within a given territory and over a given human population, and to serve human life; (2) by providing (professedly) public goods to at least some of the population in a contractlike exchange: goods for legitimacy (agreement to its claims). The kind of goods that the state provides are cast in terms of the theory of justice that the state embodies, and the provision of just services constitute, in part, the state's claim to legitimacy.*

This definition has advantages over other definitions of the state. Some contemporary definitions stress the state's responsibility to provide specific goods, such as welfare and education, to the population. By that standard, almost all regimes in history were failed states until the nineteenth century. Others stress the state's responsibility to respect human rights, a definition that would disqualify most regimes until after World War II. Others neglect the human aspect of governance, leading to a disregard for governments' records of mass atrocities. The definition developed in this section is historically flexible while still allowing us to assess the quality of statehood in different times and cultures against a common standard.

Similarly, many definitions of the state focus explicitly on the "nation-state" or the "modern state" or the "industrial state," as if the definition of government changed according to the extent of territory, temporal location, or socioeconomic circumstances with which the state is associated. I have attempted to develop a definition of statehood thin enough to apply equally well to great powers, weak states, microsovereignties, city-states, and multinational empires; to modern and premodern polities; and to industrial and traditional societies, and yet thick enough to say meaningful things about when states fail. The dimensions or aspects of statehood outlined here could, in theory, be applied to any form of sovereign human political authority. It is not a definition of any particular kind of state. We need a definition at this level of generality in order not to prejudice a theory of state building toward any particular kind of state from the outset (although later we will consider unique aspects of building a liberal, democratic state).

[4]

State Failure

There is little consensus about what constitutes a "failed state." As a consequence, "state failure" as it is used in the literature is often an underspecified term. Helman and Ratner, whose 1992 article *Saving Failed States* set the research agenda for the field, did not offer a robust definition of a failed state beyond one which is "utterly incapable of sustaining itself" and "simply unable to function as [an] independent entit[y]."[1] Some scholars use an implicit "know it when you see it" definition. A failed state is thus one that does not uphold public order or deliver basic services to its citizens, and/or one in which the rule of law has broken down and private actors exercise coercion with impunity; in which economic activity has slowed, halted, or even reversed; in which indicators of human development, such as infant mortality, life expectancy, access to water and electricity, and literacy are among the worst in the world; and/or one which cannot exercise sovereign authority within its territory. The problem with this definition is that there are so many criteria that are so flexible, and scholars freely use an "and/or" approach to the criteria, so that the number of failed states can be nearly zero if the criteria are strictly applied, or several scores of them, if they are loosely applied. The concept often is stretched so far as to lose its meaning or restricted so narrowly as to be rarely applicable.

An early and influential attempt to define and measure state failure came from the State Failure Task Force, a US government-funded research project starting in 1994 to assess the causes of state failure and help

---

1. Helman and Ratner, "Saving Failed States," 3–20.

policymakers identify cases. The task force defined four types of state failure events—revolutionary war, ethnic war, adverse regime change, and genocide—and measured the extent of failure for each case in each type of failure. The task force's data set still represents the largest and most comprehensive effort to operationalize and measure state failure, and has helped advance the field considerably. Of particular note for this book, the task force differentiates state failure both by degree and by type: it considers both that there are different kinds of state failure and that they fail in different degrees. However, the task force focuses almost entirely on violent failure. Only the "adverse regime change" type of failure incorporates variables that measure the collapse of democratic institutions and the growth of autocracy. None of the data sets measure economic performance, the delivery of public goods, or regime legitimacy.[2]

Scholars generally followed the task force's lead. William Zartman's analysis is typical. Zartman defines the state as "the authoritative political institution that is sovereign over a recognized territory," which he claims incorporates three aspects of statehood: sovereignty, institutions, and coercion. He then defines collapsed states are ones that "can no longer perform the functions required for them to pass as states." We would expect him to define three types of collapse: a failure of sovereignty, institutional capacity, and security. Zartman fails, however, to match these attributes of statehood to types of failure and collapse. In fact he notes that a state can collapse from paralysis, territorial insecurity, loss of symbolic power, loss of legitimacy, socioeconomic failure, and breakdown of law and order. Zartman does not draw a clear line from what a state is to how states fail. He resorts to listing many bad things that happen in and to weak and failing states, and offers his list as a definition. It is unclear from Zartman's definition which states count as collapsed or why.[3]

Sebastian von Einsiedel does not advance the argument beyond Zartman's analysis. He defines the state from three viewpoints: as a social contract, a coercive force, and a legal entity. Like Zartman, he fails to link his definition of the state to types of state failure. He reviews and rejects attempts to construct a typology of state failure and offers a definition that state failure is "a continuum of circumstances that afflict states with weak institutions—ranging from states in which basic services are neglected to the total collapse of governance."[4] Einsiedel's definition captures the considerable ambiguity surrounding the concept of state failure without clarifying it. What his definition gains in generality it loses in underspecification: it is neither operationalizable by scholars nor usable by policymakers.

2. Marshall, Gurr, and Harff, "Political Instability Task Force."
3. Zartman, "Introduction: Posing the Problem of State Collapse," 1–14.
4. Einsiedel, "Policy Responses to State Failure," 13–35.

Jean-Germain Gros has advanced the argument by offering a typology of state failure. He begins by adopting an incorrect version of Weber's definition (omitting, like others, that the state *successfully claims* the monopoly on the legitimate use of force). He adds that contemporary states also attempt to provide a range of services, so that states today are also institutions that perform extractive, regulatory, and redistributive functions. He then defines state failure as the failure to uphold the social contract, understood largely as the delivery of security and public goods. He rightly avoids measuring statehood against the standard of Western public goods, noting that it would automatically categorize poor states as failed, even if they are well governed. There is a spectrum of weakness, failure, and collapse along which states can be measured. He identifies five types of state according to the degree of their failure: anarchic, phantom, anemic, captured, and aborted. His analysis is an advance on Zartman's and Einsiedel's, but it still contains difficulties. His typology of state failure is unrelated to his definition of the state. As a result, he claims to distinguish between degrees of failure, not types of failure based on what parts of the state have failed. But then, in his analysis, he begins to make distinctions between types of failure, not degrees—for example, talking about the difference between states afflicted by insurgency and those that are not, or states that are institutionally weak versus those that are effective but ruled autocratically. Ironically, his typology is most convincing when it departs from his argument about quantities of failure and addresses these qualitative differences among failed states. He also distinguishes between types of failure and causes of failure—a distinction not always recognized in the literature.[5]

Robert Rotberg follows Gros in developing a typology of failed states based on their degree of failure. He distinguishes only three degrees of failure: *weak* states, *failing* states, and *collapsed* states. His analysis is more consistent in focusing solely on the degree of failure, not the kind of failure, and thus is better at illustrating the weakness of that approach. While helpful, one problem with this distinction is that actual failed states rarely fail equally across all institutions and sectors of governance; concomitantly, no matter how one defines each level or degree of failure, one can usually find exceptional cases of states that appear collapsed by some criteria but merely failing by other.[6]

These analyses have failed because they treat state failure as a singular phenomenon that occurs at varying degrees of intensity. The policy community has largely followed these analyses. For example, the Fund for Peace's Failed State Index examines several criteria, aggregates them

---

5. Gros, "Towards a Taxonomy of Failed States," 455–71.
6. Rotberg, "Failure and Collapse of Nation-States," 1–50.

into a single number, and ranks all failed states on a single scale. The resulting rankings illustrate the problem with treating state failure as a singular phenomenon. Sudan, Zimbabwe, Guinea, Burma, and North Korea were all ranked "critical" in the 2010 ranking. But so were Somalia and the Democratic Republic of the Congo. The biggest problem in the former group of states is tyranny. The biggest problem in the latter group is chaos. One group suffers from too much power and authority in the government; the other from too little. Or, to take another example, both Haiti and Afghanistan are also listed as "critical." One is entirely at peace but suffers from chronic institutional breakdown; the other is in the midst of a shooting war.

The point is not to criticize the Fund for Peace, whose work has been a valuable and helpful contribution to the discussion. But it is not clear how useful it is to lump tyrannies and anarchies together, or states suffering from war and violence together with those suffering from endemic institutional weakness. Somalia simply did not fail in the same way that North Korea did. The challenges in Haiti are fundamentally different from those in Afghanistan. And because they are so different, policymakers and scholars seeking to address state failure, rebuild failed states, and prevent state failure in the future need a better conceptual tool for understanding it in the first place. Charles Call has gone so far as to proclaim the "failure of the 'failed state' concept."[7] He argues that the concept aggregates diverse states with widely differing challenges, leads to a cookie-cutter approach to state building, hides from the inherently political questions of democracy and democratization, conflates state building with peace building, and rests on a paternalistic and condescending attitude toward the developing world. Other scholars have expanded on this last point, accusing the West of deploying the concept of "failed state" as a way of "blaming the victims" for their condition without any reference to the historical process—Western imperialism—that contributed to their failure,[8] passing judgment on the developing world for "deviancy" and "aberration,"[9] and justifying intervention in failed states.[10]

More constructive literature has begun to disaggregate the concept of state failure into various typologies. Call, for example, proposes a fourfold typology, differentiating between collapsed states, states with weak formal institutional capacity, war-torn states, and authoritarian states[11]; or, in a separate article, between security, legitimacy, and capacity gaps.[12]

7. Call, "Fallacy of the 'Failed State,'" 1491–1507.
8. Jones, "Global Political Economy of Social Crisis," 180–205.
9. Morton, "'Failed State' of International Relations," 371–79.
10. Boas and Jennings, "'Failed States' and 'State Failure,'" 475–85.
11. Call, "Fallacy of the 'Failed State.'"
12. Call, "Beyond the 'Failed State,'" 303–26.

Others have proposed various typologies of failed states, distinguishing between failures in security, representation, and welfare;[13] capacity and will;[14] authority, legitimacy, and capacity;[15] or public finance as distinct from capacity.[16] These typologies are an improvement over the older literature because they capture the insight that different states fail in different ways and that a key to understanding various subtypes of failure is to look at different aspects of statehood.

However, these typologies have weaknesses. For example, Call's list of states that face a legitimacy gap are stable autocracies, but his prescription for how to close the legitimacy gap addresses the problem of elections in postconflict societies. Call's legitimacy gap is thus ambiguous, encompassing states actively looking for alternative sources of legitimacy in the aftermath of war and dictatorships resistant to change. These are two very different scenarios that call for different responses by state builders. In addition, Call has no category for economic failure and no prescription for rebuilding collapsed economies. Milliken and Krause do, but they only conceive of legitimacy in terms of representation, limiting its applicability. Stewart's introduction of "will" is an important contribution, but he couples it with an overly broad concept of "capacity" to capture every other aspect of statehood. Additionally, Call and most others treat failure as a binary variable: failure has either occurred or it has not, making operationalization and measurement of failure rough, arbitrary, and often inaccurate.

More broadly, it is unclear how these typologies have been derived. They appear to be little more than assertions about what makes up statehood, without an investigation into the political theory literature that addresses that very question. A review of political theory yields a richer and more robust understanding of statehood on which to refine and build a typology of state failure.

Drawing on the definition of the state developed in the previous chapter, we can more easily see that there are different kinds of state failure because states can fail in any one or more of the five dimensions of statehood. Failed states can exhibit violence, injustice, incompetence, privation, or barbarity—a failure of, respectively, security, legitimacy, capacity, prosperity, or humanity. Thus there are five types of state failure: *anarchic, illegitimate, incapable, unproductive, and barbaric.* An anarchic state is one in which there is no security. An illegitimate state is one in which the

13. Milliken and Krause, "State Failure, State Collapse, and State Reconstruction," 1–21.
14. Stewart, "Weak States and Global Threats."
15. Carment, Yiagadeesen, and Prest, "State Fragility," 349–73.
16. Cliffe and Manning, "Practical Approaches," 163–84.

people no longer believe the state's claims about justice. An incapable state is unable to deliver public goods and services. In an unproductive state there is little to no reliable production and exchange of material goods and services and the government cannot extract sufficient resources. A barbaric state treats its own people as an enemy and systematically murders large numbers of them as a matter of policy. This typology improves on recent efforts to develop a typology of failed states by incorporating insights for political theory to develop a fuller and more robust understanding of statehood.[17]

For example, Haiti in 1915 was anarchic, incapable, and poor; it was probably illegitimate; but it was not inhumane. Haiti in 1993 was still incapable and poor, but no longer anarchic. Croatia in 1996 was recovering from an anarchic situation, but it struggled with few, if any, other kinds of failure. Afghanistan, as I argue in chapter 7, is unique in that it failed across all dimensions of statehood—what we could call "comprehensively failed." Some states show only weakness across most dimensions of statehood, with perhaps one or two dimensions failing.

THE ANARCHIC STATE

Three considerations describe security failure and explain how state builders must approach it: the historical pathway to security collapse, the perception of the local population, and the probability of recidivism.

First, there are different historical pathways by which security breaks down. Different pathways yield different dynamics of failure with which state builders have to cope. Probably the easiest security failure occurs in new states recently freed from imperial control that do not yet have strong security institutions. New states often have just fought a war for independence, have a well-armed citizenry but poor command and control over security forces, and are still developing judicial and correctional

17. It would be possible to refine and build on this typology further. The five types of failure can occur independently or (more typically) in combination, yielding thirty-two possible combinations of one or more types of failure, each of which could be described. Furthermore, failure is not simply an "on/off" event, as if states were either entirely failed or not at all. We could reintroduce the idea of different degrees to which states fail, combining Rotberg's three degrees of failure with the five types of failure, which would then generate ninety-six possible combinations. Obviously, this is unwieldy and, considering that the number of types may equal or surpass the number of actual failed states, unnecessary. More usefully, we might develop a data set of state failure, measuring each of the five dimensions described here and then examine the data for patterns to see if failed states cluster together in any particular combinations and explore if types of failure are correlated. That would be a fruitful avenue of research, but it is unnecessary for my purposes.

[58]

institutions. However, citizens in a newly independent state enjoy a greater sense of unity than citizens in a state recovering from civil war, and they are unlikely to fight one another or outside powers that have helped them. In the four cases of state building in newly independent states—Cuba in 1898, South Korea, Namibia, and Timor-Leste—the internal threat environment was relatively benign.

A more challenging type of security failure is present in states recovering from civil war, the most common type of security failure with which state builders have had to cope since the Cold War. Civil war continues to damage a state's security environment even after organized political violence has stopped. Security forces are often degraded in terms of personnel and equipment and too militarized for normal civilian policing. Civil war and its aftermath provides cover for violent criminal activity (the distinction between criminals and insurgents is often a key problem for counterinsurgents) and encourages the spread of weaponry throughout society. Post–civil war societies typically are home to several heavily armed groups. Civil wars can embitter citizens of a state against one another and make political compromise much more difficult. A culture of impunity for past war crimes and casual violence may prevail in the absence of strong transitional justice mechanisms, emboldening past perpetrators to commit future crimes. In post–civil war situations, citizens are likely to feel insecure because of crime and lawlessness, the prospect of renewed fighting, and the presence of well-armed militias nearby. It is not always clear if the war has ended or simply entered a lull.

The most challenging security failure is present in states with an ongoing civil and/or interstate war. This includes ongoing civil war in which international military forces are not targeted by combatants, including Angola, Cambodia, Liberia in 1993, Rwanda in 1993–4, the Democratic Republic of the Congo in 1999, and Sudan since 2005, and cases in which they are, including Iraq, Afghanistan, the Democratic Republic of the Congo in 1960, South Vietnam after 1962, Nicaragua in 1927, Haiti from 1918 to 1920, and Somalia in 1993.[18]

---

18. Another category is at least conceptually possible: state building in the midst of an interstate war *without* an overlapping civil war. The category is a null set. Italy and South Vietnam are the only cases that might be considered state-building operations in the midst of an interstate, not civil, war. However, in Italy state builders only operated in the areas of liberated Italian territory; they never attempted state building in areas still contested by the interstate war. The security environment for the state builders in Italy was thus quite permissive. The nature of violence in Vietnam was complex, involving an interstate conflict between the United States and South Vietnam against North Vietnam; to the extent that it also involved violence from indigenous South Vietnamese insurgents, it was also a civil war among the Vietnamese people, and thus fits the civil war model.

States defeated in interstate war present a unique situation. Histori-cally, states defeated in interstate war and targeted for a state-building mission, including Germany, Japan, and Italy, have presented a permis-sive security environment to state builders in that local citizens did not violently resist the occupiers. Security remains fragile in such cases: the destruction of its own security forces renders the state unable to provide security at home; at the same time the state's defeat erodes its legitimacy and can embolden domestic opponents to move against the regime.[19] But in these cases, there is no civil war and no organized resistance to the victorious power. However, state builders in these cases can face a differ-ent kind of security challenge: upholding basic law and order. States de-feated in interstate war may experience a complete breakdown of public order. The military has been defeated and delegitimized, and police may be simply unwilling or unable to enforce order for a time after the re-gime's defeat, as apparently happened in Iraq in 2003. In those situations the security environment can turn rapidly from permissive to anarchic.

The second consideration that defines security failure is the perception of the local population of the international power. Local citizens might be especially welcoming of state builders who arrive to help in the after-math of a liberation struggle for independence against an imperial power. On the other hand, some may resent an armed state-building mis-sion as an infringement on their newly won and jealously guarded inde-pendence, as was partly the case in Cuba in 1898 and perhaps in Timor-Leste in 1999. In the case of a state defeated in interstate war, some local citizens might be resentful of the occupying power and inclined to resist it, as was the case in Iraq. Others may be resigned to the presence of the occupier as the only way of restoring their country, as appeared to be the case in West Germany and Japan.[20] Citizens in a state recovering from, or in the midst of, a civil war are especially prone to react in diverse ways to an international intervention depending on whether they be-lieve the international actors are neutral or, if not, whose side they are on.

Third, armed conflict often recurs. The conditions that prevail in the aftermath of conflict are conducive to more conflict: the simple fact that security failure has happened at all makes future security failure more likely, especially if the underlying causes of conflict (such as the alloca-tion of resources) remain unresolved. One of the key dilemmas facing state builders is that they do not know in advance if a war has really stopped or if it is only in a short hiatus. In fact, the security situation in a failed state replicates the dilemma of Schrödinger's cat: it is impossible

19. Fazal, "State Death in the International System," 311–44.
20. Edelstein, "Occupational Hazards," 49–91; Edelstein, *Occupational Hazards*.

to say definitively if a war has ended until after a prospective state builder has made a choice either to intervene or not. By choosing, the state builder has "opened the box." The state builder's own actions and behavior crucially affect whether the war is definitively over or not. Another way of putting it is that the historical situation continues to evolve after an intervention begins. The clear implication for international state builders is that they must continuously evaluate the security situation after an intervention begins to monitor the true extent of security failure and be prepared to rapidly change their security strategy accordingly. All states in which armed state-building operations were attempted experienced massive security failures prior to the intervention (except Haiti in 1993 and Iraq in 2003). But in some cases anarchy continued during the intervention (such as in the Democratic Republic of the Congo in 1960, Angola, and Afghanistan), while others saw relative order restored quickly (such as in West Germany, Bosnia, and Namibia). Whether or not security failure continues *during* an armed state-building operation is a crucial variable for state builders. A mismatch on this dimension of state building virtually guarantees failure, as happened in Liberia in 1993, Angola, and Rwanda.

THE ILLEGITIMATE STATE

In the illegitimate state people stop believing the state's claims, or no longer agree with the state's theory of justice: its claim to legitimacy is no longer *successful*, in Weber's terms. There are two ways the claim to legitimacy could fail. First, the state might appeal to norms of justice that are no longer accepted by the wider society; the state's idea of justice may come to differ from those of major social influencers or simply from the everyday experience of most people. Second, the state's appeal to widely accepted norms may not be credible if its claim is systematically inconsistent with its actions. In either case, citizens in the illegitimate state no longer identify with it. They are no longer willing to invest in its success or align themselves with its efforts or identify with its claims. There is widespread disenchantment with the state. A civil war or insurgency—types of security failure—usually stems from a prior failure of legitimacy among part of the population. A consistent and steady failure to provide services can gradually undermine the state's legitimacy, while ethnic cleansing or genocide—what I call a barbaric failure, below—can destroy it much more quickly.

This type of failure is harder to measure and often shows up only retrospectively with other types of failure. We can measure the loss of legitimacy directly through public opinion polling—which is usually

[61]

unavailable in failing states—or, anecdotally, through incidents of civil disobedience; media reports; local editorials (if allowed); sermons; reports from refugees, expatriates, emigrants, and civil society groups; and through the growth of alternative sources of power. Indirectly, we can measure a loss of legitimacy through proxy variables, most of which are associated with the other dimensions of statehood.

This type of state failure encompasses failures of democracy. States that invoke democracy as their legitimizing theory of justice weaken their claims to legitimacy if they restrict the types of people who are allowed to participate in politics, the means of peaceful public contestation, or both. Democratic states loose legitimacy if they ban certain groups—such as an ethnic or religious minority—from full citizenship, censor the press, control information, deny free expression and free association, restrict candidates for office, or simply do not hold or respect the outcome of elections.

THE INCAPABLE STATE

The incapable state is incapable of upholding its part of the social contract. It is unable to deliver the sort of public goods that its supporters expect. Because the contract is often mediated through institutions that perform functions and provide goods, the incapable state is characterized by weak or collapsed institutions that lack the equipment, training, skilled personnel, or leadership to function.

For most modern states, this type of failure is much easier to measure than a legitimacy failure. Most modern states aspire to provide their citizens with a package of goods ranging from welfare, education, and health care to infrastructure, housing, and electricity. Their failures show up clearly in the statistics of social and human development; these same statistics often serve as benchmarks of progress (or regress) for development, state building, and foreign assistance programs. Institutional failure thus is correlated with low literacy; low school enrollment rates; low life expectancy; low levels of access to roads, electricity, water, and sanitation; high rates of disease and mortality; and other familiar indicators. We can also measure a state's ability to extract revenue from the economy as a percentage of GDP.

Scholars and state builders should be careful before assuming that the public goods provided by secular industrialized rich states are the only ones that matter. Not all states aspire to provide the same package of goods. Other public goods are less tangible. For example, Afghanistan, even after the Taliban, constituted itself as an "Islamic republic" and continued to pay imams and mullahs from the public treasury: Afghans

[62]

expected the state to play a role in providing spiritual services. Other states may aspire to provide a sense of nationhood or unity for their people, or to promote local and indigenous culture against global influences. Such services may in fact be more important to the legitimacy of some states than modern infrastructure or reliable retirement insurance. Measuring these aspects of the social contract is harder than measuring the above indicators.

THE UNPRODUCTIVE STATE

The unproductive state has failed in its role as an economic actor. An economic state failure can take a number of different forms. The unproductive state may be unable to extract enough resources to function because of institutional decay, general privation, or a failure to enforce tax compliance or collect customs revenue. The state then falls into a vicious cycle: the poorer it is, the less able it is to enforce its writ and collect further resources. The unproductive state may be unable or unwilling to use its resources for their intended purposes because of massive corruption. It may do proactive harm to broader economic forces by fostering— through war, confiscation, or maladministration—a societywide economic failure characterized by rent seeking and resource looting rather than the production and exchange of material goods and services.

Economic failure may be correlated with a high dependence on natural resources or international aid as in the case of "rentier states."[21] States that derive most of their revenue from windfalls and outside sources can deliver generous subsidies to powerful supporters and need not encourage production and exchange of goods and services. They also lack the incentive to tax their citizens; without taxation, the state is less likely to be held accountable by citizens or feel beholden to them. The state's primary constituency becomes the operators of the resource-extraction industry or international donors instead of the citizens of the state. In this scenario—which has played out often enough that scholars coined the term "resource curse" to describe it—a primary economic link between state and society is broken and the two grow increasingly isolated from each other.[22] Some rentier states are able to resist the trap and do not fail; and states with large natural resources may have an above-average GDP. But over time such states often are unable to translate gross wealth into

---

21. Beblawi, "Rentier State in the Arab World," 85–98; Beblawi and Luciani, *Rentier State.*
22. Ross, "Natural Resource Curse," 17–42; Ross, "Political Economy of the Resource Curse," 297–322.

[63]

productivity, higher standards of living, or reliable revenue because of poor diversification, corruption, a weak rule of law, or a lack of redistributional social programs. Because of their wealth these states may survive for decades, but they cannot be said to be economically productive.

A more common type of economic state failure in states targeted for armed state building is the destruction of normal economic life and distortion of economic incentives because of war. War can create a specific type of economic state failure. By destroying infrastructure and suspending the rule of law, war undermines the basis for production and commerce. In place of normal economic activity, war creates alternate economic incentives—for example, smuggling, the arms trade, private security services, unregulated labor markets, and privatized or criminalized governance services.[23] These dynamics are often exacerbated in states with large amounts of natural or easily lootable resources, such as oil (Angola, Sudan, Iraq), diamonds (Sierra Leone, Liberia), or timber and poppy (Afghanistan). Such resources make it easier for armed groups to finance themselves and carry on fighting even after normal economic activity has slowed. Once vested in an economy of looting and illicit trade, armed groups tend to resist a return to peace and the end to their sources of prosperity that peace brings. By lowering the cost of fighting and raising the cost of peace, lootable resources tend to lengthen the duration of wars and entrench the power of ex-combatants after a return to peace. Such resources can even play a role in the onset of (or reversion to) a civil war. Groups with grievances can invoke a supposedly unfair distribution of natural resource wealth as a triggering mechanism for their cause and, if they capture the resource, to fund their cause.[24] Nonetheless, reconstruction can be easier and more straightforward in states devastated by war than in states with more complicated forms of economic failure. War artificially dampens economic life; the return of peace typically brings a sharp economic boom. Italy grew by more than 30 percent in 1946; Afghanistan by more than 28 percent in 2002, and Sierra Leone by more than 20 percent in 2002. (The presence or absence of such a boom can in fact be an indicator of local perceptions of whether war has indeed stopped or merely paused.) In addition, at least some economic recovery is a simple matter of rebuilding infrastructure destroyed by war, such as roads, power grids, and water facilities.

Finally, economic state failure can take the form of massive economic underperformance, manifested in widespread, extreme poverty and privation separate from—though often exacerbated by—the effects of war

---

23. Cramer, "Trajectories of Accumulation," 129–48.
24. Fearon, "Why Do Some Civil Wars Last?," 275–301; Lujala, Gleditsch, and Gilmore, "Diamond Curse?," 538–62.

or the resource curse. Some states' institutional weakness simply prevents citizens from engaging in meaningful economic activity. This type of failure is not simple poverty: Botswana is a poor but stable and functioning state. Nor are traditional societies with pastoral or subsistence economies failed states (although it is doubtful any purely "traditional society" exists any longer). States that try to transition to industrial economies and fail are: they are typically mired by large, unemployed, unskilled urban populations uprooted from rural areas and who have few economic prospects, thus becoming an outright burden and even a threat to the state. Agriculture is no longer sufficient to sustain either the state's needs or individuals' aspirations, but industry is underdeveloped and stagnant. This sort of economic state failure is often the result of long-term state weakness, shallow human and social capital, poor education, corruption, inept or negligent regulation, or a general social and institutional unpreparedness for economic transformation. These causes are often, though not necessarily, coupled with and worsened by war or resource dependency: Haiti's endemic poverty, for example, does not result from war or the resource curse.

THE BARBARIC STATE

The barbaric state actively seeks to undermine human good. The clearest expression of the barbaric state is one that deliberately murders its own citizens. It makes genocide state policy, as was the case with Nazi Germany, Khmer Cambodia, Rwanda under the Interahamwe, Milosevic's Serbia, and an unfortunately long list of other regimes. A lesser degree of barbarism is present in states that seek to undermine human good by means short of murder. For example, the barbaric state bans not only certain speech and expression (nearly all states regulate speech to some degree) but attempts to criminalize and punish mere *thoughts* and *beliefs* (expressed or not), tries to compel belief in an official ideology (like North Korea's *juche*), and regulates the conception of the good that citizens are allowed to have, as is the case with the Iranian theocracy. More typically, the barbaric state typically combines totalitarianism with murder.

The label "barbaric" is meant to identify only the very worst offenders. Most states have been cruel and brutal at different points in their history; I am seeking to identify a separate category of exceptional cruelty or systematic brutality, the cases of such widespread murder that it "shocks the conscience of the world" and stands out in history. Including this as a criterion of state failure reinforces that states fail in different ways, and there are different kinds of failed states. Highly murderous regimes can in fact be quite effective at what they do and retain a high degree of monopoly on the use of force. There is no anarchic violence or civil war in North Korea. Nazi Germany had a well-functioning bureaucracy and was successfully addressing the economic challenges of the Great Depression.

This may be a controversial criterion by which to measure state failure because people and governments disagree about what constitutes human good. However, as I argued earlier, we can formulate a minimum, least-common-denominator, universal definition of human flourishing. Governments that promote, or at least do not harm, the minimal bases of human life retain a crucial aspect of what it means to "govern" a human community. Governments that deliberately and systematically murder or oppress their own citizens, for example, are not "governing" by any reasonable definition of the word. That the governments in question would disagree and claim that their policies promote someone's good is irrelevant. A subset of the population of these states may even view the oppression and murder of another part of the population as a legitimate service—the service of "ethnic cleansing." That does not obligate the international community to agree or to recognize the legitimacy of such a state. The growth of international humanitarian norms suggests that respect for basic human functioning serves as a "standard of civilization" by which to judge the fitness of regimes to be recognized as governments.[25] As Augustine rhetorically asked, long before Charles Tilly: "Remove justice, and what are kingdoms but gangs of criminals on a large scale?" Today we might ask: Remove a concern for human life, and what are statesmen but successful war criminals?

Some scholars may be uncomfortable with the value judgment implied by the label "barbaric," or argue that I am smuggling implied liberal premises into my argument. Such critics would be right that I am both making a value judgment and appealing to liberal norms; however, both, in my view, are strengths, not weakness, of my argument. My aspiration is that this book will be relevant for policymakers—specifically for liberal state builders—who must make regular value judgments by reference to liberal norms as a part of their normal responsibilities. Viewed from the policymakers' decision point, social science is not more insightful by aspiring to a fictional neutrality between murder and government, it simply sacrifices what relevance it might have for real human life.[26] For critics who insist on attempting such neutrality, this aspect of my theory is severable from the rest, which can still function without recognizing the human dimension of government.

25. Donnelly, "Human Rights," 1–23; Gong, *Standard of "Civilization."*
26. In other words, I am not "smuggling" liberalism into my theory; I am parading it.

The Dynamics of State Failure during State Building

State failure has a self-reinforcing dynamic. State failure sharpens the security dilemma at a personal level. It makes it harder for actors to reach mutual agreement on a theory of justice to legitimize collective action. By increasing selfishness and eroding norms and trust it also undermines the basis of institutional functioning and economic activity. Finally, at its worst, state failure rewards force and encourages raw coercion as a matter of course.

The vicious cycle affects the behavior of actors within a failed state. For example, war damage changes economic incentives and encourages illicit smuggling and looting. It also shortens the time horizon within which actors calculate the costs and benefits of their choices: immediate gains and losses far outweigh distant ones because of actors' uncertainty about their circumstances or even their survival in the medium and long term.

The insight is generalizable: all types of state failure increase uncertainty, shorten decision-making time horizons, impose higher costs on cooperation and higher benefits on the pursuit of self-interest. Importantly, this dynamic continues to hold even after a state-building operation is initiated. Local actors form beliefs and make choices regarding the international actors from within the vicious dynamic of state failure. They rarely unanimously bandwagon with the outside power to cooperate with the state-building program. Rather, they approach the state-building program by examining how their interests will be affected by it and choosing whether to cooperate with, co-opt, obstruct, or fight the outside power accordingly.

This aspect of state failure is underexamined in the literature. Michael Doyle, Ian Johnstone, and Robert Orr argue that state building is an "obsolescing bargain" in which an outside power has maximum leverage just prior to an intervention when it can still withhold investing resources without loss and when local actors are readiest to agree to conditions to secure international support. After an intervention begins, the outside power becomes more invested in ensuring success and therefore less and less able to extract itself, while local actors are more and more emboldened to use outside resources for their own gain.[27]

These concepts help describe the dynamics of state failure during a state-building operation, but they do not exhaust the range of possible problems. Local actors' pursuit of self-interest at the expense of state-building goals can lead to co-optation and conflict, but it can also lead to

---

27. Doyle, Johnstone, and Orr, *Keeping the Peace.*

free-riding. There is a moral hazard implicit in state building: outside actors are attempting to do what a failed state apparently could not. Local actors can then become insulated, for a time and to varying degrees, from the risks of governing, providing security, taxing, administering public services, or being accountable for the state's performance. With decreased risk but increased potential rewards from the state-building operation, they may choose to free-ride on the operation.

What determines local actors' choices? What causes some to cooperate, some to try to co-opt, some to free-ride, and others to fight? I propose to apply balance-of-power theory to the dynamic among local actors and between local and international actors to generate insights about what influences locals to cooperate with, free-ride on, or fight against state-building efforts.

Balance-of-power theory helps generate insights for the dynamic among actors in a state-building operation. State failure is the status quo in the context of a state-building operation. Local and international actors approach the conditions of state failure and state building with different perceptions, positions, and identities. International actors are a revisionist power because they seek to change the conditions of state failure. Warlords, black marketers, arms smugglers, organized criminal syndicates, and others who benefit from the conditions of failure will seek to preserve the status quo (sometimes by taking over state institutions to retain their illicit power). They are likely to perceive the state-building operation as a threat to their interests and adopt a basically unfriendly stance toward international actors. The footprint and duration dilemmas are especially sharp with respect to status quo powers.

State builders' problems are not limited to status quo powers that oppose the state-building program. State builders can also run into difficulties when buck passers free-ride on international resources. Local actors who advocate for reform, such as local democrats, loyalists of a regime in power prior to a civil war, and technocrats are likely to perceive the state-building program as consistent with their interests. They are likely to adopt a basically friendly stance toward the state builder but "pass the buck" for hard choices and tradeoffs to international state builders. The state builders' provision of resources can encourage local actors to withhold theirs, further undermining the development of the state. Local security forces can become risk averse because they can rely on the protection of better-armed and better-trained international security forces. Bureaucracies and other government institutions may actually degenerate further because they develop a destructive dependency on donor aid and outside consultants. Local investors and entrepreneurs may wait to see how economic opportunities are reshaped by donor activity before committing their own money and time, in which case donor aid does not prime the pump so much as it becomes the well. In a sense, state builders face another form of the footprint and duration dilemmas with local allies: the larger the footprint and the longer the duration, the greater the risk, not of opposition, but of apathy and moral hazard.

A crucial distinction for state builders is whether a majority sectarian group is a revisionist or a status quo power. In Iraq the majority Shia population was a revisionist power because they had been out of power under the Ba'athist regime and thus did not oppose the US-led coalition, while the minority Sunnis did. In Afghanistan ethnic minority groups that had opposed the Taliban, including the Tajik and Hazara, tolerated the state-building operation, while much of the counterinsurgency campaign was designed to keep as much of the plurality Pashtun population as possible from defecting and joining the insurgency to regain lost status. A state-building operation in which a majority group is a status quo power is not impossible—the UN seems to have managed the Serb population in Kosovo, for example—but it is surely easier when they are revisionist.

I have argued that local actors' basic disposition toward a state-building operation—friendly or unfriendly—is a function of their identities, positions, and perceptions. But describing their basic disposition does not yet answer the most crucial questions. Within a basically friendly disposition, local actors still have a range of possible behaviors, some helpful for the state-building program and some not. What causes some actors to cooperate instead of pass the buck? Similarly, within a basically unfriendly disposition, actors can chose degrees of opposition to state builders. What causes some to obstruct instead of oppose violently? I argue in the next chapter that those choices are at least partly a function of the state builder's strategy and its appropriateness to the conditions of state failure. State builders that do too much—whose strategy is too intensive for the failed state's needs—incentivize free-riding and buck-passing. State builders that do too little impose few costs on opposition to the state-building program and generate few benefits from it, thereby emboldening opposition and risking defection by local allies.

[5]

State Building

What is the right strategy for outside powers to turn violence into peace, injustice into justice, weak institutions into strong ones, poor countries into prosperous societies, and barbaric regimes into humane ones? Strategy is "the art of a commander-in-chief" and a "plan for successful action" in circumstances of "competition or conflict," according to the Oxford English Dictionary. According to the US Army, "*Strategy* is the art and science of developing and employing armed forces and other instruments of national power in a synchronized fashion to secure national or multinational objectives."[1] Or, more broadly, according to the Department of Defense, strategy is "a prudent idea or set of ideas for employing the instruments of national power in a synchronized and integrated fashion to achieve theater, national, and/or multinational objectives."[2] "Prudent" is the operative word: strategy is *practical wisdom* that guides actions to achieve defined results. Simply put, strategy is about problem solving. It is a plan for harnessing resources and executing action to achieve a desired goal.

The problem to be solved is state failure: extreme levels of violence, injustice, institutional breakdown, poverty, or barbarism. Although tactical and programmatic considerations also affect the outcome of a state-building operation, I focus on strategy because it is the necessary condition for success: as Sun Tzu is supposed to have said, "Strategy

---

1. US Department of the Army, *FM 3–0: Operations (2001)*, paragraphs 2–4. In the 2008 revision to *FM 3-0*, the Army replaced its definition with the definition that appears in *Joint Publication 1-02*.
2. US Department of Defense, *Joint Publication 1–02*, p. 294.

without tactics is the longest road to victory; tactics without strategy is the noise before defeat." Sun Tzu may have been exaggerating—strategy may be a necessary but not sufficient condition for success, and strategy without tactics may actually be the longest road to eventual defeat—but the right strategy surely increases the chances of success.

Surprisingly, there have been relatively few attempts to answer this set of broad questions. The literature on state building and peace building has focused heavily on case studies limited to single countries (with a major focus on Bosnia) or single sectors (especially the security sector). There is another portion of the literature approaching the problem from a so-called critical perspective, asking not about the causes of success and failure but questioning the assumptions and the merit of the entire project.

In this chapter I develop two different ways of defining strategies of state building. First, a strategy might be organized around an overarching goal that commands the state builder's priority of effort, such as security or liberalization (not to be confused with a set sequence). Second, a strategy might be organized around the degree of an intervention's invasiveness, that is, state builders could partner with local institutions, such as through security assistance programs, or simply take over, such as through a transitional administration. I develop each way of thinking about strategy and derive from them hypotheses about what causes success in armed state-building operations.

PRIORITY OF EFFORT

One way of understanding strategy is in reference to the goal it is designed to achieve. What is the goal of state building? The answer depends on one's understanding of statehood and of the processes of political change. At the risk of repeating some of the previous chapter, we again have to ask, what is the state, and how do states grow and change? The focus is not on how states fail, but how they are built. In this section I sketch four possible approaches to state building, drawn from the major theoretical paradigms of international relations.

Realist State Building

A realist approach to state building begins with a realist appraisal of statehood. The state is primarily a coercive force whose success depends on its ability to marshal material resources—guns and money—to enforce its exclusive sovereignty over a given territory. In this view,

[71]

domestic state building is a function of eliminating internal challengers,[3] and international armed state building will enable and contribute to this process.

This is not a straightforward matter of handing over cash and weapons to a favored local recipient, however. Like the relationship between allied states, the relationship between an intervening power and the nascent, emerging state must rest on shared interests. That is, they must both believe that cooperation increases their individual chance of survival and the growth of their power. This is most likely to happen when both actors face a common perceived threat and believe their alliance will help balance that threat.[4] Without that belief, the receiving state is likely to manipulate the intervening state into giving as much assistance as possible while avoiding the costs of cooperation. Thus, the threat environment is a key variable that explains state-building outcomes.[5]

Following a similar logic, that state building is a negotiation between self-interested actors, Barnett and Zurcher argue that there are four possible outcomes: cooperative, co-opted, captured, and conflictual state building. Cooperative state building is optimal and results in success. In co-opted state building, state and subnational elites agree to perform the rites of state building ceremonially in exchange for the continued inflow of outside resources; state builders agree to provide resources and claim incremental successes in exchange for leaving the basic structures of society more or less intact. In captured state building, the receiving state takes control of the state-building agenda and is able to manipulate the intervening power to get its money and support without having to pay the costs of state building. Conflictual state building is when the receiving state overtly resists the intervention. Barnett and Zurcher argue that co-opted state building is the likeliest outcome because local, state, and subnational elites all get to claim a victory.[6]

The realist approach broadly favors a strategic emphasis on security, with the additional detail that any state-building operation should be undertaken only for states that share interests with the intervening power. The problem, as with the "security first" approach, is that realist state building is not necessarily liberal state building. Strong local actors capable of commanding enough guns and money to eliminate internal opponents and set up a state structure that can enforce its writ are not necessarily Jeffersonian democrats.

3. Tilly, "War Making and State Making"; Tilly, *Coercion, Capital, and European States*.
4. Walt, *Origins of Alliances*, chap. 2.
5. Edelstein, "Occupational Hazards"; Edelstein, *Occupational Hazards*.
6. Barnett and Zurcher, "Peacebuilder's Contract."

Institutionalist State Building

An institutionalist approach to state building starts with an appreciation for the institutional features of the state to be rebuilt. Institutional design was an underemphasized aspect of statehood in comparative political science for decades, overlooked in favor of economic and social factors believed to be more fundamental to state behavior. Since the 1980s scholars have sought to "bring the state back in" to their analysis as an independent variable and an autonomous actor,[7] leading to some increased awareness that the type and shape of the state mattered. Domestic state building, in this view, involves careful attention to the design of constitutions, bureaucracies, and legal codes. International state building is largely an exercise in technical assistance, transmitting expertise and knowledge about the effects of different institutional choices,[8] and helping states design institutions that contain conflict, regularize political contestation, and balance power internally.

An institutionalist approach also emphasizes the roles of international institutions in the conduct of a state-building operation. International institutions help lower the costs of international cooperation and increase transparency, information sharing, and predictability.[9] International state building operations are typically multilateral efforts that require cooperation through the agency of international institutions, including the UN, World Bank, and IMF, suggesting that the institutionalist approach is relevant to state building.

The institutionalist approach would naturally lead to a strategic emphasis on building public institutions, investing in capacity building, and enhancing the rule of law.[10] Like the "institutionalization first" strategy, the institutionalist approach has drawbacks. It treats institution building as an apolitical, technical exercise and ignores the norms and the dynamics of power inherent in the attempt to transplant institutions from one society to another. It may also overstate state builders' ability to transmit institutions into the receiving state.

Liberal State Building

According to liberalism, the state is a tool for securing human liberty and, thereby, international peace.[11] Liberals do not deny that the state is

7. Evans, Rueschemeyer, and Skocpol, *Bringing the State Back In*; Nordlinger, *On the Autonomy of the Democratic State*; T. Skocpol, "Bringing the State Back In."
8. Fukuyama, *State-Building*, chap. 2.
9. Keohane, *After Hegemony*, esp. chaps. 4–7; Oye, *Cooperation under Anarchy*, chap. 1.
10. Paris, *At War's End*.
11. Doyle, "Liberalism and World Politics."

a coercive force but insist that it must serve some other purpose to secure the legitimacy that defines statehood. Statehood does not consist in the raw exercise of power, after all, but the publicly accepted exercise of power, and a commitment to human liberty is among the most successful grounds for legitimizing state power in history. State building, both domestic and international, requires holding elections and creating legal protections for individual political and economic liberties in exchange for citizens' loyalty to the state.

Scholars have noted that, in addition to its other virtues, liberalism seems to decrease the probability of war among liberal states, further bolstering liberalism's claim to be an effective tool of state building. Democratic leaders tend to select wars they feel confident of winning to protect their electability. To that end, they also devote more resources to wars once started and thus make unattractive targets for other regimes.[12] Democracies are less able to conceal their true capabilities, intentions, and resolve because they are open societies. Democracies are thus less able to bluff and less likely to initiate an unnecessary crisis, knowing that their true intentions and capabilities could be exposed, but they are also capable of giving a highly credible signal of true hostile intent if and when they are resolved on war.[13] Finally, these dynamics operate to create peace between two democracies because democratic leaders tend to perceive other liberal regimes as unthreatening but illiberal ones as untrustworthy.[14] The process of becoming more democratic may be temporarily destabilizing,[15] but once states consolidate democracy, they are more stable and less likely to fight other democracies.

Liberalism would naturally encourage a strategic emphasis on holding elections, writing liberal constitutions, and liberalizing economic governance. Its great strength is the wide support it can engender among a population, especially between formerly warring factions. Its popularity is so strong, in fact, that in every single case of international state building since the Cold War local parties have turned to elections, majority rule, and representative institutions as the preferred mechanism for peace building and political reconstruction. Its weakness, like the "liberalization first" paradigm, is that is can be destabilizing in the short term and naïve about the ability of postconflict societies to manage their own security or rebuild their own institutions.

12. Mesquita et al., "Institutional Explanation of the Democratic Peace."
13. Schultz, *Democracy and Coercive Diplomacy*.
14. Owen, *Liberal Peace, Liberal War*.
15. Mansfield and Snyder, *Electing to Fight*.

Constructivist State Building

In the constructivist paradigm, the state and the international system are socially constructed realities whose content and definition depend on the collective beliefs and perceptions of the people and states who inhabit them.[16] Constructivists would agree with the basic insight of liberals—that the state rests on norms for its legitimacy—but do not look only to liberal norms. State building is a matter of persuading people to believe in a common vision of the state and to behave accordingly. Meeting basic needs, such as for security and jobs, does not create legitimacy, in this view; rather, meeting those needs simply gives people the opportunity to formulate norms and aspirations, the fulfillment of which becomes their next demand on the state.[17] Just as states use "soft power" in relations with each other,[18] they must also use the same tools domestically to persuade people to accept its claims. International state building is a process of facilitating the transmission of those beliefs.

There are a number of difficulties with constructivist state building. One difficulty is that liberal constructivist state building must involve pushing the process of belief formation in the direction of Westphalian and liberal norms, which may not enjoy local sympathy or find a compatible conceptual framework on which to be grafted. Another is that orchestrating human perceptions and beliefs is notoriously hard, doubly so for actors foreign to the cultural context that they hope to change. The tools of belief formation and propagation—information operations, psychological operations, influence operations—are blunt and relatively in their infancy compared to conventional tools of diplomacy and military operations. Finally, constructivist state building cannot happen in a vacuum: blunt hard facts about material reality are often more influential in the formation of beliefs and perceptions than any influence operations that lack a foundation in such facts. Changing reality—a decidedly realist undertaking—is a vital part of changing perceptions.

Nonetheless the constructivist paradigm usefully highlights the importance of "winning hearts and minds." Just because it is hard and, by itself, insufficient does not lessen its importance: influencing perceptions and beliefs to be consistent with state builders' efforts can be an effective and even vital part of a state-building operation. Just as attempting to change perceptions without changing facts is a waste of

16. Ruggie, *Constructing the World Polity*; Wendt, "Agent-Structure Problem"; Wendt, "Anarchy Is What States Make of It"; Wendt, *Social Theory of International Politics*.
17. Inglehart and Welzel, *Modernization, Cultural Change, and Democracy*.
18. Nye, *Soft Power*.

words, so changing facts without some attention to publicizing the change can be a waste of manpower and resources.

First Hypothesis

Combining these four perspectives on state building, we see that state building is more likely to be successful when the intervening state and receiving state share interests, particularly interests shaped by a common threat perception; when both states are embedded within a network of effective and well-coordinated international and domestic institutions to regularize the process of state building; when the state-building project enjoys the consent of the local population and promises to increase citizens' political and economic liberty; and when both states hold the same vision for the kind of state they are trying to build.

These favorable conditions rarely all hold simultaneously, which is why state building is hard and often fails. In the absence of ideal circumstances, which conditions are most important? Which are necessary, and which are merely nice to have? What should a state builder pay most attention to in suboptimal conditions? The question is important because the answer becomes the conceptual groundwork for an intervening power's basic approach, or strategy, of state building. However, as I argued in earlier chapters, the answer differs in different states. If states fail in different ways, state builders should adopt different strategies to fix them.

The four paradigms I have discussed suggest four basic strategies of state building, centered around four different organizing goals. State building is: (1) enforcing order, (2) building institutions, (3) spreading liberty, or (4) winning converts. There is an echo here of the strategies reviewed in our earlier discussion of sequencing: the first three clearly parallel the security, institutionalization, and liberalization strategies. I argued that it is wrong to frame strategies of state building in terms of the right *sequence* of efforts, but it does make sense to talk of the *relative priority of effort*. State builders typically do several, if not all four, of the major state-building activities; but they also usually prioritize one as the main effort. I argued earlier that no single *sequence* is right for all failed states; here I argue that different *basic goals* may be appropriate in different circumstances.

Thus we can develop a typology of strategies of state building.

We can formulate a hypothesis based on this discussion and elaborate several specific implications of it.

H.1: Armed state building is most likely to succeed when state builders prioritize a goal that is tailored to address the specific type of state failure that exists in the target state. Therefore:

TABLE 5.1. Statehood, State Failure, and State Building

Aspect of Statehood	Type of State Failure	IR Paradigm	Strategy of State Building
Security	Anarchic	Realist	Enforce order
Legitimacy	Illegitimate	Constructivist	Win converts
Capacity	Incapable	Institutionalist	Build institutions
Prosperity	Unproductive	Liberal	Spread liberty
Humanity	Barbaric	Realist	Enforce order

Armed state building in an anarchic state is more likely to succeed when state builders prioritize security and stabilization.

Armed state building in an illegitimate state is more likely to succeed when state builders prioritize winning local converts to the state-building campaign through liberalization and civil society building.

Armed state building in an incapable state is more likely to succeed when state builders prioritize capacity building and institutionalization.

Armed state building in an unproductive state is more likely to succeed when state builders prioritize economic reconstruction and liberalization.

Armed state building in a barbaric state is more likely to succeed when state builders prioritize security and transitional justice.

My review of the literature on political development lends at least an initial plausibility to this set of hypotheses. They are not reliant on a single variable. They incorporate a wide range of variables that define the conditions on the ground, the state-building strategy, and the degree to which there is a match between them. They do not assume there is a set sequence that must be followed. They recognize that causation does not flow one way: they argue that the state-building strategy must be responsive to local conditions—the relationship between strategy and conditions needs to be dynamic and two-way. A change in conditions *or* a change in strategy will change the outcome of the state building effort.

DEGREE OF INVASIVENESS

Another way of operationalizing "strategy" is to observe a basic choice international actors have to make about how they will go about improving the aspects of the state that failed. State builders face a choice about the degree of invasiveness and administrative control they will assume. State builders can choose to: (1) monitor, observe, and encourage reform; (2) build things and train and equip people; or

[77]

(3) administer, control, or assume executive authority for operations. I refer to these as, respectively, an Observer, Trainer, or Administrator strategy. This distinction is largely omitted in the literature on state building and peace building.[19]

State builders choose one approach over another depending on the quality and availability of local capacity and on the extent of their own aims and ambitions. In states with some residual capacity to guide their own reconstruction and stabilization, such as Croatia, international state builders do not need to step in and assume control. Similarly, especially in the immediate post–Cold War missions, international state builders had a more modest vision of what their intervention should aim to achieve. The interventions in Namibia and Nicaragua, for example, confined themselves largely to observing and monitoring reform efforts and elections preparations.

By contrast, in states that have largely ceased functioning, international state builders may have little choice but to assume control once they have decided to attempt a state-building mission, such as in East Timor after the devastation wrought by the withdrawing Indonesian security forces. Similarly, if state builders deliberately set out with high ambitions, like the United States in Germany and Japan after World War II, they may argue that a high degree of control is the best guarantor of success.

Second Hypothesis

We can formulate another hypothesis and series of particular statements from this discussion.

H.2: Armed state building is most likely to succeed when state builders adopt a higher level of invasiveness for higher degrees of state failure and higher state-building ambitions. Therefore:

> Armed state building is more likely to succeed when state builders adopt an observer strategy for states that retain the capacity to guide their own reconstruction, or states for which international actors have low ambitions.
> Armed state building is more likely to succeed when state builders adopt a trainer strategy for states that lack some capacity to guide their own reconstruction and for states for which international actors have modest ambitions.

19. In fact, the distinction is significant enough to cast doubt on including such different missions, like the observer mission in Namibia and the transitional administration in East Timor, as objects in the same research program. The methodological objection is not prohibitive—the framework I develop here attempts to show how both can fit within a broader study—but it needs to be addressed more directly than it typically has been. (See appendix A for more detail.)

Armed state building is more likely to succeed when state builders adopt an administrator strategy for states that have ceased to function and states for which international actors have transformative ambitions.

One advantage of operationalizing strategy this way is that by categorizing strategies by their level of intensity, we see that the footprint and duration dilemmas, discussed in chapter 2, are not unique to military deployments and may be relative to the degree of need in the target state. I agree with Edelstein's argument that larger, more invasive military forces deployed for longer periods of time may incur local resentment, outstay their welcome, or provoke the local population to stop cooperating with the mission. On the other hand, smaller forces with less ambitious mandates may be less effective at accomplishing state-building goals.[20] I extend that insight to all aspects of a state-building strategy. A large presence of international civilians, a more invasive state-building mandate, the establishment of an international transitional administration, international control over reconstruction planning, or international control over transitional justice all face the duration and footprint dilemmas. The closer international state builders come to an Administrator strategy the more acute the footprint and durations dilemmas become.

However, the footprint and duration dilemmas may be mitigated if the Administrator strategy is justified by the degree of state failure in the target state. Edelstein argued that state building and occupation are more likely to succeed if local actors feel the need for international help. I agree, and extend that insight to all areas of state building. Local populations are likely to be more welcoming of international administration the more broken their state's institutions, economy, and mechanisms of legitimacy are, or the more barbaric a former regime was. I do not argue that state builders are able to escape the duration and footprint dilemmas completely, but I argue that the variable I have identified—the match between strategy and circumstances—helps explain how those dilemmas can be mitigated.

Similarly, we can better see how the dynamic of power balancing between local and international actors is affected by the match, partial match, or mismatch between state-building strategy and degree of state failure. State builders are revisionist powers that threaten the interests of warlords, illicit smugglers, and other status quo powers but encourage bandwagoning and free-riding from like-minded but weak reformers and local democrats. An overbearing state-building strategy may provoke the worst behavior from both groups. State builders who do too

20. Edelstein, "Foreign Militaries."

much—who adopt a strategy that is more invasive than necessary, for example, an Administrator strategy when only an Observer strategy is called for—are more likely to provoke a backlash from status quo powers. They are also more likely to enable free-riding from local revisionist powers that would otherwise have the incentive and means to do for themselves what the international actors are doing. An overbearing strategy hastens the dynamic of the footprint and duration dilemmas, risking backlash and free-riding from local opposition and local allies, respectively.

By contrast, state builders also run a risk at the other end of the spectrum if they implement a strategy that is not intensive enough for the degree of state failure. If they adopt an Observer strategy when a Trainer strategy would be more appropriate, or if they adopt an appropriate strategy but fail to implement it with sufficient resources, they can embolden status quo powers to mount a resistance against a weak international presence. They can also prompt local allies to defect and bandwagon with (or simply surrender to) status quo powers if the international actors do not appear to have the competence, will, or resources to implement an effective state-building program.

A Third Hypothesis

H.1 and H.2 are mutually exclusive; one hypothesizes that success is a function of state builders' goals, the other, invasiveness. But we can conceptualize strategy as encompassing both goals and invasiveness. In this view, state builders adopt one of the three levels of invasiveness in each of the five dimension of statehood discussed in the previous chapter. In this view, a state-building strategy is composed of the state builders' approach to each of the five dimensions of statehood, and the approach can occur at a variety of levels of invasiveness.

This approach to strategy yields a final hypothesis:

H.3: Armed state building is more likely to succeed if state builders adopt a strategy that corresponds to the *type and degree* of state failure: more invasive efforts for aspects of statehood that show a greater degree of failure and less invasive in areas that show less failure.

Operationalizing strategy this way has several advantages. The more broken any dimension of statehood is, the greater intensity of effort international state builders will have to make in that area. State builders should apply attention, resources, and effort to the parts of the state that are broken, and should apply more efforts the more broken the state is. The areas of greatest failure are likely to be the most important for the ultimate outcome of the state-building effort. By disaggregating state

[80]

TABLE 5.2. A Typology of Strategies of State Building

	Security	Legitimacy	Capacity	Prosperity	Humanity
Observe and Encourage	Traditional peacekeeping, monitor ceasefire	Monitor elections, press, sermons, etc.	Monitor public administration reform	Monitor budget, encourage transparency	Monitor human rights
Train and Equip	Security assistance	Civil society empowerment	Technical assistance	Technical assistance	Civil society empowerment, technical assistance to commission or tribunal
Administer and Control	Peace enforcement, combat operations, military government	Nation building	International administration	International administration	Regime change, purge of former regime elements

building into the five dimensions of statehood, we better see the necessity of constructing a well-rounded strategy that takes into account all ways in which the target state has failed.[21]

That does not mean all aspects of a strategy fit neatly into a harmonious whole. Some aspects of a state-building strategy may exist in tension with other aspects. Fostering a process for relegitimizing the state—for example, by elections—can be disorderly and even destabilizing. Prompting economic growth can be socially disruptive and tax

21. The international environment also affects the outcome of an international state-building operation, suggesting a possible sixth area that strategy should address. My theory does capture external influences—not as a separate category but as those external factors show up in the five dimensions of statehood and state failure. For example, Pakistan retains significant influence over the outcome in Afghanistan. However, that is largely captured by looking at the security dimension. Pakistan's influence is felt mostly as a drag on security because of its support for militants and through lax border enforcement. Thus, reestablishing security in Afghanistan requires kinetic operations against (Pakistani-supported) insurgents and reestablishing security along the Pakistani border. Pakistan's influence might also show up as an effort to subvert the legitimacy of the Afghan government through propaganda or civil unrest, in response to which state builders (both international and domestic) would have to bolster Kabul's legitimacy through, for example, holding elections, using Islamic and nationalist rhetoric, and strengthening tribal ties. A sixth category of analysis—the international community's recognition and construction of a state's sovereignty—might capture these dynamics more directly, but it would erode the parsimony of an already complex theory.

the capacity of weak institutions struggling to keep up. The time- and labor-intensive process of rebuilding institutional capacity can take resources away from quicker and more immediate programs, such as humanitarian relief.

But the fact that there is tension among the goals is not cause for simply jettisoning some in order to focus on others, or to relegate some goals to a later date in the name of "sequencing." The misguided effort to find a master sequence of state building, as I argued in chapter 2, is a recipe for a lopsided strategy, institutional delay, and a high risk of failure. State building necessarily must involve a strategy geared to address failures in all five dimensions of statehood, even with tensions among them. The art of statecraft, as applied to state building, means living with tensions and enabling skilled administrators to reconcile them on a day-to-day basis based on the realities on the ground.

[6]

Strategies of State Building

In this chapter I describe strategies of state building for each of the five dimensions of statehood. In each dimension, I describe strategies of state building in each of the three ascending levels of invasiveness: Observer strategy, Trainer strategy, and Administrator strategy. Using empirical data from a variety of cases of state building, I describe how state builders either succeeded or failed to apply a strategy tailored to address the dynamics of state failure they confronted, and I trace the process by which the match, partial match, or mismatch in strategy resulted in success or failure.

REBUILDING SECURITY

In this section I describe the Observer, Trainer, and Administrator strategies of rebuilding security. I argue that the different strategies are appropriate in different situations, depending on the degree of security failure in the target state. In the previous chapter I described how different historical pathways to security failure generally lead to different degrees of failure. Newly independent states emerging from imperial rule and states conclusively defeated in interstate war represent the easiest security environment. States emerging from civil war represent a harder security environment. And states in the midst of an ongoing civil war represent the most difficult security environment. (And those in which international military forces were targeted by combatants represent the most challenging subtype.) I also argued that because the causal mechanism linking historical circumstances to security outcomes—local perceptions—is also affected by other factors, and because it is not always clear if a war had ended or not, state builders should also examine the degree and consistency of any ongoing political violence to determine the extent of security failure.

Observer Strategy. Permissive security environments—probably most common in newly independent states emerging from imperial rule—are marked with tension and uncertainty but not widespread or systematic violence. In these cases international state builders can adopt a relatively straightforward strategy. International military forces, as a trusted, neutral, third party, can observe the security situation, facilitate communication between actors (citizens and former imperial forces), design and oversee confidence-building measures, verify compliance with a ceasefire, and oversee disarmament and demobilization. The presence of a trusted international force as an honest broker in this environment can reduce risk by increasing information and predictability in the security situation. The international deployment in Namibia in 1989 is an example of a well-calibrated monitoring mission—by following the South African police force to observe their activities—in an unstable security environment that contributed to successful state building.

Trainer Strategy. States emerging from civil war present a more challenging security environment. Typically parties have agreed to a ceasefire but may not be able to enforce complete compliance within their ranks. Security forces are unable (or unwilling) to provide security, and ex-combatants turned into criminal forces threaten the state's stability. These cases are distinguished from anarchic failures because there is no longer (or not yet) a state of war: the overall level of organized political violence has fallen to the point that peaceful political bargaining and economic reconstruction can resume. In this environment, the most successful security strategy would, in addition to the normal observer functions, encompass the full range of what the UN calls "security sector reform" and what the US military calls "security assistance." Security sector reform, according to *UN Peacekeeping Operations: Principles and Guidelines*, includes efforts to restructure, reform, and train police and military forces: strengthen the national judiciary and penal system; promote legal and judicial reform; and support legislative development.[1] Security assistance, according to the US Army's *Field Manual 3–0: Operations*, is providing equipment and training to foreign militaries, including through foreign military sales, the International Military Education and Training program, and arms exports.[2] Rebuilding security services involves training, equipping, and even paying new soldiers and policemen; reforming

1. United Nations, "United Nations Peacekeeping Operations."
2. US Department of the Army, *Field Manual 3–0: Operations*.

the management and oversight of the security services; and (what seems to be often missing) strengthening the armed forces' loyalty to the state. Along with technical assistance to civilian administration, these state-building programs are labor intensive and expensive. Strong and sustained donor commitment are required for successful security assistance and security sector reform. Security sector reform and security assistance help strengthen the security institutions of the state, consolidate a cease-fire, and allow political and economic reconstruction to move forward.

The state-building operations in Nicaragua (1989–92), El Salvador (1991–95), Mozambique (1993–95), and Guatemala (1997) are examples of post–Cold War UN security sector reform in countries recovering from civil war that resulted in at least shallow successes. Those missions involved disarming militias, observing ceasefires, and encouraging reform. They generally deployed fewer than 5,000 troops (up to 6,500 in Mozambique), or fewer than 10 per 10,000 civilians. They also tended to be among the shortest state-building operations, averaging less than two years. The mandates of international forces most closely resembled traditional UN peacekeeping operations; they edged over into state-building operations because of their role overseeing elections, repatriating refugees, and monitoring disarmament and demobilization. The UN has subsequently incorporated increasingly substantial security sector reform efforts into recent missions, including in Bosnia (1995–present), Kosovo (1999–present), and Timor-Leste (1999–2005). There are several other examples of international security assistance that effectively built up local security forces and reversed a security failure while failing to achieve overall success because of a failure to rebuild the state's legitimacy or capacity or strengthen civilian rule over the armed forces, demonstrating that successful state building requires an effective strategy across multiple dimensions of statehood, not just the security dimension. The United States trained security forces and imposed stability on the Dominican Republic (1916–24) and Nicaragua (1927–33) only to watch the local security forces seize power and establish dictatorships under Rafael Trujillo and Anastasio Somoza, respectively. More recently (and successfully) the British turned around the failing mission in Sierra Leone in part by establishing the International Military Advisory and Training Team to train Sierra Leonean security forces, and US efforts to accelerate the training of the Afghan National Security Forces after 2006 have significantly improved the chances of at least a shallow success there (see chapter 7).

Administrator Strategy. States in the midst of an ongoing war present the most challenging security environment for international state builders—what I have called an anarchic security failure. In these cases, international state builders typically intervene in an ongoing civil war in an attempt to stop the war and build the conditions for sustainable

[85]

peace. The intervention sometimes becomes an occasion for interstate war between the international actor and one of the parties to the local conflict. (In rare cases anarchic failure takes the form of a simple interstate war in which an outside power seeks to effect regime change and subsequently build a new state in place of the old; anarchy can swiftly resolve into peaceful occupation if the war concludes decisively.) If the international community attempts a state building operation in an anarchic environment, it must simultaneously undertake security sector reform *and* be willing and able to administer the security sector: until new local security forces are capable, international forces must assume responsibility for enforcing public security. The deployment must be large, well-armed, and well-resourced, and willing to choose sides and undertake offensive operations, including foreign internal defense and counterinsurgency operations. It must either have a credible local partner or be willing to impose a military government or transitional administration.

The international community has failed in nearly every case in which it has attempted a state-building operation in an anarchic security environment, including in Nicaragua (1927), the Democratic Republic of the Congo (both 1960 and 1999), South Vietnam, Angola, Somalia, Rwanda, Liberia (1993), and Iraq. In the five post–Cold War UN operations—Angola, Somalia, Rwanda, Liberia, and the Congo (1999)—failure was a straightforward result of an inappropriate mandate backed by too few soldiers: failure was directly attributable to a wrongheaded security strategy. The depth of state failure was greater than the invasiveness of the state-building operation: international actors were not ambitious enough. As a result, local status quo actors faced low penalties for opposing the state-building operation and high costs for cooperating. They predictably moved against the operation (not by fighting international soldiers but simply by reneging on agreements and renewing violence). Local allies remained weak and unable to implement the state-building program on their own without more robust international support. In those operations, the UN generally deployed a force with a peacekeeping mandate and attempted to remain neutral. It deployed about the same number of troops, or troops per civilians, as it did in the successful observer missions, deploying fewer than 10 per 10,000 civilians in all cases but Somalia—an inadequate strategy considering the comparatively worse security environment. The missions also tended to be nearly as short-lived as the earlier successful observer missions, when they would have needed to spend much *more* time to make progress on the comparatively harder security situation. In all five cases the United Nations either did not attempt to revise its strategy or, in the cases of Angola and Rwanda, made only token efforts at revision that did not fundamentally alter the strategy of intervention. (Successful revision is possible, as I demonstrate in the case studies of Sierra Leone and Afghanistan.)

In the other cases of state building in an anarchic environment, the international community came closer to deploying an adequate security strategy but failed because its efforts were too little or too late, and because of inadequate strategies in other dimensions. The United States effectively contained the Sandino rebellion in Nicaragua in 1933 (and also trained competent security forces) but failed to shore up the legitimacy of the Nicaraguan state or invest in the capacity of the civilian control over the military, and its state-building effort was undone by the rise of the Somoza dictatorship three years after withdrawal. The UN's failure in the Congo in 1964 fell along similar lines, as General Mobutu seized power in 1965. The US-trained Army of the Republic of Vietnam (ARVN) was more capable at the end of the Vietnam War than at the beginning, and by some accounts was able to hold its own during the North Vietnamese offensives in 1972, but the United States and its local allies failed to invest adequately in the South Vietnamese government's legitimacy. They largely abandoned democratization after 1967 and failed to address widespread corruption and incompetence in the South Vietnamese government. The failure of legitimacy undermined whatever security gains they had made, and the collective failures led to South Vietnam's defeat. The United States (eventually) tamped down the insurgency in Iraq in 2007, and the Congolese conflict of the 1990s and 2000s eventually petered out during the United Nations mission there, but both missions failed to prevent humanitarian atrocities that occurred on their watch and seem unlikely to lead to stable liberal governance in either country.

There are only three cases—all marginal—of possible successes in an anarchic security environment. The United States effectively defeated the Second Caco Revolt in Haiti from 1918 through 1920. Coupled with relatively effective civilian administration and supervised elections, Haiti enjoyed just over a decade of peace after the US withdrawal. The United Nations deployed almost 16,000 troops to Cambodia in 1992 to oversee elections and administer a transitional administration. Despite the Khmer Rouge's ongoing insurgency, elections were held and fighting eventually stopped. Scholars are divided as to whether the Cambodian intervention was a success or not because of the erosion of democratic liberties there since the mid-1990s. Finally, I argue in chapter 7 that Afghanistan may be an emerging shallow success, although the ultimate outcome is still uncertain.

Generally, it appears that state builders come closer to success in anarchic environments if they are not mandated to maintain neutrality, that is, if they are willing to take sides and engage in military operations to enforce peace. For example, the UN attempted to remain neutral in Angola, Rwanda, and Liberia and was consequently ill-postured to respond when spoilers resorted to violence. In other cases, including Iraq, Afghanistan, Nicaragua (1927), and Sierra Leone, state builders took sides. They did not succeed in every case, but arguably they performed better. It is also noteworthy that failure appears more often a result of a too-modest approach rather than the opposite. State builders rarely commit the error of being too aggressive. Even Germany and Japan, extreme outliers in the number of troops deployed and degree of control exercised by the occupation governments, did not provoke local opposition or insurgencies.

Iraq would seem to be an example of an aggressive security strategy that provoked local opposition. However, the perception that the Coalition Provisional Authority adopted an overbearing posture in Iraq likely stems more from the circumstances surrounding the beginning of the operation (invasion and forced regime change) and the occupation's early missteps, not the conduct of the state-building operation itself. If the state-building operation (as opposed to the military campaign that preceded it) was implemented with more troops, not fewer, and the CPA had tools to enforce order, it might have preempted the collapse of civil order, accelerated reconstruction, and prevented, or at least mitigated, the growth of the insurgency. Much of the later opposition perhaps was not provoked by an overly aggressive strategy *during* the state-building

TABLE 6.1. Matching Strategy to Degree of Security Failure

Degree of Failure	Strategy of State Building
Weak–Unstable	Observe
Newly independent states	Deploy peacekeeping force
Security forces minimally capable	Monitor ceasefire
Combatants cooperative with DDR	Facilitate DDR
	Monitor security forces
Failed–Violent	Train/Equip
Recent civil war	Provide security assistance
Security forces incapable, underpaid, untrained	Train/equip local security forces
	Embed international with local forces
Widespread, overt, organized criminality	
Collapsed–Anarchic	Administer
Ongoing war	Deploy peace enforcement force
Combatants resistant to DDR	Execute combat operations and foreign internal defense
	Establish military government / transitional authority

operation as by the circumstances of its initiation followed by its ensuring *weakness*.

This discussion of security strategies illustrates an example of my
main argument. State-building operations do not always need more
troops and more time. Several missions have succeeded quickly with few
troops, but only when they took place in a permissive security environment: resources are not the single master variable. And, contrary to critics
who argue that the security environment is the key variable, we also saw
that in other cases the international community came close to meeting
the demands of even an anarchic environment but still failed because of
inadequacies in other aspects of their strategy. The match between
strategy and circumstance across all five dimensions of statehood—not
just security—is key.

Rebuilding Legitimacy: Is It Possible?

Rebuilding a state's legitimacy is perhaps the thorniest issue in state
building. A state's claim to legitimacy necessarily takes place in that
state's cultural and historical context. Successful claims to legitimacy
must be framed in terms that appeal to indigenous concepts and ideals.
International efforts to build legitimacy directly blurs the distinction between state building and nation building. State builders typically rely on
more indirect measures to encourage and facilitate legitimacy-building
processes. How?

For the sake of simplicity, we do not need to explore the mechanisms
for rebuilding legitimacy according to all possible ideologies. This book
focuses on liberal state building, in which states seek to legitimize themselves by practicing democracy. This focus is justified because, in fact, in
every post–Cold War case local actors have demanded some form of democracy as the basis for political reconstruction, a trend that shows no
sign of abating. While states can be legitimized by a variety of ideologies,
for our purposes we can focus on the effort by state builders to foster
democratic governance in weak states.

The effort raises several questions: Can democracy succeed anywhere,
in any culture, or is it limited to "Western" societies and their offshoots?
How does democracy come about? What are the prerequisites to its success? How does democracy relate to indigenous forms of legitimacy?
Most important for our purposes, how can outsiders give support to a
state transitioning to democracy?

First, can democracy succeed outside of Europe and the Americas?
The empirical evidence is straightforward and overwhelming: democracy is more likely in Europe and the Americas, but it emphatically does

TABLE 6.2. Democracy in the World, 2010

	Total States	Democratic States**	Percentage
Europe, Americas, and Offshoots*	88	62	70.1
Africa and Asia	105	33	31.4
Total	193	95	49.2

*Includes the Caribbean, Australia, New Zealand, Russia, and Cape Verde.
**Polity IV score of 7 or higher, or rated "free" by Freedom House.
Source: Freedom House, Polity IV Project.

exist and function elsewhere. According to the Polity IV Project, which rates states on a scale from autocratic (-9) to democratic (9), 24 states outside of Europe and the Americas had a score of 7 or higher (full democracy) in 2008, including Benin, Timor-Leste, Kenya, Lebanon, Madagascar, Mali, Sierra Leone, Turkey, Zambia, Botswana, Ghana, Indonesia, Lesotho, the Philippines, South Korea, Senegal, the Solomon Islands, Comoros, India, South Africa, Japan, Mauritius, Mongolia, and Taiwan. The Polity IV Project excludes states with a population of less than 500,000, excluding some 30 states. Among those, at least nine more are non-Western states rated "free" by Freedom House in 2009, including Tuvalu, Nauru, Palau, the Marshall Islands, Micronesia, Kiribati, Sao Tome and Principe, Vanuatu, and Samoa. All told, there are 33 non-Western democracies in the world, with about 31 percent of the 105 states in Africa and Asia accounting for 35 percent of democracies worldwide. Democracy is more likely in Europe and the Americas, which account for about 65 percent of democracies in the world, but it can without doubt exist and function elsewhere.[3] I belabor this point because, although it may sound like a truism to scholars, it is still not widely accepted by policymakers.

How does democracy come about? As discussed, there is a large literature on democratic transitions that is largely inconclusive (complicated by the fact that in the research, some scholars write about democracy as a facet of "modernization," others are writing about democracy and state

3. An unexplored connection may exist between the size of a polity and its likelihood of democracy. Anecdotally, it seems that a disproportionately large number of small states are democratic. Because international relations theorists tend to exclude micro-sovereignties from their studies—exemplified by the Polity IV Project—they have overlooked the association. I hypothesize that democracy lowers the cost of statehood by eliminating the need to enforce a given theory of justice, censor the press, screen public officials, or field a large domestic intelligence capacity. Elections can be expensive, but they are not as costly as tyranny. Small states with few resources find it easier to exist as a democracy.

building, and still others are writing about democratization in the wake of civil war). The renowned Yale emeritus professor Robert Dahl offered the classic, and still one of the most thorough and convincing, explanations for the emergence of democracy in 1971. He argued that democracy requires a system of mutual guarantees for both government and opposition to engender the trust necessary for peaceful competition and transfer of power. Democracy is most likely to emerge successfully from a peaceful evolutionary process that gradually transforms a previously legitimate regime into a legitimate democracy; wars and revolutions make democratic consolidation harder. Social and economic power should be diffused throughout society, rather than concentrated; and there appears to be a minimal subsistence threshold of economic development below which democracy is highly unlikely to work. Class and cultural homogeneity is an advantage; if (as is more likely) there are subcultural cleavages, democracy works best if no subculture constitutes a majority, if cleavages do not run across regional lines, and if no subculture is permanently out of government. Especially relevant for state building, Dahl argued that democracy is more likely if any foreign control is weak and temporary.[4]

Dahl's argument remains influential, but it is not without critics. Adam Przeworski subsequently argued that the study of transitions has some general methodological problems. He argues that social, economic, and institutional conditions are only constraints on what is possible in a given historical situation, not determinants of outcomes. Studies like Dahl's that focus on the external conditions could only be probabilistic and could not definitively explain transition outcomes. Individual choices, and the strategic situation in which they are made, matter too. Transitions do not happen simply when one regime loses legitimacy but when another possible regime gains more legitimacy than the present one. As a result, analyses that model the costs and benefits actors face in a nondemocratic regime contemplating transition to democracy shed some light on transition outcomes. Actors face considerable uncertainty about the future in a democratic regime. Institutions that permit uncertainty about policy outcomes without threatening the interests of key actors and groups—such as an effective justice system administering the rule of law impartially—are thus crucial to a successful transition.[5]

Additionally we might note, as Przeworski argues, that democracy lasts when it offers the major political forces in society a truly fair chance to compete, such that it evokes self-interested and spontaneous compliance with the rules of the game; but that such an arrangement is increasingly

4. Dahl, *Polyarchy*.
5. Przeworski, "Some Problems in the Study of the Transition to Democracy."

difficult in times of economic transformation.[6] Dietrich Rueschemeyer, Evelyne Huber, and John Stephens argue that democracy depends on three balances of power: among classes, between state and society, and among surrounding states. In addition, political parties are crucial for consolidating democracy.[7] Juan Linz and Alfred Stepan argue that consolidated democracies are supported by robust civil society, political society, rule of law, bureaucracy, and economic society.[8] Przeworski, et al. argue that democracy is more likely to survive in affluent societies; but that even without affluence, education and a balance of power between competing groups can improve democracy's prospects.[9] Carles Boix argues that democracy is more likely in societies with low income inequality, high capital mobility, and a balance of power between major groupings in society.[10]

This is only a tiny representative sample of the enormous literature on the causes of democracy. Huntington lists twenty-seven different variables that different scholars have argued contribute to democracy or democratization, including a high level of wealth, Protestantism, a British imperial heritage, ethnic homogeneity, income equality, a market economy, high levels of literacy, occupation by a prodemocratic foreign power, and ethnic heterogeneity.[11] Huntington suggests, and the literature increasingly has agreed, that democratization is the result of many causes, that no single factor explains the advent of democracy in all places at all times, that there are different causes in different countries, and that there are many possible roads to democracy. He then argues that the "third wave" of democratization from 1975 to 1990 was caused by five variables: authoritarian governments were increasingly viewed as illegitimate because of poor performance; the economy grew dramatically in the decades prior to 1975, raising expectations and literacy; the Catholic Church reformed, introducing a spirit of openness in many countries; external actors, including the United States and Europe, were increasingly focused on democracy and human rights; and the pattern of democratization was easily transmitted because of advances in communications technology.

If there is no single cause of democracy, can we identify typical prerequisites that must be in place before democracy can take root? The problem with the discussion about the prerequisites for democracy is that so many of the alleged prerequisites are not unique to democracy: they are

6. Przeworski, *Democracy and the Market*.
7. Rueschemeyer, Huber, and Stephens, *Capitalist Development and Democracy*.
8. Linz and Stepan, *Problems of Democratic Transition*.
9. Przeworski et al., *Democracy and Development*.
10. Boix, *Democracy and Redistribution*.
11. Huntington, *Third Wave*.

prerequisites for competent statehood of any type. For example, democracies are more common among rich states, and some scholars argue that greater levels of prosperity make democracy easier to consolidate. However, it is likely that greater levels of prosperity make almost any form of government easier to consolidate because the state will have more resources to extract and use to enforce its writ and provide goods. Similarly, strong institutional capacity within the machinery of government can help democracy because strong institutions contribute to political stability, which in turn promotes democracy. Again, institutional capacity and political stability probably would help reinforce whatever regime is in power and can benefit from competent institutions.

The question of prerequisites becomes insightful when we ask what prerequisites are *unique to* democracy, *distinct from* other legitimizing theories of justice. We can rephrase the question this way: What conditions make people more likely to believe that democracy, and not another theory of justice, legitimizes the state? Notably, the question is about beliefs, and thus about culture. The unique prerequisites for democracy are about what people believe and the availability of cultural resources (e.g., social capital) to enact those beliefs.

Huntington goes so far as to say that the connection between people's beliefs and democracy is so clear and strong as to constitute a near tautology, and he calls for more explanation.[12] But it is not clear why he thinks a variable with so much explanatory power is inadequate. Rather, we should draw out the causal mechanism that ties beliefs, habits, and culture to democratic outcomes. Research on civic culture is relevant in this context. Robert Putnam in his pioneering study *Making Democracy Work* argued that "civic-ness," "civic virtue," or "civic community" helps foster democracy. He described civic community as a type of human association marked by civic engagement, political equality, solidarity, trust, tolerance, and voluntary associations. At root, he is talking about the "character of the citizens." He argued that politics flow from the character of the people. Putnam measured civic-ness with four independent variables: the number of voluntary, nonpolitical associations; the size of the newspaper readership; voter turnout at national referenda; and the incidence of preference voting (patron-client networks) in general elections. Taken together, Putnam argued that these variables were sufficient to measure how fully a polity embodies the ideals of engagement, equality, solidarity and so forth. Putnam's variables are best seen as proxies for an underlying reality that cannot be measured by social science—the reality Putnam hints at in his reference to citizens' "character." Sports

12. Ibid.

clubs don't make democracy, but they indicate the presence of beliefs, habits, and relationships that do.[13] A robust civil society and habits of association are unique prerequisites for democracy. Putnam's argument makes intuitive sense: if democracy is rule by the people, democracy succeeds where the people have habits and beliefs that reflect equality, trust, tolerance, and sociability. Notably, it is precisely these traits that civil wars—which often preceding state-building operations—tend to destroy. I take up the question about how (or whether) outsiders can build such habits in the next section.

Lastly, how does democracy relate to other forms of legitimacy? Building democracy is not the only way to rebuild a state's legitimacy, even if international state builders sometimes seem to think so. Legitimacy comes from accepted theories of justice as articulated by influential groups or people over whom the state seeks to exercise authority, including religious and academic groups, tribes and clans, businessmen, investors and entrepreneurs, unions, trade guilds, professional associations, media, farmers' groups, and nongovernmental organizations. In short, legitimizing theories of justice to which the state makes an appeal can come from the entire range of actors encompassed by the term "civil society." (The difficulty with the concept of "civil society" is that it exists as a singular entity only in the abstract realm of social science. In the particulars of actual cases, there is never an actor self-consciously representing him or herself as an agent of civil society, only an actor identified by one of several concrete roles or groups that social scientists lump together under the umbrella of "civil society.") In many cases, claims about justice are framed as comprehensive claims that exclude other possibilities. Theocratic claims are not consistent with libertarian ones, for example. Democracy is best seen as a process by which such claims compete peacefully. Seen in this light, democracy can be consistent with other claims to justice, and can serve simply as a vehicle by which other claims about justice are articulated and enacted in the public sphere—which perhaps explains democracy's success in adapting to cultures outside of Europe and the Americas, and the readiness with which formerly warring parties almost without exception have looked to democracy to rebuild their state's legitimacy since the Cold War. The obvious corollary is that other theories of justice have to accept the rules of the democratic game. Some do not and accuse democracy itself of being a comprehensive theory that excludes other possible comprehensive theories. Theocratic claims about justice may bristle at submitting the will of God to a popular vote, for example. The lesson for state builders is that the "thicker"

13. Putnam, Leonardi, and Nanetti, *Making Democracy Work.*

democracy is—the more invasive and detailed the rules of the game are, the stronger the anti-comprehensiveness is—the stronger this criticism can be. This seems especially true with regard to religious claims: the more strongly democracy implies secularism, the more opposition it will provoke from religious groups.[14] The "thinner" democracy is, the easier it will be for non-Western cultures and formerly warring parties to adopt it and the easier it will be for international state builders to promote it.

Given that democracy is at root a matter of beliefs and culture, can outsiders promote democracy, especially in a postwar context? Can they do anything to foster civil society, civic culture, habits of association, and beliefs about justice? The empirical record demonstrates that the answer is yes: four of the thirty-three non-Western democracies were objects of a state building campaign, and several more achieved independence and democracy following a period of trusteeship or colonial rule by a Western power—to say nothing of how some Western states helped spread democracy *within* the West. I belabor this because although it is an established fact, it is not widely accepted or believed by policymakers. A more interesting question than "Can the West spread democracy?" is "How, under what circumstances, at what cost, and by what means, can outside powers foster or promote democracy in another state?"

Larry Diamond argues bluntly that outsiders cannot "impose a preference for democracy where it does not exist."[15] At best, the international community can approach the problem only indirectly, by shaping circumstances favorable to local democratic advocates, who must be already on the scene before the international community becomes involved. The research and practice of democratization has followed much the same course as the earlier efforts toward modernization and development. Initially, in the 1960s, the United States and other donors focused heavily on promoting democracy indirectly by promoting socioeconomic development. They believed the claims of modernization theory that democracy is a natural outgrowth of economic development and modernization. After a period of decline in the 1970s, fed in part by the development failures of the 1960s in postcolonial states and the war in Vietnam, democracy assistance became prominent again in the 1980s and especially 1990s, this time more in the area of building institutions. Indeed, in many ways it was more accurately seen as governance assistance than democracy assistance, as the United States and other donors began to invest in poor states' judicial systems, police forces, legislatures, local

14. Rawls, *Political Liberalism*; Sandel, *Liberalism and the Limits of Justice*; Sandel, *Democracy's Discontent*.
15. Diamond, "Promoting Democracy."

and municipal governments, and civilian control over the military. But, again with echoes from the debates on modernization and development, democracy assistance was often premised on a "democracy template" that assumed, among other things, that there were set stages of political development with autocracy at the bottom and democracy at the top. As that model has worn away, democracy assistance programs have finally come to acknowledge the role of power in making democracy possible; the plurality of paths toward democracy; and the importance of local conditions.

Nonetheless, democracy assistance remains largely a matter of technical assistance, training, and capacity-building programs for a host of institutions, especially electoral authorities, political parties, legislatures, judicial institutions, media, and "civil society" groups.[16] These types of assistance cannot manufacture civic character where there is none, but they can transfer money, technical know-how, and encouragement; provide a safety net that allows democratic advocates to take risks with fewer costs; facilitate networks; give the local population an opportunity to build a storehouse of experience in democratic politics; and tilt the playing field to democrats' advantage. In other words, international democracy assistance can *increase the power* of local democrats (through money, equipment, and human capital) relative to undemocratic actors and groups. This can be a crucial form of assistance, because democracy—like any other competing theory of justice—must not simply be attractive but be *more attractive than* rival theories of justice in order to be adopted, and its advocates and institutions must have the power and clout to win in a competition with other theories.[17] Democratization involves adopting new power relationships throughout society, which necessarily threatens elites of the previous undemocratic system, who will naturally resist. Outside assistance that increases local democrats' power makes democratization more likely to succeed.

Rebuilding Legitimacy: Programs and Policies

In this section I discuss the available programs and policies that an international state builder can pursue to rebuild an illegitimate state's legitimacy. In so doing, international state builders are also investing in the legitimacy of the intervention itself, which some scholars have identified as a key variable for state-building operations. The two—the legitimacy of the target state and the legitimacy of the intervention—are

16. Carothers, *Aiding Democracy Abroad.*
17. Przeworski, *Transition to Democracy.*

closely connected. The legitimacy of the intervention affects efforts to rebuild the legitimacy of the target state. Local populations may simply refuse to cooperate with the legitimacy-building programs of an intervention that they view as illegitimate—for example, by boycotting elections sponsored by a military occupier, as Iraqi Sunnis did in 2005. The reverse may happen as citizens show an eagerness to participate in relegitimizing their state under the auspices of an intervention they believe is necessary and legitimate, as for example Afghans did in their 2004 elections. In turn, the legitimacy of the target state can redound to the legitimacy of the intervention. An intervention that was initially viewed as illegitimate (or simply inept) can increase in legitimacy if legitimacy-building efforts for the target state are successful, as may be the case in Iraq in the later years of the US intervention or in Sierra Leone after the British intervention. And an intervention that was initially perceived to be legitimate by the local population can be dragged down if the host government loses legitimacy, which was part of the downward spiral in South Vietnam. Thus, legitimacy-building programs and policies are all more likely to succeed if the intervention itself is viewed as legitimate, and less likely to succeed if it is not.

Observer Strategy. In a state with weak legitimacy, there is a basic agreement on a path for political reconstruction to which the major parties are adhering. Such agreements can fall apart quickly because of a lack of trust, poor information, or because of the logic of strategic action. A postconflict peace agreement is a type of prisoners' dilemma. Actors take risks when they cooperate with a peace agreement because they don't know if all actors will cooperate, and each actor stands to lose if he or she invests resources in a failing process. Defectors stand to gain by hedging against failure, whether or not others cooperate, making defection the most rational course of action. International state builders change the logic of the situation, even with a minimal monitoring mission in which they simply observe and report on compliance with any power-sharing or consociational agreement, implementation of elections, and state-society relations. An international civilian monitoring mission increases transparency, disseminates reliable information, acts as a trusted neutral third-party, facilitates communication between parties, and adjudicates disputes. The international intervention reduces the risks of cooperating and the likelihood of failure, thus increasing the incentive to cooperate. Finally, reducing risks, increasing the incentive to cooperate, and providing reliable information are all ways of increasing the power of local democrats who are working to implement the agreement against spoilers who want to defect. International observers equip local democrats with better information and a more conducive environment in which to work.

The interventions in Namibia, El Salvador, Nicaragua, and Mozambique are examples of successful monitoring missions appropriately calibrated to states with weak but slowly consolidating legitimacy. In those states peace agreements generally held and the parties were broadly cooperative. The international community appropriately did not assume executive authority, administer elections, or undertake large civilian training missions.

Trainer Strategy. In some states, an agreement has not yet been reached, or it is in the process of falling apart; these are states with failing legitimacy. Some actors are unable to overcome the barriers to peace and are unable or unwilling to implement some provisions of an election, despite a clear preference not to return to war. As opposed to states with collapsed legitimacy, actors in these states have the ability to put forward and agree, at least on paper, on general principles for relegitimizing their state; as opposed to states with merely weak legitimacy, they are unable or unwilling to fully implement their plan. In this environment, international state builders must do more than monitor and report, but they do not need to assume control of the legitimizing process. Specifically, state builders should become directly involved in negotiations over the terms of peace agreements, providing expertise based on prior experience with postconflict agreements. State builders may need to directly administer elections to ensure they happen and are considered free and fair by local actors. More broadly, state builders should broaden participation in the peace agreement by empowering civil society, for example through funding and training in advocacy. Because civil society is a key source of legitimacy, more active involvement by civil society actors can alter the terms of a peace plan, broaden the base of support for it, and increase the likelihood that it will be implemented. For example, warring parties may reach an impasse over who should become the executive of a postconflict state. Religious groups or tribal elders might intervene and work to decentralize the government and deconcentrate power away from the executive, which reduces the risks to the warring parties if they fail to place their candidate in the office and could help clear the logjam. In the language of much of the literature on peace agreements, international state builders must work to increase local "ownership" of the process.

The failed interventions in Cuba uniquely illustrate the importance of legitimacy even in isolation from a concurrent security crisis. The United States adopted an appropriate security strategy in both the 1898–1902 and 1906–9 interventions. No fighting broke out during the interventions and basic public order was maintained throughout. The United States even administered elections in each case to reestablish political institutions accepted by the local population. In the first Cuban intervention the United States oversaw local elections in May 1900, the election of delegates to a constitutional convention in September of the same year (the convention itself in November), a presidential election in 1901, and legislative elections in 1902. Cubans appear to have accepted the legitimacy of a democratic form of government. Political parties formed and contested the elections. But what legitimacy the United States built up with elections, it undermined with the Platt Amendment, a law imposing a series of restrictions on Cuba that amounted to a violation of its sovereignty and denial of its independence (an example of how the legitimacy of the intervention and the legitimacy of the target state are tied). Don Thomas Estada Palma, the Cuban president who took office in 1902, was tainted by having to govern within the Platt restrictions and began to rely on the security forces to support his reelection after the United States withdrew. When the Liberal opposition, which advocated immediate repeal of Platt, believed, with reason, that there would be no fair elections in 1906, they broke into open revolt. Despite both parties' apparent acceptance of democratic elections as the means to legitimize their state, they were unable to fully implement or adhere to the democratic rules of the game because the US-sponsored electoral process failed to create a group of Cubans invested in the democratic process, willing and able to insist on and administer a new round of elections: in other words, the United States failed to train Cubans in the democratic process needed to sustain the legitimacy of their new state. Importantly, the security failure was triggered by and occurred after the legitimacy failure. The US security strategy effectively kept the peace during the intervention, but its inept support for the legitimacy of the Cuban state undermined its efforts.

The United States reintervened in Cuba in 1906 to put down the revolt and attempt to reestablish the political bargain it had brokered in 1902. The second intervention differed from the first in a number of ways. It was a civilian rather than military government—headed by an American provisional governor reporting through the War Department's Bureau of Insular Affairs, not a military governor reporting to the general staff—but it was direct rule nonetheless. It was also much smaller, involving only 3,000 Marines and soldiers, in contrast to the 45,000 present in 1898. The United States also improved its security strategy: where the first intervention had been essentially a monitoring mission, the second intervention undertook to train and equip a professional Cuban security force. The revolt quickly ended and the Cuban parties agreed to reestablish the political process, a sign that the legitimacy situation had not completely collapsed. US officials drafted a new electoral code and held presidential elections in 1908, which the Liberals won, and US forces departed the next year. Nonetheless, the second intervention was undermined much the same as the first, by a failure of legitimacy. Revolts again erupted in 1912 and 1917, first by disenfranchised black Cuban veterans of the war against Spain, then by Liberals after another dubious Conservative electoral victory. Despite US efforts and Cubans' avowed acceptance of democratic norms, it was clear that the Cuban democratic process had failed to live up to its own promises. Significant segments of the Cuban population did not believe the Cuban government's claim to democratic legitimacy was credible—in the case of Cuban blacks, because the regime was not inclusive enough, and in the case of Cuban Liberals, because the regime did not permit meaningful or consequential public contestation.[18]

Administrator Strategy. Some states are simply viewed as completely illegitimate by the people who live in them, and no local actors are able or willing to establish a credible way forward. In these cases, international state builders, if they decide to attempt a state-building operation under these extremely unfavorable circumstances, must decree a way forward, even in the absence of a formal agreement with local parties. The strategy can only be implemented by a military government or international transitional authority. This strategy is counterintuitive in that it seems to work against the goal of local ownership, which is usually necessary for legitimacy. However, the concern over local ownership is only relevant in cases where there are local actors willing and able to take ownership of the legitimizing process. The international community cannot give ownership to a population that cannot or will not take it, that is, when legitimacy and the means of creating it have completely collapsed.

There are very few examples of international state builders attempting this strategy of state building. It seems to violate norms of self-determination and state sovereignty. Notably, however, the few examples are of successful interventions. Following Japan's unconditional surrender that ended World War II, the chauvinistic nationalism and racist imperialism that had underpinned the Japanese's state's legitimacy for the previous generation was completely destroyed, and there were no local actors capable of leading a relegitimizing process. The United States proceeded to remake Japan's political system at will. US officials wrote Japan's new constitution and a US Army general, Douglas MacArthur, governed Japan until 1949. A country with literally no experience with democracy—its previous high Polity IV score was 1—was made into a liberal democracy by fiat. The Americans' sole concession to Japanese conceptions of legitimacy was to permit their retention of the emperor, but he was stripped of his powers. The singular exception highlights the otherwise categorically sweeping powers the Americans arrogated to

18. Boot, *Savage Wars of Peace*; Langley, *Banana Wars: United States Intervention*; Musicant, *Banana Wars: A History*.

[100]

TABLE 6.3. Matching Strategy to Degree of Legitimacy Failure

Degree of Failure	Strategy of State Building
Weak–Fragile Consensus • Agreement on political reconstruction in place and holding • Civil society supportive of agreement	Observe • Monitor elections • Monitor compliance with power sharing or consociational agreement and establishment of transitional authority • Monitor state–civil society relations
Failed–Widespread Disenfranchisement • Agreement not yet in place • Agreement in place but parties unwilling or unable to implement some provisions • Some civil society actors unsupportive of agreement	Train/Equip • Give technical assistance to elections • Broker talks for power sharing or consociational agreement • Give technical assistance to transitional authority • Train and support civil society actors to speak out freely for their views
Collapsed • No agreement on political reconstruction • Actors incapable of holding elections • Civil society not consulted	Administer • Establish path of political reconstruction by international decree • Administer elections • Disempower elites of old regimes in favor of reformist elements in civil society

themselves in remaking Japan into a democracy. It is no exaggeration to say that the United States reshaped local norms to legitimize the Japanese state according to democratic theory of legitimacy and that they were able to do so because there was no competing alternative. The breadth of ambition is only less impressive than the success with which democratic Japan has endured for more than six decades.[19]

An example of a more troubled, but still successful, internationally imposed legitimizing agreement is the Dayton Accords ending the war in Bosnia. Following the fratricidal civil war in Bosnia between Croats, Serbs, and Bosnian Muslims, there was no locally credible means of legitimizing a Bosnian state. NATO, led by the United States, forced the parties to the negotiating table following military action in 1995 and left the parties with little alternative to signing the Dayton Accords. Dayton

19. Dobbins, *America's Role in Nation-Building*; Dower, *Embracing Defeat*; Wolfe, *Americans as Proconsuls*.

established a multiethnic consociational democracy in Bosnia enforced by a de facto international executive authority in the Office of the High Representative created to implement the agreement. The implementation of Dayton and the performance of the High Representative have been the subject of much scholarly criticism, but the basic fact remains that Bosnia has remained at peace and democratic practice has been ongoing for fifteen years under Dayton and its institutions. Bosnia has held a half-dozen national elections since 1995 and was rated "partly free" by Freedom House in 2011. Political violence has not resurfaced despite the drawdown from 60,000 international military personnel in 1995 to just 1,200 in 2012, suggesting that Bosnians have come to accept new democratic norms of legitimacy and that their state is not simply held together by external fiat, contrary to the claims of some critics.[20]

Despite these examples of success we can note several of failure in the context of completely collapsed legitimacy environments. The most illustrative is Somalia. Somalia has been without government since the fall of the Barre government in 1991. Several agreements have been signed; none have held. The state-building intervention there from 1993 to 1995 failed in part because there was no agreement among warring parties, no transitional government with which the international state builders could work, and the international community did not fill the void by decreeing a path of political reconstruction and establishing an international transitional authority. There was no legitimate claimant to statehood, and the state builders did nothing to create one.

REBUILDING CAPACITY

Rebuilding weak and failed states' institutional capacity has received a significant amount of attention in recent decades. I noted in chapter 1 that many scholars' and policymakers' definition of "state building" was, effectively, institution building. Because of the close link, and because international organizations like the World Bank have been attempting to strengthen weak states' institutions since at least the 1980s, there is a large amount of work on institutional capacity building. Less noticed is how institutional capacity building fits in with the broad project of state building. Scholars and policymakers have also neglected the

20. The literature on Bosnia is massive. See, for example, Berdal and Economides, *United Nations Interventionism*; Chesterman, *You, the People*; Dobbins, *America's Role in Nation- Building*; Doyle and Sambanis, *Making War and Building Peace*; Durch and Schear, "Faultlines"; Fleitz, *Peacekeeping Fiascoes of the 1990s*; Muehlmann, "Police Restructuring in Bosnia-Herzegovina"; and Paris, *At War's End*.

relationship between institutional capacity building and international transitional administration, which I view as the same basic activity at different levels of intensity. In this section I combine the discussion of rebuilding the state's capacity with a discussion about rebuilding the state's ability to extract resources, because the relevant strategies of state building are effectively identical.

Observer Strategy. A state with weak capacity still functions at a minimal level. In this situation, international state builders should deploy an observer mission to monitor civilian administration and encourage reform. The international community succeeded in Croatia, Namibia, and Nicaragua (1989) despite deploying relatively light civilian monitoring missions to those states. They succeeded because those states needed less help. The institutions of government in Croatia, Namibia, and Nicaragua functioned at a higher level than most postconflict, failed, or poor states. For example, they each collected 30 percent or more of GDP in taxes and had a life expectancy above sixty years. A light civilian monitoring mission was all that was required.

Trainer Strategy. A state whose institutional capacity is failing or has failed has ceased performing some key functions. Some bureaucracies may have broken down or effectively stopped delivering services, while others are still operating. Skilled personnel are in short supply, and equipment is outdated, broken, or unavailable. In this situation international state builders should deploy a technical assistance and capacity-building mission. Technical assistance and capacity-building programs traditionally have included efforts to train civil servants, provide equipment, and rebuild infrastructure. Since the end of the Cold War, practitioners have noted the importance of fostering organizational culture, imparting a sense of mission to civil servants, helping management cultivate a "mystique" about their organizations, streamlining procedures, executing budgets, facilitating networks of communication, and reorienting institutions to be performance and customer focused.[21] Of all state building activities, this is among the most expensive (aside from the cost of military operations), so this strategy requires sizeable and long-lasting donor commitments.

The current state-building operation in Liberia may be an example of a successful technical assistance and capacity-building strategy, although it is too early to say with certainty how successful it is. Liberia was wracked by civil war from 1989 to 2003, with only brief pauses during the 1990s. Despite a previous history as one of the better-performing governments in Africa, by 2003 it had dropped to the ranks of one of the poorest and least developed. The international intervention that began in

21. Hilderbrand and Grindle, "Building Sustainable Capacity."

2003 was marked by several notable features. The UN Mission in Liberia's (UNMIL's) mandate included provisions to help reestablish a "functioning administrative structure at both the national and local levels" and "consolidate government institutions, including a national legal framework and judicial and corrective institutions."[22] The mandate amounted to a fairly strong directive to restore the government's institutional capacity, a much more direct mandate to focus on institutional strengthening than the typical mandates during the 1990s. The World Bank established a number of capacity-building projects in Liberia, including programs supporting the Liberian Ministry of Finance, the Institution of Public Administration, the General Auditing Commission, and the Extractive Industries Transparency Initiative.[23] Donors funded capacity-building and other programs with over $1.5 billion in official development assistance between 2004 and 2007: at $120.44 per person per year, it is one of the better-funded state-building operations. The UN deployed 455 international civilians as part of UNMIL, a massive number for a country of Liberia's size (Sierra Leone, with a million more people, had almost a third fewer international civilians in its UN mission; the Democratic Republic of the Congo, sixteen times larger in population and twenty-four times larger in landmass, has only twice the number of international civilians). Partly as a result of international capacity-building efforts, Liberia has shown one of the strongest and broadest postconflict improvements in governance of post–Cold War state-building operations, according to the World Bank's Governance Indicators. While still weak, every aspect of governance—voice and accountability, political stability, government effectiveness, regulatory quality, control of corruption, and the rule of law—has improved since 2003. Liberia leapt from the seventh to the thirty-third percentile for control of corruption in that timeframe. Liberia's success shows what international technical assistance and capacity building, armed with a proper mandate and adequate funds and personnel, can accomplish.

Administrator Strategy. An incapable state is one whose institutions have largely ceased to function and that does not provide services to the people. In this situation, breakdown is so widespread and incapacity so pervasive that a technical assistance mission would be ineffective, like the proverbial effort to bail out the ocean with a thimble. If international state builders embark on a state-building effort in an incapable state, they should explore the feasibility of an international trusteeship, transitional administration, military government, or

---

22. United Nations Security Council Resolution S/RES/1503 (2003).
23. World Bank, "In Liberia, World Bank Support."

temporary international executive authority. The international community is likely to make the most progress by directly administering as many of the state institutions as it can, primarily as a means of providing on-the-job training for the local population.

We need to distinguish this strategy for rebuilding collapsed capacity from the parallel strategy to administer the security sector in anarchic security environments. In an anarchic security environment, international state builders must assume responsibility for enforcing public security, which may or may not involve establishing a military government depending on whether or not there is a local civilian authority with which to partner. By contrast, in an incapable state, international state builders must assume responsibility for providing governance, which *necessarily* means assuming functions of sovereignty that the local state cannot perform. In this view, international administration of the civilian organs of government can take the form of a temporary civilian authority or a military government. It may be confusing to view a military government as part of a strategy to rebuild a state's civilian capacity, but that is precisely what military governments do. They are not fundamentally about a *security* strategy but a *civilian* strategy to get civilian institutions of government functioning again.

It is also important to recognize that temporary international authority is simply the logical extension of a train-and-equip strategy. Both involve international state builders providing resources that the failed or collapsed state lacks: in the case of a merely failed state, it is a lack of training, equipment, money, or certain skills. In the case of a collapsed state, it lacks everything, including leadership, or what the military calls command and control. Military government and international administration are simply the temporary provision of command and control until local capacities are up and running.

The international community tends to be hesitant to adopt this option, although there are a number of historical examples of it. Examples of civilian authority include the US authority in Cuba in 1906, the Coalition Provisional Authority in Iraq in 2003, the UN Transitional Administration in East Timor (UNTAET) in 1999, the UN Transitional Authority in Cambodia (UNTAC) in 1992, the UN Interim Administration Mission in Kosovo (UNAMIK) in 1999, and the Office of the High Representative in Bosnia in 1996. Examples of a military government include the US military governments in Cuba in 1898, the Dominican Republic from 1916 to 1924, and in West Germany, Japan, Italy, and South Korea in 1945. Interestingly, most of these interventions were at least shallow successes. They also appear to be more difficult to end. The post–World War II occupations lasted longer than the average state-building mission, as did the interventions in the Dominican Republic, Kosovo, and Bosnia. Once

[105]

international actors begin providing governance directly, they face two tasks at once: governing, and training local officials to take over governance at the earliest possible time. The former will take precedence over the latter in the crush of day-to-day operations, delaying the transition to local rule. Local actors, for their part, may not have a strong incentive to take over from international actors—the free-rider problem—if they believe the international actors are providing for free what would cost locals considerable time and effort to do and if locals see benefit to allowing international actors to remain accountable for tough decisions.

The operation in Timor-Leste is illustrative. Timor-Leste voted for independence from Indonesia in August 1999. Indonesian security forces embarked on a campaign of organized violence the next month that destroyed much of the Timorese infrastructure. Timor-Leste was already one of the poorest, least developed societies on earth. The Indonesians' departure, similar to the Belgian withdrawal from the Congo in 1960 or the American denazification program in West Germany in 1946, immediately deprived the state of almost all its most senior, skilled, and experienced civil servants and government officials. Under the circumstances, the United Nations believed it had little choice but to assume the role of the sovereign government of Timor-Leste from 1999 to 2002 (again paralleling state builders' actions in the Congo and West Germany, among other cases). According to its mandate, UNTAET was "endowed with overall responsibility for the administration of East Timor" and "empowered to exercise all legislative and executive authority, including the administration of justice." It was to "provide security and maintain law and order throughout the territory of East Timor" and "establish an effective administration."[24] The UN special representative, Sergio Vieira de Mello, ruled by decree, reminiscent of Brigadier General Leonard Wood in Havana one hundred years previously. UNTAET comprised more than 700 international civilians and more than 1,700 local civilians, backed by more than 6,200 soldiers. Parliamentary elections were held in 2001, and the UN handed sovereignty over to the new Timorese government the next year.

Since then the country has generally been stable, despite a brief and minor flare-up of violence in 2006. Another round of elections was successfully held in 2007. The country began its independent life in 2002 with a Polity IV score of 6, which has since improved to a 7. Real GDP per capita has grown by 1.75 percent since 2000. Timor-Leste remains one of the poorest states in the world, and government performance has generally been bad and has not improved, according to the

24. United Nations Security Council Resolution S/RES/1272 (1999).

TABLE 6.4. Matching Strategy to Degree of Capacity Failure

Degree of Failure	Strategy of State building
<u>Weak–Limited Functioning</u>	<u>Observe</u>
• Institutions minimally functioning	• Monitor civil service and bureaucracy
<u>Failed–Partial functioning</u>	<u>Train/Equip</u>
• Some institutions nonfunctional	• Provide technical assistance
	• Train civil servants, government officials
<u>Collapsed–Incapable</u>	<u>Administer</u>
• Most/all institutions nonfunctional	• Establish international transitional authority

World Bank's governance indicators. At least one scholar and participant judged that UNTAET made some poor decisions early on—overly centralizing control and neglecting Timorese actors and institutions (again the difficulty of governing and training in governance simultaneously)—which may account for the Timorese government's below-par performance. But considering the absence of widespread political violence, the state's continued independence, the continuation of democratic practice, and decent economic performance, Timor-Leste is a clear example of successful state building. It seems hardly fair to conclude that the UN "built state failure" in Timor-Leste.[25]

The intervention in the Dominican Republic illustrates how an international administration can fail if implemented poorly. The Dominican Republic was chronically unstable, insolvent, and provided little in the way of services to the population. The United States imposed a military government on the Dominican Republic in 1916 to preempt suspected European intervention and preserve the US monopoly on the route to the Panama Canal. The military government, backed by only three thousand Marines, divided the Dominican Republic into military districts and assigned a Marine commander to act as the civil governor of each area. The Marine governors administered their areas through Marine provost marshals posted in towns and villages. At the national level Marines assumed control of key ministries, and at the local level Marines were given powers to investigate, prosecute, and judge crimes against the occupation. The US military government "would assume complete control of Dominican finances and would supervise law enforcement, the judiciary, and internal administration . . . [while] the ordinary administration of both civil and criminal justice would remain the responsibility of

25. Chopra, "Building State Failure."

Dominican courts and officials."[26] American personnel saw to a wide range of civilian tasks: they ensured that "roads [were] built, jails cleaned up, sanitation imposed, hospitals updated, taxes overhauled."[27] In addition, the Marines disarmed the population and formed and trained a new constabulary to replace the old army.

If the United States imposed a military government on an incapable state, why did the state-building effort ultimately fail? Two reasons stand out: first, the United States had an inadequate security strategy—the Dominican military proved disloyal to the civilian authority—but also the US military government itself was inadequate. It did not have a plan to train Dominicans or invest in the Dominican economy. Aside from bringing in US Department of Agriculture advisers to teach Dominicans better farming techniques, "the Marine brigade in the Dominican Republic had no organized, nationwide program for improving the economic and social condition of the people."[28] And crucially, it also neglected to build the capacity of the Dominican government. The Marines "observed Dominican civil officials in the performance of their duties," and "supervised the Dominican officials responsible for local police, schools, road maintenance and other municipal functions."[29] The Marines "observed" and "supervised," but did not train, the Dominican bureaucracy. If the military government had invested more in the Dominican economy and the bureaucracy, the military might not have thought that it had the support to turn against the civilian government in 1930.

Are there examples of cases when international state builders should have established an international authority but refrained? By most measures, including life expectancy, infant mortality, per capita GDP, and government revenue as a percentage of GDP, Liberia, the Democratic Republic of the Congo, Angola, Sierra Leone, Haiti, Somalia, and Afghanistan were comprehensively incapable states that did not provide services to their populations, and they may have been good candidates for an international transitional administration. The state-building operation in Haiti from 1915 to 1934 was a shallow success, but the operation in the same state from 1993 to 1996 was a failure: in the former operation, the state builders assumed de facto responsibility for administering civilian governance, whereas in the latter they failed to deploy a robust civilian assistance mission, let alone establish a transitional authority. In Liberia (1993), Somalia, the Congo (1999), and Angola ongoing violence exacerbated the breakdown of civilian governance. The inadequate military deployments were

26. Fuller and Cosmas, *Marines in the Dominican Republic*, 25.
27. Boot, *Savage Wars of Peace*, 170.
28. Fuller and Cosmas, *Marines in the Dominican Republic*, 59.
29. Ibid, 55–56.

matched by inadequate civilian missions, which together led to some of the most spectacular state-building failures in history. Local allies were left with little to no resources with which to advance the state-building agenda; local opponents faced little to no penalty for reneging on agreements. The collapse of those states across multiple dimensions of statehood suggest that if the international community was to have succeeded in building those states, it should have contemplated a civilian transitional authority backed by a substantial military force. I am not advocating such a policy so much as saying that such a policy would have been necessary for success once the international community chose to undertake a state-building mission under circumstances of complete institutional breakdown. An equally defensible position, considering the costs of a successful intervention, is to argue that the international community should not attempt state-building operations under those circumstances at all.

Investing in Prosperity

In the previous chapter I described how failed states can display a variety of symptoms of economic failure. Poverty by itself should not be considered an economic failure, but economic underperformance resulting from war, destruction, maladministration, corruption, distorted incentives, looting, or overreliance on natural resources should. State builders' specific programs and policies should be tailored to the unique circumstances of economic failure, but it is not my intent to dwell on specific programs and policies—what we might call the tactics of state building. Rather, my focus is on state builders' broader strategic options. Should economic reconstruction be led by local or by international actors? That in turn depends on a prior question: Do local actors have enough resources and expertise, or do they need a temporary injection of international money and know-how?

Observer Strategy. International state builders can successfully adopt an observer strategy only in states that have experienced very little economic failure, have ample resources, are already committed to a reform program, and have the human capital and technical expertise to implement it. Few states targeted for state building fit into this category. They have to have failed dramatically in some other category to draw international attention yet somehow have escaped the normal economic consequences of such failure—a rare combination. Croatia in 1996 is a good example. Its failures were of security and legitimacy: Croatian Serbs did not trust the state to guarantee their safety during the transition of their areas back to Croatian sovereignty because of the recent war, nor did they accept the legitimacy of the Croatian state. The Croatian economy,

[109]

however, weathered the war well. GDP per capita was $5,699 (in 1990 constant dollars), the absolute highest figure for any state in the first year of a state-building operation. Government institutions continued to function well: the state collected over 37 percent of GDP in revenue that year. State builders accordingly did not focus attention on the Croatian economy. Donors gave a mere $28.51 per person per year during the intervention and for the decade afterward, compared to $267.10 in next-door Bosnia. State builders instead focused on implementing a brief but robust strategy to secure and relegitimize the state, imposing a transitional administration over a few select areas backed by more than eight thousand troops. The strategy was a success, and the Croatian economy grew strongly through the next decade without donor help. It simply needed less assistance in the first place.

Trainer Strategy. Almost all states targeted for state building are in significantly worse economic shape than Croatia was. Two types of economic failure together present the next level of economic failure and both require substantial financial and technical assistance from international state builders to fix: war-devastated and resource-cursed states. In these states an effective strategy of state building involves technical and financial assistance to rebuild infrastructure and train and equip economic officials—but need not involve the direct administration of reconstruction programs by international actors who might sideline or undermine local actors.

State builders rebuilding war-devastated states have two advantages. Postwar economies typically boom when peace returns, and much reconstruction is a straightforward matter of rebuilding infrastructure. The boom gives state builders time and momentum and can provide the target state with needed tax revenues to begin locally initiated rebuilding projects. Rebuilding infrastructure is, compared to other economic development programs, fairly simple and uncontroversial—more so than budgetary planning, reforming a central bank, revamping legal and regulatory codes, or other more complex economic state-building policies. Infrastructure projects are both a direct economic stimulus that provides jobs and cash for the construction sector and an investment in economic capacity that increases the state's potential growth rate. A postwar boom and a well-financed slate of infrastructure projects cannot make up a full reconstruction strategy, but they can carry a state a long way from its wartime nadir. They should be complimented by a technical assistance package that is backed by sufficient donor pledges to train and equip local citizens to lead the reconstruction effort.

A separate but related challenge arises in states whose economies are malformed by overreliance on natural resources or states in which lootable resources make up a large amount of the state's economic activity. In practice, these states rarely become targets for state building unless they are also war-torn states. Examples include Angola and Iraq (oil), Liberia and Sierra Leone (diamonds), and Afghanistan (poppy). In these states state builders face all the same challenges of rebuilding war-torn states, and must also encourage diversification, law enforcement, and natural resource stewardship.

These states illustrate another point about economic state building. In both cases—of war-ravaged and resource-dependent states—a reconstruction strategy must be closely aligned and coordinated with a capacity-development strategy. The two aspects of state building are closely related. The difference is that capacity-building involves all institutions of government and some aspects of civil society and the non-profit sector, whereas reconstruction programs involve the economic institutions of government—including the central bank, a tax collection body, regulatory agencies, state-owned enterprises, and others—and the private sector. State building in both sectors involves increasing the capacity of local institutions, training and equipping locals to govern or produce more effectively, rooting out corruption, and improving institutional stability. The two aspects of state building are especially intertwined in the effort to counteract the distorted economic incentives created by wartime. Wartime economies create incentives for smuggling and black market transactions: they drive economic activity into illicit channels and push entrepreneurs and organized criminal groups together. Once entrenched, such interests can endure after war has ended so long as they can continue to make a profit. Reversing this dynamic involves both increasing licit economic opportunities—which is part of a reconstruction strategy—and also increasing the state's capacity for law enforcement—which is part of the capacity and even security strategies.

Finally, the key element of a Trainer strategy, as opposed to the Administrator strategy, is working with and through local capacity where it exists. Issuing aid directly to the people or through donors and contractors replaces and thereby undermines the state's institutions, undercutting the long-term goal of state building. Channeling aid through institutions of the state that have been vetted for integrity and transparency helps the state develop its capacity in the public finance system, including managing the treasury, planning and executing a budget, raising revenue, issuing public debt, and managing state assets, another example of how the capacity-building and reconstruction strategies are mutually reinforcing.[30] States that are not completely collapsed retain some institutional capacity, which state builders should view as their most important resource for state building.

30. Carnahan and Lockhart, "Peacebuilding and Public Finance."

Administrator Strategy. In some states economic failure has reached the point that the state is no longer able to lead or even participate, initially, in the reconstruction process. Economic failure of this type typically results not from war (or not only from war) but from long-running neglect, institutional breakdown, and the absence of basic human capital. This type of economic failure is harder to fix because it is not a matter of reversing war damage or riding the wave of a postwar boom. It requires implementing difficult, and often controversial, structural reforms, increasing the capacity of key economic institutions through intensive training programs, rooting out corruption, establishing normal economic incentives, and even growing a culture of trust, enforceable contracts, and commercial dispute resolution under the rule of law.

This strategy of state building is closely related to the Administrator strategy in capacity development and in fact may require many of the same steps. International actors may need to temporarily administer key institutions, such as the central bank, the public treasury, and the mint as a stopgap until locals are able to do so; even then, an embedded technical-assistance presence may be required. When locals are unable to coordinate a large donor effort or draft a useable reconstruction blueprint, international actors should do so. This is roughly the strategy that international actors successfully pursued in Afghanistan, absent the formal trappings of an international transitional administration.

Restoring Humanity

States that become the object of a state-building operation are typically emerging from (or in the midst of) war or regime change, or both. They have often been the site of war crimes, human rights abuses, repression, tyranny, or, at the worst, totalitarianism, ethnic cleansing, or genocide. Rebuilding a state's respect for human dignity in the aftermath of barbarism is a both a matter of preventing future inhumanity and coping with the past. Preventing future inhumanity is accomplished by ending war, rebuilding the rule of law, and refounding the state's legitimacy on a broadly accepted democratic basis, which we have dealt with above. In this section I will discuss specific steps relevant to a state's human rights situation and with coping with the past—or transitional justice.

There is a wide literature on the comparative merits and weaknesses of truth-and-reconciliation commissions, war crimes tribunals, and blanket amnesties. It is unlikely that any one institutional form is the best means for reestablishing a state's respect for human dignity in all states, and I therefore do not recommend, for example, a truth-and-reconciliation commission in a merely failed state versus an international tribunal in collapsed state. The choice about the form and content of transitional justice is tightly connected to a new regime's emerging legitimacy, and therefore it should emerge from local views and beliefs. Local citizens are likely to judge a new regime's claim to legitimacy by how credibly it deals with past atrocities. Democratic legitimacy is easier to adopt the "thinner" the concept is—that is, the more flexible and responsive to local circumstances. Similarly, transitional justice works best when it is responsive to local concerns and beliefs. As such, international state builders probably do not have a role in prescribing one form of transitional justice over another. At best, they can advise about the merits of tribunals compared to commissions and amnesties, but it seems that transitional justice mechanisms are likely to succeed best when they are most responsive to local wishes.

Observer Strategy. In states with a poor human rights record, the government is publicly committed to protecting human rights and preventing future atrocities, but it may be unable or unaccustomed to doing so. Security services might bully citizens, journalists, and dissidents out of habit developed under a prior regime. Courts and legislatures might not yet have created the legal instruments necessary to protect human rights simply out of a lack of internalizing their responsibility for doing so. Broadly, the state has not yet reoriented its security and judicial services away from solely protecting itself and toward protecting its people. The state is negligent, not barbaric. Rebuilding a state with habitual disregard for human dignity involves monitoring and reporting on the human rights situation, providing public information about human rights, and encouraging ongoing reform. International state builders are primarily in the position of teachers.

Trainer Strategy. A state that has failed to protect human rights is still struggling to overcome current and past inhumane acts. There may be a recent history of war crimes and human rights abuses for which there was no accounting, an ongoing culture of impunity among political and military elites, and a trend toward repression. These states may publicly claim to be committed to protecting human rights and accounting for past crimes, and even create institutions dedicated to human rights, but they take few steps because doing so would threaten current elites.

Rebuilding these states involves more than monitoring and reporting. International state builders need to take a more active role, primarily by partnering with local advocates and institutions dedicated to human rights and transitional justice. Elites in these states permit such advocates and institutions to exist but do not give them resources or support. The international community can fill that role by training human rights

[113]

TABLE 6.5. Matching Strategy to Degree of Human Failure

Degree of Failure	Strategy of State Building
Weak–Negligent • Government unable or unaccustomed to protecting human rights	Observe • Monitor human rights • Provide public information about human rights • Encourage ongoing reform
Failed–Repressive • Past history of mutual war crimes and ethnic cleansing, ongoing culture of impunity and recriminations • Current trend towards repression	Train/Equip • Empower civil society • Train human rights advocates • Support truth and reconciliation commissions • Give technical assistance to investigations
Collapsed–Barbaric • Totalitarianism • Genocide	Administer • Effect regime change • Establish international tribunal

advocates and journalists, giving technical assistance to human rights organizations, transitional justice commissions, or war crimes investigators, and targeting capacity-building programs to the justice sector. As with the effort to promote democratic legitimacy, the goal is to increase the power of local advocates against their rivals. This strategy of state building is necessarily political and not neutral; over time, some elites are likely to feel threatened by the international presence. This strategy must be matched by an appropriate security strategy to protect local and international human rights workers and by a legitimacy strategy that accounts for the legitimate interests of elite actors. If elites threatened by the effort to protect human rights and account for the past come to believe *all* aspects of the state-building operation are stacked against them, they are likely to take steps to organize violent opposition to the international presence; if, however, they believe that the political process is fair and legitimate and affords them the opportunity to protect themselves, they may channel their opposition through the peaceful political process.

Administrator Strategy. Some states should be considered collapsed if they deliberately and systematically destroy some or all of their people's human functioning as a matter of policy, even if their bureaucracies function at a high level. Policymakers should not feel obligated to consider such regimes states at all but simply organized groups of thugs, terrorists, or murderers. It should be clear that in these states—totalitarian regimes and perpetrators of genocide—no amount of technical assistance or civil society empowerment will rebuild the state's humanity. If international state builders choose to undertake a state-building operation in

[114]

a barbaric state, the first step is regime change, followed by a purge of former regime elements from national life.

This is less a strategy of *state building* than an argument about just war. War is sometimes the necessary prerequisite before a state-building operation can take place. Specifically, the military overthrow of a barbaric regime is necessary before any attempt can be made to improve a state's governance. This is a commonsensical point: before the Allies could try the Nazi leaders at Nuremberg, they first had to defeat the Wehrmacht. The Allies stopped the Holocaust not through empowering civil society advocates but by overrunning the concentration camps. More recently, before the United States and United Nations could establish the Afghan Independent Human Rights Commission, they had to defeat the Taliban regime. Regime change as a precondition for improving a state's human rights record is not unheard of. The international community accomplished it in West Germany, Japan, Italy, Afghanistan, Iraq, and arguably Bosnia and Kosovo (by defeating and eventually catalyzing the fall of the Serbian government). International actors did not overthrew those regimes *in order to* improve the human rights situation in each state—obviously many motives were at work in each case—but regime change was necessary before any attempt could be made to improve human rights in those states. The ability to rebuild respect for human rights was a consequence, not necessarily a motivating cause, of the military campaigns.

Several cases are instructive because of what the international community failed to do, and what the consequences were. The Khmer Rouge genocide in Cambodia was stopped not by the UN intervention there, but by the Vietnamese invasion of Phnom Penh a decade previously. Similarly, the Hutu genocide against Rwandan Tutsi ended not through any effort of the infamously ineffectual UN peacekeeping force but because the Rwandan Patriotic Front (RPF) invaded Rwanda, defeated the Interahamwe, and overthrew the government. But the most instructive case is the ongoing effort by the UN to stop a genocide by appealing to the government responsible for it, in Sudan.

War erupted in 2003 between the government of Sudan and its allied Janjaweed militias on one side, and an array of Darfuri rebel groups in western Sudan on the other. Many observers accused Sudanese forces and allied militias of deliberately targeting Darfuri civilians and estimated that four hundred thousand civilians died in the conflict. Several outside observers, including then-US Secretary of State Colin Powell, characterized the Sudanese government's actions as genocide against the people of Darfur. Sudan was also among the most oppressive regimes in the world: in 2003 Sudan had a Polity IV score of -6 and was rated by Freedom House as "not free." In response to the Sudanese government's barbarism, the African Union and the United Nations attempted to

[115]

deploy a robust but traditional peacekeeping force to Darfur. The AU helped broker a peace agreement in 2006, and the UN deployed the UN/AU Hybrid Mission in Darfur (UNAMID) in 2007 with a mandate to provide security, protect civilians, and facilitate implementation of the peace agreement.[31] However, far from seeking regime change in Khartoum, the arrangement looked to the government of Sudan as a prospective partner in peacekeeping efforts, an incredible provision that simply overlooked the realities of the war. Even allowing for the fact that the UN cannot be expected to overthrow the government of a member state, the mandate contained no provision similar to the revised mandate in Sierra Leone that instructed the force to take sides and combat the Revolutionary United Front (RUF) if necessary. UNAMID's mandate pretended that it could partner with a cooperative Sudanese government to reverse the barbarism that the government itself was perpetrating. Unsurprisingly, fighting continued in 2008, and UNAMID admitted on its own website in 2010 that "UNAMID's full deployment has been hampered by a lack of cooperation from the Government of Sudan," and in 2012 that it operates "in the face of bureaucratic and armed obstruction."[32] The UN Secretary General noted that there were continuing military operations between Sudanese forces and rebels in Darfur in early 2010, and reported that there was "increasing intercommunal violence and banditry" in the area.[33] The UN effort in Sudan is premised on a completely inappropriate strategy across almost all dimensions of statehood; at root is the failure of outside powers to seek regime change in Khartoum, without which there is unlikely to be progress in any area. The killing may end (probably because Khartoum believes it has achieved its objective of protecting the state's territorial integrity, not because of the AU or UN forces), but there almost certainly will be no accountability for the genocide and no softening of the government's totalitarian rule. It may be that effecting regime change in Sudan is impractical or undesirable for other reasons; if so, the international community should also recognize that it is simply unable to make sustainable progress halting genocide or rebuilding the humanitarian situation there either.

30. Carnahan and Lockhart, "Peacebuilding and Public Finance."
31. United Nations Security Council Resolution S/RES/370 (2007).
32. United Nations, "UNAMID Background." The former quotation is no longer on the website.
33. United Nations Security Council Resolution S/RES/50 (2010).

[7]

Five State-Building Case Studies

In this chapter I test my theory against five cases of armed state building. I use the five dimensions of statehood to structure and focus each case. First, I describe the general background to the case. Second, I describe the degree of failure in each dimension of statehood. Third, I describe the state-building strategy employed (if any) in each dimension of statehood, and assess whether or not it addressed the dynamics of state failure in that dimension of statehood. Fourth, I employ process-tracing methodology to illustrate how the strategic match or mismatch caused the outcome observed in the case.

I chose cases that demonstrate variance in my independent variable. My independent variable is the match, partial match, or mismatch between the armed state-building strategy and the type and degree of state failure. I have chosen one case that demonstrates a match between strategy and conditions across all dimensions of statehood (West Germany, 1945–55); one that partially matches (Nicaragua, 1989–92); and one that demonstrates a complete mismatch across all dimensions (Liberia, 1993–97). I have also selected cases that illustrate variance on the independent variable *within* the case—that is, cases in which the international community changed its strategy in the middle of the intervention—and I demonstrate how that change affected the outcome. I show how the international community's adoption of a more aggressive and robust military approach in Sierra Leone in 2000 turned a failing mission into a

TABLE 7.1. List of Qualitative Case Studies

Germany	Europe	Post–WW II	Full match
Nicaragua 1989	Americas	Post–Cold War	Partial match
Liberia 1993 Liberia 2003	Africa	Post–Cold War	Full mismatch Change in strategy
Sierra Leone	Africa	Post–Cold War	Change in strategy
Afghanistan	South Asia	Post-9/11	Partial match Change in strategy

success. Finally, I contrast the strategy of state building in Afghanistan before and after 2006. My cases also reflect a diversity of time periods and geographical regions.

METHODOLOGY

I measured state failure, state building, and outcomes independently to guard against measurement bias and a possible endogeneity error. I measured state failure with a wide range of metrics, including battle deaths before and during an intervention; GDP per capita; previous high GDP; changes in Polity IV score; government revenue as a percentage of GDP; the World Bank's governance indicators; the UN's human development index; and a range of socioeconomic indicators, including life expectancy and infant mortality. Not all data were available for all cases.[1]

I measured state-building strategies by examining the state builder's mandate or stated purpose and by examining the number of military

1. Security indicators are derived from the Correlates of War data set and the Uppsala Conflict Data Program. COW is available at http://www.correlatesofwar.org/. It is described in Sarkees and Wayman, *Resort to War*. I consulted the inter-, intra-, non-, and extra-state war lists in the COW data. For the Uppsala Data Conflict Program, see *UCDP Battle-Related Deaths Dataset v.5–2011*. Historical data on GDP and GDP per capita was derived from Maddison, *Historical Statistics of the World Economy, 1–2006 AD*. Historical data on government revenue was derived from Mitchell, *International Historical Statistics: 1750—2005*, 3 vols. Contemporary data on GDP per capita was derived from the IMF's *World Economic Outlook Database*, April 2012. The World Bank's governance indicators are found in Kaufman, Kraay, and Mastruzzi, *Worldwide Governance Indicators*. Contemporary data on government revenue, as well as data on infant mortality and life expectancy and other socioeconomic indicators recorded in tables in this chapter, are derived from the World Bank's *World Development Indicators Database*. Polity IV scores are drawn from Marshall, *Polity IV Project*. (Full information can be found in this book's bibliography.)

[118]

personnel it deployed (as well as the ratio of troops to population and troops to land mass), the duration of their deployment, and the amount of donor assistance given (calculated as well as the ratio of dollars per capita per year during the intervention and for ten years afterward). I also examined how these resources were employed—specifically, whether they were used to observe, train, or administer, and in which sector of statehood they were employed—by reference to general histories of each case.

I discuss how I measure outcomes in appendix B.

WEST GERMANY, 1945–1955

The armed state-building operation in West Germany from 1945 to 1955 is an example of a full match between the strategy of state building and the type and degree of state failure. It is also one of the most clear-cut and comprehensive successes in the history of state building.

The armed state-building operation in West Germany is unique, or nearly so, in several respects. The intervention followed a total war fought between the world's great powers. The intervention started in the aftermath of one great power rivalry, and took shape in the shadow of another one. It took place in a state that failed because of its comprehensive defeat in interstate war. Ethnic cleavages, civil war, and insurgency played no role in the situation. It is the third most populous state in which an armed state building operation has been attempted (after Japan and the Democratic Republic of the Congo in 1999) and is an extreme outlier in terms of the peak troop strength deployed during the operation.

Some scholars treat West Germany's (and Japan's) uniqueness as grounds for dismissing its applicability to today's armed state-building operations. They appear to treat West Germany and Japan as a data set with a population of two that can be safely set aside because the unique circumstances are unlikely to be replicated in today's environment. Such reasoning is wrong, especially because Germany is a clear and undisputed success story.[2] Precisely because it is both unique in some variables and a

2. It is sometimes said that Germany and Japan are the "exceptions that prove the rule." That argument is a logically incoherent misuse of a common phrase. An "exception that proves the rule" is more accurately called an "exemption that illustrates the broader principle," e. g., a sign proscribing parking on a street during certain times implies that parking is allowed at other times. The way the phrase is usually used—meaning "evidence in favor of an argument is actually evidence against it because of its uniqueness"—is nonsense. As Sir Arthur Conan Doyle has Sherlock Holmes say, exceptions do not prove rules; they disprove them. There is no reason Germany and Japan should be dismissed out of hand as cases from which lessons might be drawn for international state building.

[119]

success, Germany is a key test of the scope conditions and generally applicability of my theory. If my theory can explain Germany's success in terms that also explain the outcomes of other cases, it will be a strong indicator that my theory has broad applicability and that Germany's success can be replicated elsewhere.

Background

Through a series of wars and diplomatic maneuvers King Wilhelm of Prussia unified most German-speaking polities in Europe and proclaimed himself Kaiser Wilhelm I of Germany in 1871. The new nation-state, with a large landmass, sizeable population, exploitable resources, and rapidly industrializing economy, quickly became a great power in Europe and competed with France, England, and other states for influence, colonies, and wealth. After being narrowly defeated in World War I, Germany became a republic but retained its territorial integrity and great power potential. The republic suffered from a collapsed economy, weak institutions, and political extremism from the right and left. A dubious electoral victory by the National Socialist Party in 1933 led to the imposition of single-party rule—its Polity IV score dropped from 6 to -9 in a single year. Remilitarization fueled economic recovery, enabling the National Socialists to consolidate power, remove dissidents, and launch a war of conquest across Europe in 1939. In the process the party's leaders erected one of the most autocratic and barbaric regimes in history.

After nearly six years of fighting, the German government was defeated and overthrown, principally by the United States, United Kingdom, and the Soviet Union, concluding World War II in Europe. Germany was initially divided into four zones of occupation under the United States, United Kingdom, France, and the Soviet Union. The United States, United Kingdom, and France eventually merged their zones of occupation and formed the Federal Republic of Germany (West Germany) in 1949, but state building in the west predated the formal creation of the state by several years. The US zone was governed through the Office of Military Government, United States, which reported to the four-power Allied Control Council. The ACC broke down in early 1948, a casualty of the Cold War. After the Federal Republic was created a year later, OMGUS was replaced by the civilian High Commissioner for Germany.

The Allies' mandate for the occupation, governance, and reconstruction of Germany was captured in a series of documents that were not always consistent with each other. The documents universally agreed that, as the Potsdam Agreement put it, "supreme authority in Germany is exercised" by the Allied governments and the occupation authority. The Joint Chiefs of Staff Directive 1067 instructed US officers that "you are, by virtue of your position, clothed with supreme legislative, executive, and judicial authority in the areas occupied by forces under your command." The goal was to "prevent Germany from ever again becoming a threat to the peace of the world [through the] eventual reconstruction of German political life on a democratic basis," according to the final version of JCS 1067.[3] Officials disagreed about postwar economic policy and other issues, but there was no disagreement about the basic approach of assuming responsibility for governing Germany.

State Failure in West Germany

West Germany had enjoyed strong political institutions and a robust economy before World War II, but both had been almost completely destroyed by the war. It was an open question as to how realistic the project to reconstruct Germany was.

Security. Security in Germany was weak at the time of the surrender, but it had not completely collapsed. An estimated 4.2 million Germans had been killed in the war. Fighting, especially in the final months, was brutal. Because of the depth of bitterness and the German forces' seeming inexhaustible will to resist, US forces prepared to meet continued guerilla resistance after the official surrender. Some Nazi leaders did indeed begin planning a guerilla campaign—the Werwolf plan—but in practice it did not materialize. The armed state-building operation in West Germany took place in a relatively violence-free security environment, a crucial "dog that did not bark" that was key for the Allies' ability to draw down their military presence quickly. The situation was far from stable—the absence of German security forces and the widespread unemployment, hunger, and privation almost certainly made crime and banditry a serious problem—but neither was it completely anarchic. There were no widespread reprisals by German civilians against former regime elements, no guerilla movement against the Allies, and no civil war between Nazi diehards and reformists to determine the state's future shape.[4]

Legitimacy. The legitimacy of the German state had completely collapsed. Kaiser Wilhelm's state had staked its legitimacy on being the political expression of German-speaking people. The National Socialists narrowed this ideal further by redefining "German-ness" and excluding

---

3. The key clause about "the reconstruction of German political life on a democratic basis" is absent from earlier versions of JCS 1067, including the draft version republished in US Department of State, FRUS, *Conference at Malta and Yalta*, 143–54, reflecting the ongoing debate within the US government over the Morgenthau Plan and the ultimate fate of Germany.

4. Dobbins, et al., *America's Role in Nation-Building*, chap. 2.

Jews, Roma, Poles and other Slavic peoples, and other groups. The war and ensuing partition into East and West Germany discredited such racialist and ethnic-nationalist grounds for the German state. The only other recent German political experience was with democracy under the Weimer Republic, but it was precisely the failure of that democracy that led to the rise of the Nazi Party and Germany's present ruin. Germany had few resources with which to relegitimize the state.

Capacity. The institutions of the German government had completely collapsed, and the government was not capable of delivering goods and services. Infrastructure and public facilities were so destroyed that the country had an infant mortality rate comparable to that in Côte d'Ivoire or the Democratic Republic of the Congo today. GDP per capita—which was still rising until 1944—fell almost two-thirds from a peak of $6,084 in 1944 to $2,217 two years later (in 1990 constant international dollars), almost instantly impoverishing the German middle class. Banks and citizens, who held 450 billion Reichsmarks of government debt from the old regime, were bankrupt, and it was uncertain at the outset what the value of the currency was or even what currency was in use. Schools had closed; when they reopened, they lacked textbooks because of the Allies' prohibition on books printed by the old regime. Housing was inadequate and up to twenty million displaced persons were homeless or without shelter. Famine threatened millions with starvation. On top of the war damage, the initial wave of denazification instantly removed hundreds of thousands of civil servants, bureaucrats, teachers, and other government officials tainted by association with the National Socialist Party from public employment, leaving only the inexperienced to operate the machinery of government.[5]

Prosperity. There are no reliable statistics about the German government's revenue in 1945 or for several years afterward. Mitchell estimates that Germany collected 16.46 percent of GDP in revenue in 1950, about the level many poor developing states aspire to after years of capacity building and reconstruction. Because of the government's total breakdown in 1945, we can assume that its revenue generation had also totally collapsed.

Humanity. The German government under the National Socialists set a new standard for barbarity. Its crimes are infamous and hardly need repeating: it launched a war of aggression that ultimately killed millions of human beings, including several million systematically murdered in death camps. It waged genocide against Jews, Roma, and others. It conscripted millions of civilians and prisoners of war into slave labor. Its

5. Ibid.; Ziemke, *US Army in the Occupation of Germany.*

form of tyranny and oppression was so thorough and complete as to occasion the coining of a new term—totalitarianism—to describe it. The Nazi government's atrocities came to define *war crimes* and *crimes against humanity* for later generations. The National Socialist regime's actions were so blatantly inhuman that they compelled the international community to recognize a responsibility to prevent such atrocities in the future, captured in the Genocide Convention of 1948.

State Building in West Germany

The most appropriate strategy of state building would involve a military deployment to monitor the security situation and train a new security force; the establishment of an international transitional authority to restart the institutions of government and establish a relegitimizing process by decree; and, following regime change, an effort to purge elements of the former barbaric regime from national life. The Allies followed this strategy in virtually every respect, and succeeded strongly.

Security. The Allies imposed a military government on West Germany backed by between 1.6 and 2 million troops, easily the largest troop deployment in any armed state-building operation in history. The number is deceptive, however, because the Allies began rapid demobilization following Japan's surrender. There were 342,000 troops in West Germany in July 1946, about 200,000 by the end of 1946, and 135,000 by the summer of 1947. The United States organized a 30,000-strong constabulary to carry out police duty during the drawdown. Troop levels reached a low of 79,495 assigned to the entire European Command area of operation in 1950 before rebounding amid Cold War fears. The Allies did not need 2 million troops to rebuild Germany, especially considering the lack of unrest or insurgency against the occupiers, so the drawdown could occur without materially hurting the state-building effort.[6]

The high numbers are misleading in another sense. Despite a greater number of resources, the US troops did not have a particularly aggressive *mission* in West Germany after the surrender—especially compared to the role of US troops in South Vietnam, Iraq, or Afghanistan, or UN troops in Sierra Leone or in the Democratic Republic of the Congo in 1960. The massive US force in West Germany was essentially a giant monitoring and training mission to ensure the Germans adhered to the terms of the surrender; accordingly they—like the UN would in later monitoring operations—oversaw the demobilization and disarmament of the remaining German forces. The US constabulary force trained a

6. Dobbins, et al., *America's Role in Nation-Building.*

[123]

new German police force to focus on routine police duties. It is true that the Allies did not know what the security environment would be; according to Dobbins, US forces expected to encounter partisan resistance and planned accordingly. Although counterfactuals are always speculative, it is probable that the Allies' initially overwhelming force, and their preparations to meet partisan resistance, helped render such resistance futile and thereby preempted any from emerging.

Legitimacy. As East Germany increasingly became a satellite of the Soviet Union, West Germany embraced a new source of legitimacy as part of the Western democratic alliance against Communism. West Germany did not simply find legitimacy in democracy, although that is part of what happened: it found legitimacy in its new regional and global role as a member of the "free world," a key player in the nascent European-wide economy, and eventually as a full (rearmed) member of NATO. As such, the German state turned to democracy and economic liberalism to play the role that fascism had played in the Third Reich: a legitimizing public philosophy that gave the state purpose and direction at home and abroad.

The Allies planned and facilitated the transformation. Both the Potsdam Agreement and JCS 1067 explicitly named "the eventual reconstruction of German political life on a democratic basis" as a goal of the occupation. Local elections in small towns were held in January 1946. In the summer elections were held to state constitutional conventions, and in spring 1947 state legislative elections were held. In July 1948 state legislatures elected a parliamentary council to draft a new national constitution, and nationwide general elections were held in August 1949 to seat the new parliament. The democratic transformation was only the first step in reshaping Germany's new regional role as a partner in the democratic world. West Germany was increasingly integrated into the Western European economy through the European Recovery Program (the Marshall Plan) starting in 1948 and the European Coal and Steel Community starting in 1951. The Allies permitted West Germany to rearm and become a full member of NATO in 1955. By the end of the occupation, West Germany had crafted a new identity as a partner in the democratic West. In response to the German state's total collapse of legitimacy, the Allies had helped find a new foundation on which to build.

Capacity and Prosperity. The Allies established a military government and directly administered the German government until 1949 (indirectly until 1955), staffed by some 12,000 soldiers and civilians in the American sector alone (ranging up to 62,000 in West Germany as a whole).[7] In late

7. Zink, *United States in Germany.*

1945 military occupation teams fanned out across the country and embedded themselves as overseers of local administration in every town with more than twenty thousand people. They appointed mayors and administrators, set and enforced curfews, organized food supply and rationing systems, collected weapons and contraband, provided support for public health and safety, restored and operated utilities, cared for refugees and displaced persons, and cleared rubble.[8] Reconstruction programs were backed by $38.3 billion (in 2009 constant dollars) in economic and military assistance from the end of the war through the middle of the 1960s.[9] The effort to restore the capacity of the German state was comprehensive, but at the local level it was also short-lived. Shortly after local elections had put in place German government officials untainted by Nazism, the US began pulling back the military occupation teams from the lowest administrative units and replacing them with small liaison teams charged with observing and reporting on, but not administering, the German civil administration.[10] Starting in 1947 the Allies began creating institutions for economic administration across the zones of occupation. At the national level, the Allies created selected central institutions and continued to exercise full or partial control until 1955, by which time the German government was on a trajectory to become one among the most efficiently administered states in the world.

Humanity. The Allies effected regime change, tried the former regime's leaders for war crimes, and sought to purge the previous regime's influence from society as a whole. The Nuremberg Tribunal operated for just under one year, from October 1945 to October 1946 (a model of efficiency compared to later international tribunals). It indicted twenty-four top Nazi leaders, tried twenty-one, convicted eighteen, sentenced twelve to death, and executed ten. The broader denazification effort necessarily made use of local German courts created for the purpose because the Allies were unable to process the sheer number of potential defendants. The German courts were reportedly more lenient than the Allies had wanted, and historians often note that denazification ended up being far less pervasive than was initially intended, and therefore characterize it as a modest effort. It is true that only about 24.4 percent of Germans chargeable under the Law of Liberation from National Socialism and Militarism were ever tried, and only 3.2 percent were convicted. But historians are comparing denazification to its initially ambitious aims, not to transitional justice initiatives in other postwar societies. The 3.2 percent amounted to over

8. Ziemke, "Improvising in Postwar Germany."
9. USAID, *US Overseas Loans and Grants.*
10. Nelson, *History of US Military Forces in Germany.*

117,000 people convicted of war crimes, a staggering number compared, for example, to the handful prosecuted by the special court for Yugoslavia. Denazification in West Germany was one of the most ambitious and pervasive efforts to rehumanize a state and society blighted by barbarism in the history of armed state building, even allowing for how far it fell short of its original ambitions.

Result

The military campaign against the National Socialist regime followed by the denazification program and war crimes trials decisively altered the balance of power within Germany away from the former regime elements. Virtually all Nazi leaders with the will and capacity to resist the occupiers were dead, imprisoned, on trial, in hiding, or delegitimized. The Allies' overwhelming power and extensive controlling mandate at the outset of the operation made resistance futile. The armed state-building operation took the form of an irresistible leviathan against whom no opposition was possible—perhaps one reason why the Werwolf plan never came into effect. More important in the long run, the relegitimation campaign altered the public identities available for Germans such that the place from which opposition might be mounted—former regime loyalists and fascists—no longer existed. The combination of power and norm shifting simply removed potential opposition from the field. The Allies found a unique solution to the balance-of-power problem in the conditions of state failure: the imposition of complete hegemony. The result was cooperative state building.

Given the Allies' overwhelming power, the greater danger may have been free-riding and passing the buck by Germans sympathetic to the state-building campaign. The Allies might have become trapped governing Germany indefinitely—as, indeed, some feared might happen—if Germans were kept dependent on Allied aid. The debate surrounding the Morgenthau Plan reflected these concerns, and the ultimate rejection of the Morgenthau Plan in favor of the Marshall Plan by 1947 reflected the Allied consensus to empower Germany as a partner rather than rule it as a province. Three moves illustrate the Allied consensus. The withdrawal of military government teams from localities as early as 1946 and the shift toward liaison instead of direct control after local elections reflected the Allies' early recognition that they must empower Germans to participate in governance. Second, the structure of Marshall Plan aid compelled Germans to participate in economic reconstruction as well. The aid was not administered by US or Allied decision makers but disbursed to recipient governments through the Economic Cooperation

Agency, to which recipient governments sent envoys. Decision making on economic matters was thus put into the hands of Germans who had to make decisions cooperatively with the French and other recipients. Third, the training of new German security forces and, more so, its eventual rearmament and incorporation into NATO (unthinkable in 1945) demonstrated the Allies commitment to German empowerment. The Allies' motives, especially regarding German rearmament, stemmed from Cold War concerns, but regardless of motive it effectively prevented German free-riding.

The Allies applied an appropriate and well-calibrated strategy of state building across all five dimensions of statehood in West Germany. As a result, West Germany is the paradigmatic example of success in armed state-building operations. It did not revert to Nazism; there was no insurgency against Allied forces; and it enjoyed political stability for the decade following its resumption of sovereignty. The economy grew strongly during and after the intervention, averaging almost 8 percent annual GDP per capita growth, and West Germany recorded a sustained positive change of 19 points in its Polity IV score, reflecting its transition from Nazi tyranny to liberal democracy.

NICARAGUA, 1989–1992

Nicaragua is an example of a partial match between the international strategy of state building and the type and degree of state failure in the target state. The mission resulted in a shallow success.

Nicaragua was one of the first post–Cold War UN interventions that evolved past traditional peacekeeping. It blended a political mission with military operations in a state recovering from civil war. The mission in Nicaragua was clearly a departure from past precedent. It was distinct in several respects from deployments in, for example, Cyprus, South Asia, and the Sinai in which peacekeepers monitored cease-fires between belligerents in an interstate war and played little or no political role. But because it occurred early in the development of complex peacekeeping, liberal peace building, and international state building, it was also a small and disjointed mission compared to later operations. If the UN attempted a mission in a country under similar circumstances today, it would almost certainly go in with a broader mandate and higher aspirations. The comparatively small and narrow nature of the mission in Nicaragua is no reason to exclude it from our cases of state building. On the contrary, we should recognize that multilateral state building under UN auspices only became what it did because of the record of the early post–Cold War missions in places like Nicaragua,

Namibia, Mozambique, and Cambodia. The mission in Nicaragua holds more importance in the history of state building than its size would suggest.

Background

Nicaragua won independence from Spain in 1821 and from the United Provinces of Central America in 1838. Civil war, instability, and autocracy plagued the republic for much of the nineteenth and early twentieth centuries. The state's Polity IV score fluctuated between a -3 and a -8 from independence to 1978. The United States intervened in Nicaragua in the early twentieth century, as in many other South and Central American states, to impose stability, protect its economic interests, and prevent European intervention in a state that offered a potential rival route to the Panama Canal. During one especially intensive period, from 1927 to 1933, the United States was drawn into a full-blown state-building and counterinsurgency campaign involving, at its peak, some five thousand US troops. The United States brokered an end a civil war, oversaw elections in 1928, invested in Nicaraguan security forces, and fought to contain a new rebellion under the leadership of Augusto Sandino. The Nicaraguan government made peace with Sandino shortly after the US departure, which was unpopular with the military. The head National Guardsman, Anastasio Somoza, assassinated Sandino in 1934, seized power in 1937, and established a dictatorship.

The left-wing Sandinista National Liberation Front (FSLN) was founded in 1961 to carry on Sandino's legacy and oppose the Somoza dictatorship. The Sandinistas escalated their armed resistance to the Somoza regime in the 1970s, eventually toppling the Somoza regime and taking power in 1979. The establishment of the Sandinista government was, however, just another phase in the long Nicaraguan civil war. It was followed by ten more years of war with right-wing counter-revolutionary ("Contra") insurgents that killed 78,000 people, each side a proxy for the superpowers in the Cold War. The war was intertwined with similar conflicts in El Salvador and Guatemala, and drew in Honduras and Cost Rica as well. The end of the Cold War in Central America was reflected in the Esquipulas Accord of 1987, in which the leaders of five Central American states agreed to work towards cease-fires, national reconciliation, and elections. Nicaragua was the first to implement Esquipulas and reach a peace agreement with insurgents in 1989.

The parties requested the UN and the Organization of American States to oversee its implementation. The UN initially authorized the UN

Observer Group in Central America in November 1989 to verify the cessation of cross-border aid to armed groups by Central American states and the denial of safe haven for militants. ONUCA's mandate was expanded twice in the next few months to increase the UN force, enable it to facilitate demobilization, and monitor the cease-fire and separation of forces.[11] A separate mission, the UN Observer Group for the Verification of Elections in Nicaragua, was formed to oversee and facilitate the electoral aspects of the Esquipulas Accord. (This was early in the UN's foray into complex peacekeeping. The institutional architecture of integrated missions had not evolved yet.) The World Bank and International Monetary Fund became involved in efforts to reform and grow the Nicaraguan economy. Collectively, the interventions starting in 1989 mark the beginning of international state building in Nicaragua.

State Failure in Nicaragua

Nicaragua had never enjoyed a high level of security and stability. In 1989 it was recovering from a civil war that had lasted more than a decade—and that reflected a deep-rooted political conflict that dated to the founding of the republic. By the end of the civil war the security forces were militarized and widely distrusted. The Contras retained a strong, armed presence throughout the country. As is common in postconflict societies, violent criminality soon spiked after the war. On the positive side, large-scale political violence had ceased, but security was precarious.

It is not clear if the Nicaraguan state had ever enjoyed legitimacy with most Nicaraguans. The chronic instability, frequent political violence, and rigid authoritarianism characteristic of Nicaraguan political life suggests that the Nicaraguan state largely lacked a credible claim to legitimacy, and that there were no coherent, shared norms to which the state could appeal to legitimize its rule in a sustainable way. Conservatives and the military attempted to root the state's legitimacy in an appeal to the rule of law and to nationalism. Liberals and the Sandinistas attempted to root the state's legitimacy in their claim of serving the poor majority with land reform and social programs. Neither were able to consolidate their claim to legitimacy for long in Nicaragua's history, and by 1989 it was unclear what, if any, norms could legitimize the Nicaraguan state. The Esquipulas Accord and the follow-on agreements, entailing a commitment to democracy, was therefore an opportunity for a major

11. United Nations Security Council Resolutions S/RES/644 (1989); S/RES/650 (1990); S/RES/653 (1990).

change in Nicaraguan politics. It was also a plan without precedent in a country that had no experience with or heritage of democracy.

Nicaragua had a few small advantages compared to other states targeted for international state building: the government had not collapsed, and the economy was less worse off than might be expected. In terms of capacity and prosperity, the Nicaraguan state was weak but not failed. The Somoza dictatorship had been a model of efficient tyranny, as opposed to the Taliban model of mixing oppression with incompetence. After Somoza fell the Sandinista government made genuine efforts to govern the country, which kept the institutions of government in workable condition. Paris claims that government revenue fell precipitously in the 1980s because of investor flight and US economic sanctions,[12] but the World Bank records that the government still collected 30 percent of GDP in taxes in 1989, a remarkably normal figure, before falling dramatically to between 12 and 21 percent for the next decade. Life expectancy was 63.4 years and infant mortality was a relatively low (for a poor developing state), 53.4 per 1,000 live births. Nicaraguans were poor, but poverty was as much a direct result of war as of chronic underperformance: real GDP per capita had fallen by more than half during the war, partly because of a spike in inflation, suggesting a potential for a strong postwar rebound. And even after the war devastation, GDP per capita was still more than triple the worst levels of poverty in West Africa and South Asia.

Finally, the Nicaraguan state did not have a good track record of humane governance. Nicaragua had escaped genocidal levels of violence, and the Somoza dictatorship was not as thoroughly totalitarian as Germany's National Socialists or the Soviet Union under Stalin. But the alternation between tyranny and civil war left a long legacy of crime and atrocities by all sides in Nicaragua's serial civil wars.

State Building in Nicaragua

Given these conditions, the international community would have had the greatest success if it had adopted an across-the-board Trainer strategy to increase the capacity of Nicaraguan security forces, civil society, government bureaucracies, institutions of economic governance, and human rights advocates. Considering the relatively decent capacity of the Nicaraguan institutions of government, an Observer strategy toward capacity development might have been appropriate. State builders instead adopted largely an across-the-board Observer strategy with some elements of Trainer programs. Their failure to adopt a Trainer strategy

12. Paris, *At War's End*, 114–22.

may be due to the international community's residual caution against intervention, donors' unwillingness to devote resources or attention to a strategically peripheral region, and the fact that Nicaragua was one of the first state-building efforts in decades and state builders did not have the benefit of prior experience to recognize that a training effort was necessary.

The United Nations deployed just under one thousand soldiers to Nicaragua and neighboring states in 1989 to monitor the cease-fire, monitor the cessation of cross-border movement, and verify the demobilization of the Contras. The UN acknowledged that it simply did not have enough troops to carry out its mission because there were far too few troops to observe all the mileage of international borders across which militant movement could occur. Instead, the UN changed how its troops were used starting in 1991, reorienting them away from direct observation toward liaising with the host nation security forces to help them patrol their own borders more effectively. In this way the UN was gradually moving toward a Trainer strategy by the end of the Nicaraguan intervention. ONUCA also oversaw the demobilization and disarmament of some 22,000 insurgents in Nicaragua and Honduras.[13] Partly because of international efforts, the war ended definitively. Security, however, remained fragile because violent crime rose sharply in ensuing years as demobilized ex-combatants without employment turned to crime to earn a living—a pattern that would become familiar in subsequent postconflict state-building operations. The international community's failure to develop a full training program for soldiers and, especially, policemen was a significant lost opportunity.

The Nicaraguan parties had agreed to participate in competitive, open, multiparty elections to relegitimize the Nicaraguan state. Nicaragua had virtually no experience with credible democracy. The 1928 election overseen by the United States was among the more credible in Nicaragua's history and helped end a civil war, but it was not credible or open enough to prevent another civil war or to create a lasting regime. In response to the Nicaraguans' request, the UN deployed the Observer Group for the Verification of Elections in Nicaragua to oversee elections held in February 1990. The parties participated in the election, which was held on time. The Sandinistas lost—and accepted their loss peacefully, by no means a foregone conclusion considering violence had flared as recently several months before the election (and also considering the record of other postconflict elections in, for example, Cambodia and Angola). According to Roland Paris, "for the first time in

13. Durch, *Evolution of UN Peacekeeping*, 436–62.

Nicaragua's history, a governing party peacefully handed over power to its democratically elected opponents."[14] Widely accepted elections were also held in 1996, 2006, 2008, 2011, and 2012, with the Sandinistas returning peacefully to power in 2006.

To rebuild the Nicaraguan economy, the international community pressed the Nicaraguan government to pursue a program of liberalization. The newly elected conservative government complied by pushing through a raft of deregulation and a lowering of trade barriers. Donors responded with $11.9 billion in development assistance to Nicaragua over the next decade—at $196 per person per year, one of the highest assistance programs in any state-building operation. The reforms helped bring inflation back to normal levels. Real GDP per capita fell slightly, however, by 0.1 percent per year from 1989 to 2002. Paris lays the blame on the international state builders' premature liberalization of the Nicaraguan economy. He argues that state builders should strengthen institutions before pushing liberalization. Nicaraguan government institutions had not collapsed, but they were weak from decades of war and maladministration and appeared to be getting worse as the war wound down and the state-building process began.

Indeed, the international community appears to have invested little, if anything, in capacity-development programs in Nicaragua in the 1990s. As a result, donor aid failed to show any long-term effects in Nicaragua. Individual relief efforts never coalesced into a broader change in Nicaraguans' economic opportunities. Much of the aid was siphoned away in corruption. Nicaragua fell from sixty-first to eighty-first on Transparency International's Corruption Perceptions Index from 1998 (the first year in which it was ranked) to 2002. The international community increased its focus on capacity building during the 1990s partly in response to the missions in places like Nicaragua where it became evident that sizeable donor commitments alone could not buy peace and stability: how the money was used was equally important.

The international community did not become involved in efforts at transitional justice in Nicaragua, partly because there was no local effort to explore the issue for almost two decades after the end of the war. The Esquipulas Accords called on signatories to issue blanket amnesties for all combatants in the Central American wars. Subsequently, there was no effort to try Contra or Sandinista leaders for any war crimes, or even to investigate alleged atrocities. A national reconciliation commission was

14. Paris, *At War's End*, 116.

established in 1988 to oversee the peace agreement, not to address past war crimes. A follow-up peace and reconciliation commission was finally formed in 2007, long after the end of the international state-building effort.

Result

The international state-building operation in Nicaragua had such a light footprint that it did not significantly alter the balance of power among Nicaraguan factions and was in no danger of provoking open or violent opposition from the Sandinistas or Contras. The two sides had already come to an agreement before the international intervention began and appeared to be cautiously committed to the peace process. To the extent that either side perceived the process to be threatening to their interests, they channeled their opposition into widespread corruption, seeking to use the opportunities of peace and international aid for private profit. Demobilized militiamen with no employment prospects were perhaps the force most threatened by the state-building program, and the spike in criminality in the 1990s likely reflects the form their opposition took. The international state builders' failure to invest in capacity building and the rule of law permitted such opposition to take place. The result was compromised state building.

The Nicaraguan intervention was a shallow success. The war ended and Nicaragua has enjoyed more than two decades of peace. The democratic process appears to have taken root and become a successful mechanism for legitimizing the Nicaraguan state. The Sandinistas, whose violent seizure of power in 1979 touched off ten years of war, accepted their loss in the 1990 and 1996 elections. When they took power in 2006, Nicaraguans accepted the result peacefully (a rather tidy comparison illustrating the different results of democratic competition versus violent insurgency). However, because the international community failed to implement a capacity-development effort or a program to train Nicaraguan police, the quality of governance declined and security remained fragile. The World Bank judged that the rule of law eroded in Nicaragua over the course of the 1990s and violent crime and corruption increased. Without improvements in the rule of law, much international aid was ineffective and corruption increased. The economy grew sluggishly, and real GDP per capita actually declined. Nicaragua is at peace, but it remains troubled precisely because of the areas in which international state builders failed to adopt a sufficiently well-matched strategy of state building.

TABLE 7.2 Indices of Socioeconomic Development, Nicaragua and the World, 1989 and 2002

	1989				2002			
	Nicaragua	Latin America/ Caribbean	World	OECD	Nicaragua	Latin America/ Caribbean	World	OECD
Life expectancy at birth (years)	63.4	67.89	65.2	74.5	70.6	72.2	67.6	77.5
Infant mortality rate (per 1,000 live births)	53.4	44.4	63.4	18.7	31.5	25.9	49.7	10
Hospital beds (per 1,000 people)	1.83	2.49	3.64	5.7	0.9	–	2.6	5.6
Immunization, measles (% aged 12–23 months)	63	76	68	83	98	93.3	72.9	91.6
Immunization, DPT (% aged 12–23 months)	66	68	69	85	85	91.4	73.8	93.6
Incidence of TB (per 100,000 people)	108	88	–	–	62	57	–	–
Sanitation facilities, % pop. with access	43	67.9	47.4	95.6	49	75.9	57.3	96.7
Water source, % pop. with access	74	85.7	76	97.4	81	90.9	83.9	98.3
Telephone subscribers (per 100 people)	1.12	5.88	9.4	37.0	3.3	16.5	17.3	49.5
Literacy rate (% age 15+)	–	–	75.7	–	76.7	–	81.8	–
GDP per capita, constant 2000 $USD	684	3,570	4,549	18,580	782	4,005	5,345	23,371
Government revenue, % GDP	29.93	19.42	–	–	14.9	19.1	24.4	25.56
Polity IV score	–1	–	–	–	8	–	–	–

Note: Blank cell indicates unavailable data.

Sources: World Bank, Polity IV Project, World Health Organization.

[134]

SIERRA LEONE, 1999—2006

The armed state-building operation in Sierra Leone is an example of an initially mismatched strategy that changed over time to a fuller match between strategy and circumstances. It illustrates nicely how the change in strategy led to an improved outcome. The armed state-building operation in Sierra Leone, which is a likely success, is still very recent and any conclusions about its success must necessarily be tentative, especially as we are still within ten years of the conclusion as of the time of this writing. Yet Sierra Leone is an excellent case for research on armed state building, even if conclusions have to be preliminary. Because of the course of events in Sierra Leone, the intervention there has become a useful laboratory for illustrating how a change in strategy can clearly and dramatically change the outcome of state-building operations.

Background

The United Kingdom established one of its earlier African colonies in Freetown in 1792. The city became a refuge for freed slaves, who eventually became a distinct people group—the Krio—much as the Americo-Liberians would in next-door Liberia later in the nineteenth century. There were a few revolts against British rule, but the nineteenth and twentieth centuries were peaceful and included the establishment of the earliest (and for a long time the only) university in West Africa. Independence was achieved in 1961 without a war or a national liberation struggle, an evolution rather than a revolution—ideal for the consolidation for democracy, according to Dahl's theory, which seemed confirmed after peaceful elections in 1962. The economy grew slowly but steadily, averaging 2.24 percent growth in real per capita GDP from 1961 to 1966. Elections in 1967, however, led to a series of coups and countercoups and the establishment of an autocracy. Political parties were banned and one man held the prime ministership for nearly twenty years. Sierra Leone's Polity IV score plummeted from 6 before 1967 to -6 by 1971 and -7 by 1978, where it stayed almost continuously until 1996. Economic growth slowed: for the twenty-three years between the 1967 election and the 1991 outbreak of war, real per capita GDP grew by an average of only 0.27 percent per year.

A Liberian-sponsored rebellion against the ruling All People's Congress emerged in March 1991 under the banner of the Revolutionary United Front led by Corporal Foday Sankoh. Following the government's inability to meet the RUF threat, military officers overthrew the government in 1992 and established the National Provisional Ruling

Council. The NPRC hired mercenaries and pushed back the RUF in 1995, and handed back power through elections in 1996. However, other military officers formed the Armed Forces Revolutionary Council, allied with the RUF, and overthrew the government in 1997. Nigerian forces, under the auspices of the Economic Community of West African States (ECOWAS) Monitoring Group (ECOMOG), ousted the AFRC-RUF regime and reinstated the democratically elected government. The RUF briefly seized the capital in January 1999, leading to an especially grizzly few weeks of fighting and slaughter, before being ousted again by Nigerian-led ECOMOG forces. The government and the RUF signed the Lomé Peace Accord in July 1999, following international pressure and mediation.

The Lomé Peace Accord officially terminated hostilities and established a national unity government between the RUF and the government.[15] It provided for the transformation of the RUF into a political party, permitted RUF personnel to hold public office, gave the RUF a vice presidency and four cabinet posts, established the Commission for the Consolidation of Peace, issued a blanket pardon and amnesty to everyone, and regulated the gold and diamond industry. It requested the UN—which had an observer mission in place since mid-1998—to increase its activity and monitor the cease-fire (including by chairing a joint monitoring commission), help the RUF transform into a political party, monitor elections, repatriate refugees, and advise on human rights. The UN responded by establishing the United Nations Mission in Sierra Leone (UNAMSIL) in October 1999, inaugurating the beginning of its state-building effort.

State Failure in Sierra Leone

Security. Sierra Leone was anarchic at the beginning of the armed state-building operation. Despite the Lomé agreement, fighting continued until 2002, and the government was unable to provide basic public security in much of the country. RUF fighters continued to exercise control over areas in which they were deployed, resisted disarmament and demobilization, stole food, and kidnapped peacekeepers. The government increasingly relied on informal militias to defend itself. The UN secretary-general warned that the security environment was deteriorating and noted an increase in cease-fire violations in October and November 1999.[16] In January 2000 it warned of a "rising level of lawlessness and

15. United Nations Lomé peace agreement document S/1999/777.
16. First Report of the Secretary-General on the United Nations in Sierra Leone (UNAMSIL) S/1999/1223.

banditry" and reported that ex-combatants had attacked UNAMSIL disarmament sites.[17] The UN continued to note cease-fire violations for the next several months.

Legitimacy. The Sierra Leonean state had few sources of legitimacy on which to draw. It had been created as a polity by foreign colonization and had been governed by corrupt autocrats for much of its independent existence. The civil war illustrated that at least part of the population viewed the previous regime as illegitimate; the RUF's subsequent failure at the polls in 2002 illustrated that most Sierra Leoneans did not view it as a legitimate claimant to political power either. There were few grounds on which to base an appeal to legitimacy because there were few shared norms about what constituted a valid claim. The Lomé agreement put forward a power-sharing agreement and democratic elections as the basis to relegitimize the state, a basis to which both sides agreed in public, as evidenced by the RUF's participation in the election. However, the state was unable to implement Lomé on its own, and the legitimizing agreement was in danger of collapsing in 1999 and 2000.

Capacity. The Sierra Leonean state had nearly ceased functioning by 1999. The war was a disaster for Sierra Leone and severed the ties between the government and the citizenry. The economy was devastated: real per capita GDP fell by more than half between 1991 and 1999. Crop production fell by 32 percent over the course of the decade, and the incidence of tuberculosis rose from 219 to 355 per 100,000 people from 1991 to 1999, according to the World Bank. The United Nations found in 1999 "remarkably high levels of severe malnutrition in both children and adults. . . . Malaria, respiratory infections and nutrition-related illnesses are rampant. Cases of cholera have also been reported."[18] At thirty-nine years, the citizens had one of the shortest life expectancies of any state in the world. Only 11 percent had access to sanitation and 45 percent, to an improved water source. According to 'Funmi Olonisakin, who wrote one of the definitive early books on the Sierra Leone intervention, the country "was left to cope with a generation of uneducated and unemployed but functional illiterates, many of whom roamed the country's streets . . . forming a ready pool of recruits available to the highest bidder."[19]

Prosperity. Government revenue as a percentage of GDP (excluding grants) fluctuated widely between 5 and 12 percent during the war, and was at just 7.1 percent in 1999, one of the lowest in the world and not

17. Second Report of the Secretary-General on the United Nations Mission in Sierra Leone S/2000/13.
18. Eight Report of the Secretary-General on the United Nations Observers Mission in Sierra Leone S/1999/1003.
19. Olonisakin, *Peacekeeping in Sierra Leone*, 12.

enough to support even basic state functions. And what little money the state had was not put to effective use. Olonisakin wrote that "the state coffers were looted [in the 1980s] to feed the politics of patronage. . . . With an empty state treasury, offices were gradually looted of equipment by unpaid civil servants without alternative means of livelihood."[20]

Humanity. Sierra Leone did not experience genocide or totalitarianism, but its people did endure a decade of war punctuated by war crimes and atrocities against civilians. For example, the RUF's brief occupation of Freetown in 1999 was the worst such episode, according to Human Rights Watch, during which "the rebels dragged entire family units out of their homes and murdered them, hacked off the hands of children and adults, burned people alive in their houses, and rounded up hundreds of young women, took them to urban rebel bases, and sexually abused them." According to the same report, the RUF deliberately planned such attacks on civilians as punishment for allegedly supporting the government, and chose targets at random to spread fear.[21]

State Building in Sierra Leone: Security Strategy

In light of the ongoing fighting, international state builders should have temporarily assumed responsibility for providing public security in Sierra Leone while training new security forces, empowered by a strong mandate and sufficient personnel enabling international forces to enforce the peace. Instead, the UN initially deployed something closer to a traditional peacekeeping or monitoring mission and nearly suffered a catastrophic failure within a year of deployment. However, the international community continuously adapted its security posture in Sierra Leone as conditions on the ground developed. Scholars have rightly noted the key role played by the United Kingdom's intervention in May 2000 in pushing the UN to adapt its posture in Sierra Leone. However, it is important to note that the UN was working to adapt to realities on the ground before the UK's intervention. The mission in Sierra Leone was marked by continual adaptation from the beginning to the end. As a result, the intervention was eventually successful in its security aims.

UNAMSIL's mandate was initially limited to being a security observer. It was to help implement the Lomé Peace Accord; assist with the demobilization, disarmament, and reintegration plan; monitor the cease-fire; encourage confidence-building measures; and provide support to elections.[22] Initially, the United Nations deployed a force as ill-suited to the

20. Ibid., 11.
21. Human Rights Watch, *Getting Away with Murder.*
22. United Nations Security Council Resolution S/RES/1270 (1999).

situation as the force in Liberia. It was charged with monitoring the non-existent cease-fire, observing the disarmament of rebels who refused to disarm, and supporting elections that were unlikely to be free and fair.

The security strategy was inappropriate considering the degree of security failure present in Sierra Leone. As noted, the cease-fire was not holding, and violence and banditry were on the rise. In response, the United Nations expanded UNAMSIL to 11,100 troops, increased its civilian component, and strengthened its mandate in February 2000, just one month into the operation.[23] The new mandate specified that UNAMSIL should provide security for government buildings, airports, intersections, and disarmament sites, and coordinate with Sierra Leonean security forces. The international community was slowly assuming the role of a security provider rather than a security observer.

The United Nations was adapting, but the RUF was more aggressive still. In early May the RUF attacked disarmament sites and, in a series of incidents, kidnapped over five hundred UNAMSIL peacekeepers. The UNAMSIL personnel did not use force to prevent their kidnapping, possibly out of a mistaken belief that they were not permitted to do so or because of miscommunications among the UN peacekeepers and between the peacekeepers and their home capitals, according to Olonisakin. A later UN investigation found that there was no common understanding of the rules of engagement.[24] Regardless of the reason, rumors quickly abounded that RUF troops, using stolen UNAMSIL armored personnel carriers, were advancing toward the capital and threatening to destroy the peace process and topple the government. The UN, fearing the imminent failure of its peacekeeping mission—a failure that would have been as stark and abject as the failures in Angola and Rwanda in the 1990s—urgently appealed to the United Kingdom and other countries to intervene and save the mission.

The United Kingdom intervened swiftly. A force of some 1,200 to 5,000 British troops, backed by air and naval assets, deployed to Sierra Leone. Initially, the British force's mission was to evacuate Commonwealth civilians. But David Richards, the commanding general, took initiative to expand his mission. He embedded British troops with UNAMSIL and Sierra Leonean security forces. British air and naval units conducted presence operations to demonstrate British intent to stabilize the country. Sierra Leonean forces, bolstered with British advisers, engaged the RUF and reversed the RUF's offensive. British forces secured the release of the UNAMSIL hostages and defeated RUF forces in direct engagements.

23. United Nations Security Council Resolution S/RES/1289 (2000).
24. Fifth Report of the Secretary General to the Security Council on the United Nations Mission in Sierra Leone S/2000/751.

They ended their brief combat role by mid-June but established the International Military Advisory and Training Team to train the Sierra Leone Army and police forces.[25]

Meanwhile, the United Nations again expanded UNAMSIL's authorized strength, to 13,000 troops, and took the fight to the RUF.[26] According to Larry Woods, a retired US Army officer, and Timothy Reese, an active-duty US Army officer, who together studied the history of interventions in Sierra Leone for the Army's Combat Studies Institute, "With renewed confidence UNAMSIL and [Sierra Leonean] soldiers were able to take over positions previously secured by British soldiers and began actively fighting and winning battles with the RUF."[27] The United Nations reported, with understatement, that conditions "resemble civil war."[28]

The UN responded not just with renewed military vigor but with a thorough reevaluation of UNAMSIL's organization, operations, and resources. The evaluation (undertaken at the same time the Brahimi Report on UN peacekeeping was being written) led to improvements in command and control and a change in the rules of engagement for UNAMSIL. More important, it led to a change in mandate. In August, the United Nations made official what had been clear on the ground since May: it removed all pretense of neutrality and permitted UNAMSIL "to deter and, where necessary, decisively counter the threat of RUF attack by responding robustly to any hostile actions or threat of imminent and direct use of force." It candidly and publicly admitted that there were "serious inherent weaknesses in [UNAMSIL's] structure, command and control and resources" and recommended improvements.[29] Follow-on British interventions in September and October to rescue more hostages and bolster flagging UN resolve finally broke the RUF's intransigence and permanently changed the security dynamic in Sierra Leone. The RUF signed a new cease-fire in November and began to abide by it. In March 2001, the Security Council increased UNAMSIL's authorized strength once more, to 17,500—nearly tripling its size over the course of a year and a half.[30] Disarmament finally got underway, and the civil war was official declared over in January 2002.

---

25. Wood and Reese, *Military Interventions in Sierra Leone*; Olonisakin, *Peacekeeping in Sierra Leone*.
26. United Nations Security Council Resolution S/RES/1299 (2000).
27. Wood and Reese, *Military Interventions in Sierra Leone*, 64.
28. S/2000/751.
29. United Nations Security Council Resolution S/RES/1313 (2000).
30. United Nations Security Council Resolution S/RES/1346 (2001).

State Building in Sierra Leone: Civilian Strategy

International state builders should have engaged aggressively to shore up the failing effort to relegitimize the state, laid out in Lomé; engaged with civil society to broaden participation; assumed control of state institutions to rebuild their capacity; and facilitated transitional justice with technical assistance. The UN came very close to implementing this strategy, only falling short in its effort to rebuild the state's capacity.

The Sierra Leonean intervention is usually noted mostly for the dramatic events in the security sector. The intervention came to be seen, understandably, as a sort of ideal testing ground demonstrating how a change in security strategy can concretely change the security environment. However, it is also true that UNAMSIL employed a competent civilian strategy. UNAMSIL did not fully rebuild Sierra Leone's institutional capacity or dramatically improve the population's social development, but it did reverse the country's downward trajectory and place it on a sustainable path of gradual improvement.

UNAMSIL's initial mandate did not explicitly mention rebuilding Sierra Leonean government institutions. Some aspects of the Lomé agreement implicitly involved the UN in civilian activities, including elections, reintegrating ex-combatants into society, repatriating refugees, and advising the RUF on transforming into a political party. Following the May 2000 crisis, UNAMSIL's mandate and concept of operations were revised not only to strengthen its military mission, counter the RUF, and increase its troop strength. It was also given broader and more specific civilian tasks. The UN secretary-general noted in his August 2000 report that the mandate and concept of operations changed to account for "circumstances on the ground." The new concept of operations stated that "the main objectives of UNAMSIL would be to assist the efforts of the Government of Sierra Leone to extend State authority, restore law and order and further stabilize the situation progressively throughout the entire country, and to assist in the promotion of a political process, leading to a renewed disarmament, demobilization, and reintegration programme."[31] Despite the report's claim that the mandate "remains" the extension of state authority and restoring law and order, no such provisions were mentioned in the original mandate in October 1999. The broader language was an acknowledgement of the depth of Sierra Leone's failure as a state and the incapacity of its state institutions. To implement the broader mandate, the mission increased to include a peak of 322 international civilians in March 2002.

31. Sixth Report of the Secretary-General on the United Nations Mission in Sierra Leone S/2000/832, 3.

Donors also changed course after 2000. Official development assistance to Sierra Leone was only $180.6 million in 2000, but averaged $354 million per year from 2001 to 2006, according to the World Bank. In all, donors gave $108.88 per capita per year from 1999 to 2006, almost exactly the median value for armed state-building interventions for which data is available. Sierra Leone ranks above average compared to other state-building efforts in per capita, per year assistance given during the intervention and up to a decade afterward (through 2007 for Sierra Leone), indicating a more enduring donor commitment in Sierra Leone than in other cases, like El Salvador or Haiti in 1993 when donor commitment dropped off sharply after the intervention ended.

Legitimacy. As noted previously, the Sierra Leonean state had few sources of legitimacy on which to draw. In the context of the post–Cold War consensus on liberal democracy, the Lomé agreement turned to elections and consociational democracy as means to restore the state's legitimacy among the greatest number of its citizens. The UN successfully registered more than 2.3 million voters and oversaw elections in May 2002. The RUF transformed into a political party (the RUFP), peacefully contested the election, and accepted its loss without resort to force. The state's legitimacy was as good as it had ever been.

The international community even contributed, in small ways, to Sierra Leonean civil society. For example, the peacekeeping force established Radio UNAMSIL. The radio station was initially intended to give the UN a means to communicate directly to the Sierra Leonean people and counter false information spread about UNAMSIL by the RUF. But the radio station ended up becoming one of the few national media in the country. The radio station "helped make Sierra Leone more cohesive, by encouraging open discussion."[32] UNAMSIL used the radio station as an opportunity to give Sierra Leoneans on-the-job training in journalism—a key investment in civil society capacity. When UNAMSIL withdrew, it left the radio station operating under local ownership.

Capacity and Prosperity. The international community did not implement an across-the-board effort to retrain and equip the Sierra Leonean bureaucracy and machinery of government. Instead, UNAMSIL directly undertook quick impact reconstruction and civilian projects, such as rebuilding infrastructure, schools, and religious institutions, which may explain why most of the improvement in governance and the rule of law had happened by 2004 and largely leveled off after that, according to the World Bank's indicators. The World Bank itself implemented a small institutional reform and capacity building project to "establish

32. Olonisakin, *Peacekeeping in Sierra Leone*, 107.

a functioning local government system and improve inclusiveness, transparency, and accountability of public resource management at all levels of government," but spent only $25 million on it between 2004 and 2009.[33] Nonetheless, the return of peace, UNAMSIL's and the World Bank's small efforts, and the state's increasing revenue stream were enough to allow the machinery of government to resume functioning at a minimal level.

Humanity. With the end of the civil war, Sierra Leoneans were freed from a decade of brutal conflict that often included violence against civilians. The Lomé agreement called for the establishment of a truth and reconciliation commission to implement a measure of transitional justice in a practicable manner without provoking renewed war. The commission operated from 2002 to 2004. Its final report catalogued human rights abuses in Sierra Leone since the outbreak of war in 1991, named individual perpetrators, and recommended a raft of reforms to fight corruption, protect civil rights, strengthen civilian control of the military, and weaken the executive. Additionally, the UN and the government of Sierra Leone established a special court in 2002 to prosecute high-profile war crimes. It has indicted thirteen people and convicted five. Of the remaining, three are deceased and one is at large. The court began to shut down starting in 2011.

Result

The international intervention initially adopted an insufficient strategy and thus failed to change the balance of power in Sierra Leone. The RUF, which benefited from the conditions of state failure because it gave them continued opportunities to regain power, saw the Lomé Peace Accord and the UN mission as a threat to its interests. Because the UN mission initially had a weak mandate and insufficient forces, the RUF had the opportunity to challenge the UN directly and violently. It nearly succeeded. The British intervention, followed by the increase in UN forces and expansion of its mandate, resulted in a more appropriate strategy, enabling the international actors to check the RUF and compelling the RUF to act within the strictures of the Lomé Peace Accord and the statebuilding program. The UN and British avoided free-riding by allied locals because the small size of the initial intervention, the rapid British withdrawal, and the establishment of the International Military Advisory and Training Team communicated the internationals' unwillingness to carry the burden in Sierra Leone indefinitely. The result was

TABLE 7.3. Indices of Socioeconomic Development, Sierra Leone and the World, 1999 and 2010

	1999				2010			
	Sierra Leone	Sub-Saharan Africa	World	OECD	Sierra Leone	Sub-Saharan Africa	World	OECD
Life expectancy at birth (years)	39.0	49.5	67.0	76.7	47.4	54.2	69.6	79.3
Infant mortality rate (per 1,000 live births)	144.6	96.0	53.2	11.7	113.7	77.0	41.2	6.8
Hospital beds (per 1,000 people)	-	-	-	5.8	-	-	-	-
Immunization, measles (% aged 12–23 months)	62.0	51.6	71.7	90.2	82.0	75.5	85.3	93.8
Immunization, DPT (% aged 12–23 months)	43.0	52.1	73.8	92.2	90.0	76.5	85.1	95.3
Incidence of TB (per 100,000 people)	355.0	264.0	-	-	682.0	271.0	-	-
Sanitation facilities, % pop. with access	11.0	27.3	54.9	96.3	13.0	30.7	62.5	97.7
Water source, % pop. with access	45.0	54.1	82.0	98.0	55.0	61.1	88.4	99.2
Telephone subscribers (per 100 people)	0.5	1.4	15.0	50.3	0.2	1.4	17.2	40.9
Literacy rate (% age 15+)	-	-	81.8	-	40.9	62.5	83.7	-
GDP per capita, current $USD	152.1	509.4	5,138.2	22,054.8	268.3	645.0	6,006.0	24,579.0
Government revenue, % GDP	7.1	-	-	-	-	-	22.9	23.0
Polity2 score	0	-	-	-	7	-	-	-
Voice and accountability, percentile	8.7	-	-	-	41.7	-	-	-
Political stability, percentile	1.9	-	-	-	37.3	-	-	-
Government effectiveness, percentile	4.4	-	-	-	11.0	-	-	-
Regulatory quality, percentile	9.3	-	-	-	24.9	-	-	-
Rule of law, percentile	10.5	-	-	-	18.0	-	-	-
Control of corruption, percentile	21.5	-	-	-	25.4	-	-	-

Note: Blank cell indicates unavailable data.
Sources: World Bank, Polity IV Project, World Health Organization.

conflictual state building that was successfully transformed into cooperative state building.

Sierra Leone is one of the few clear successes that showed improvement across the board in security, reconstruction, and governance.
Fighting stopped in 2002. With peace and international aid, governance
and economic performance improved dramatically. Elections were held
in 2002; Sierra Leone's Polity IV score jumped by seven points. Another
round of elections in 2007 were "largely transparent and well-adminis-
tered," according to the National Democratic Institute, and occasioned
the first peaceful transfer of power between one democratically elected
government to another in Sierra Leone's history.[34] The state's revenue as
a percentage of GDP rose from 7.1 percent in 1999 to a high of 12.4 percent in 2003, but leveled off for the rest of the decade. However, the
economy was growing strongly, so the state's revenue increased substantially in the postwar period, enabling it to assume responsibility for
an increasing number of public goods and services for the citizenry. Sierra Leone rose dramatically in voice and accountability and political
stability on the World Bank's governance rankings and posted gains in
every other governance sector as well. The economy grew strongly: real
GDP per capita grew by an average of 6.4 percent from 1999 to 2010, its
best performance in its history. By every measure, Sierra Leone was better off, and on a trajectory of continued improvement, after the intervention than before it. The area of least improvement—institutional capacity,
as measured by government effectiveness, the rule of law, and control of
corruption—is precisely the area in which the state builders' strategy
matched least well with the degree of failure in Sierra Leone, and suggests the UN may have had more success if it had established an international transitional authority similar to the ones it had established in
East Timor or Kosovo.

LIBERIA, 1993—1997

The armed state-building operation in Liberia from 1993 to 1997 is an
example of a complete mismatch between the state-building strategy
and the degree and type of state failure. Liberian security and legitimacy had completely collapsed; the state's capacity and ability to extract resources had failed, and it had an abysmal record of protecting
human rights. International state builders would have had the greatest
chance of rebuilding Liberian security and legitimacy if they had

---

34. National Democratic Institute, *NDI Final Report on Sierra Leone's 2007 Elections*.

assumed responsibility for enforcing public security and the terms of the 1993 Cotonou Agreement, which declared a ceasefire and established a transitional government (not to be confused with the 2000 Cotonou Agreement, an aid and development agreement between the European Union and developing states). Instead, the international community deployed a small mission with a limited mandate to observe a cease-fire that did not exist and help implement a peace agreement that the warring parties were ignoring. Similarly, rebuilding the capacity of the Liberian government and rebuilding respect for human rights would have required either strong and robust technical assistance and capacity-building mission, or even a partial international transitional administration—like in Cambodia the year previously. Instead, international state builders limited themselves to observing and facilitating the civilian elements of the Cotonou Agreement—repatriating refugees and assisting with elections—but did not undertake longer-term civilian assistance programs. Additionally, despite the intervention lasting four years, the international state builders never altered the basic outlines of their strategy. Unsurprisingly, the Liberian case is one of the more thorough and complete failures of armed state building.

At the same time, Liberia offers another opportunity, like Sierra Leone, to see how a changed international strategy in the same or similar context can achieve a substantially different state-building outcome. The international community returned to Liberia in 2003 for a second attempt at state building, but with a significantly different approach. I explore the differences in strategy and outcome in an epilogue to this case study.

Background

The American Colonization Society started resettling freed African American slaves on Africa's west coast in 1820. The resettled Africans assumed independence and proclaimed the Republic of Liberia in 1847. Americo-Liberians, who formed a minority governing elite, enjoyed a modicum of open and competitive politics (other Africans were excluded from citizenship until 1904) until the True Whig Party consolidated power in the 1884 election and imposed single-party rule that lasted until 1980. Liberia's Polity IV score plummeted from 4 to -3 in 1884 and gradually dropped to a -7 by 1980. The economy performed sluggishly. Real per capital GDP grew by 0.72 percent per year between 1951 and 1979. In 1980 a Liberian Army sergeant, Samuel Doe, overthrew the Americo-Liberian government and killed the president and scores of top officials. His repressive and corrupt rule was even worse than the True Whig

Party's: real GDP per capita declined by 3.05 percent per year from 1980 to 1989, and the decade was marked by several attempted countercoups and tribal violence.

In 1989 the National Patriotic Front of Liberia (NPFL), a rebel movement led by former government official Charles Taylor, invaded Liberia to topple the Doe dictatorship. The civil war outlasted Doe, who was killed in 1990, and raged between various factions that splintered off from the main combatants at various times. Between one-third and one-half of Liberians were displaced and up to twenty thousand killed by 1991.[35] The Economic Community of West Africa States Monitoring Group attempted to impose a cease-fire and help form an interim government in 1990. Despite the Nigerian-led peacekeeping force's efforts, the war continued. ECOMOG appeared to reach a successful cease-fire with the signing of the Cotonou Agreement in July 1993 (shortly proved to be illusory).

The Cotonou Agreement declared a cease-fire and pledged the parties to disarm, established a power-sharing transitional government, called for elections, and granted a general amnesty to all combatants. The agreement called on ECOMOG and the UN to monitor and help implement it, to seal borders with neighboring states, oversee disarmament and demobilization, investigate and report on violations of the agreement, help fund elections, and assist with refugee repatriation. In September the UN Security Council authorized the deployment of the United Nations Observer Mission in Liberia (UNOMIL) to help implement the peace agreement, monitor the cease-fire, facilitate demobilization, deliver humanitarian assistance, and oversee elections.[36]

State Failure in Liberia, 1993

Security. The armed state-building operation in Liberia took place in the context of anarchic state failure. Liberia had been in a civil war since 1989 and stayed at war even after the Cotonou Agreement. The civil war continued, with brief halts and stops, despite the agreement and the international interventions. Multiple peace agreements were signed throughout the decade, while at least 153,000 Liberians were killed in fighting between 1992 and 1996. Actors who disagreed with various accords and cease-fires simply splintered off, formed their own groups, and resumed fighting. The Liberian Peace Council, Independent National Patriotic Front of Liberia, and United Liberation Movement of

35. Aboagye and Bah, *Liberia at a Crossroads.*
36. United Nations Security Council Resolutions S/RES/866 (1993); S/RES/1020 (1995).

Liberia for Democracy all emerged at various points to continue fighting. The Liberian intervention of 1993 marks one of the rare cases in which the international community attempted a state-building operation in the midst of an ongoing war.[37]

Legitimacy. Liberia had enjoyed several decades of semidemocratic rule after independence. Democracy unfortunately collapsed and was succeeded by 110 years of autocratic and incompetent rule prior to the 1993 intervention. Neither traditional Americo-Liberian rule nor its alternative (the Doe regime) retained any vestige of legitimacy with Liberians. Liberians were divided by tribe and language (some twenty main groups), ethnicity (between Americo-Liberians and the rest), geography, and religion (about 40% Christian, 20% Muslim, and 40% indigenous beliefs). The Doe regime had rested largely on favoritism toward the Krahn ethnic group. As a result, the state had few, if any, shared, common norms to which to appeal. As with all post–Cold War cases of armed state building, Liberians turned to democracy and elections to provide grounds for legitimacy, and the Cotonou Agreement became the avowed basis for relegitimizing the Liberian state.

Capacity. Liberian institutions prior to the war functioned at a higher level than those of other poor developing states. By 1993 the country had deteriorated dramatically, but it was still largely on par with the rest of sub-Saharan Africa and a very slight step above the ranks of the most thoroughly failed states. The Liberian economy, despite a decade of decline, was still slightly better-off than the very bottom tier. Forty percent of the population had access to improved sanitation and 57 percent to clean water in 1990, according to the World Bank, above average for a failed state.[38]

Prosperity. Government tax revenue was 18.6 percent of GDP in 1988 before the war, according to the IMF, a respectable figure that reinforces the picture of Liberia as above average compared to other poor developing, weak states. Tax revenue plummeted to just 3.9 percent by 1997 (figures are unavailable for the intervening period), the third-worst among the forty cases of state building addressed in this book, indicative of the near-total disappearance of the state from much of Liberia during the war.

---

37. State building fails in almost all such cases (including in South Vietnam, Angola, the Congo in 1960 and 1999, Somalia, Rwanda, Nicaragua in 1927, and Iraq). Haiti in 1915, Cambodia, and Afghanistan are the only cases in which the international community achieved even a shallow success at state building in wartime, and those "successes" are not counted as such by all scholars.
38. The figure comes from an earlier version of the World Bank's "World Development Indicators Database." The newest version does not report these indices for Liberia for the given years.

Humanity. The Liberian state completely failed to protect Liberians' human rights. Liberia did not experience totalitarianism or genocide, but its civil war was widely noted as one of the more brutal and bloody of Africa's civil wars and did involve ethnic cleansing. Fighting was often along tribal lines, broadly progovernment Krahn against non-Krahn rebels, resulting in ethnic cleansing and massacres. Combatants targeted civilians, conscripted child soldiers, inflicted corporate punishment against whole towns, targeted enemies on the basis of ethnic or tribal identity, raped women, and looted goods.[39] There were no effective police forces to protect people, little in the way of a judicial system through which to seek redress, and no institutional commitments to protect human rights.

State Building in Liberia

The international community's strategy in Liberia bore no resemblance to the degree and type of state failure in Liberia.

Security. The United Nations deployed 368 military personnel—at 2 per 10,000 civilians, it was the second-smallest deployment of international forces of any armed state-building operation. The UN's excessive weakness alone goes far to explaining the failure of peacekeeping and state building in Liberia. Further, because the UN deployed no significant force, it was reliant on the 4,000-strong ECOMOG force, which brought difficulties of its own. ECOMOG was untrained and unequipped for counterinsurgency and complex peacekeeping, and its presence highlighted regional, linguistic, and tribal tensions, and may have even helped prolong the conflict.[40] (Even counting ECOMOG this only brings the ratio up to 22 troops per 10,000 civilians, below the median of 31 per 10,000 and well below the average of 93 per 10,000.) In addition to its small size, UNOMIL's mandate was inappropriate to the circumstances. UNOMIL was mandated to monitor the cease-fire, report violations, help disarmament and demobilization, and remain neutral; it was not authorized to undertake offensive operations or compel parties to abide by the peace agreement. ECOMOG operated under similar constraints. (Cotonou technically gave ECOMOG enforcement powers, but they could be triggered only after a lengthy and unrealistic judicial process of investigating and consulting with violators.) The parties resisted disarmament, and fighting continued. In response, the UN made minor changes to UNOMIL's mandate in 1995, strengthening some of its verification authorities. But it did not change UNOMIL's security strategy from observing to

39. Human Rights Watch, *Liberia*.
40. Howe, "Lessons of Liberia," 145–76.

enforcing, and no effort was made to reform or retrain Liberian security forces. UNAMSIL's mandate never contained a provision similar to UN-AMSIL's amended mandate of 2000 that allowed it to compel the RUF to abide by the peace agreement. Fighting started and stopped throughout the decade, with notable large-scale eruptions in 1996 and in 1999, shortly after the withdrawal of international forces. The small size of the force and restrictive mandate in the midst of one of Africa's most brutal and lethal civil wars was one of the most dramatic mismatches between a failed state's security situation and the international community's security strategy, and explains in large part why the war simply continued during and after the intervention.[41]

Legitimacy. The Cotonou Agreement and the international community looked to a power-sharing agreement between the warring factions and prompt elections (within seven months of the agreement) to restore the state's legitimacy. Power-sharing failed—not all factions were represented in the transitional government, and those that were did not cooperate with one another. The failure was for largely the same reason that the war continued. The combatants in the civil war did not recognize each other's legitimacy and were not prepared to compromise. Elections were repeatedly put off because of the impracticality of holding them amid an ongoing war. A transitional government finally took shape after the Abuja Agreement in 1996, and elections were hastily held in July 1997. Observers at the time declared it to be reasonably open and fair, but a consensus gradually emerged that Liberians elected Charles Taylor believing that because he was largely responsible for the war, his election would guarantee peace.[42] In effect, Liberians elected Taylor out of fear that he would resume the war if he lost—hardly the sort of democratic deliberation Liberians or the UN were hoping for. Considering the pervasive climate of fear in which the election was held, and the subsequent record of the Taylor government, the 1997 election can hardly be said to have restored the Liberian state's legitimacy.

Capacity and Prosperity. The international intervention in Liberia in 1993 did not include an effort to rebuild the capacity of the Liberian state. UNOMIL's mandate included few civilian assistance activities, such as repatriating refugees, helping deliver humanitarian assistance, and observing elections. Later UN peacekeeping mandates began to include standard language about promoting a government's authority and reestablishing civilian administration: UNOMIL's did not. With a lack of mandate, no focus on civilian assistance, and a continuing absence of

41. Alao, *Burden of Collective Goodwill*; Alao, Mackinlay, and Olonisakin, *Peacekeepers, Politicians, and Warlords*; Fleitz, *Peacekeeping Fiascoes*; Lowenkopf, "Liberia."
42. Harris, "From 'Warlord' to 'Democratic' President," 431–55.

security, the international state builders put little effort into restoring the Liberian state's capacity. Donors gave a desultory $1.3 billion for reconstruction and development over ten years, between 1993 and 2003, or $61.95 per person per year. The amount was well below that given in cases with robust capacity-development and technical-assistance programs, such as Timor-Leste ($286.67)—like Liberia, one of the poorest states in the world with a similarly low GDP per capita. The weakness of the Liberian state was undoubtedly a contributing factor to the outbreak and persistence of conflict, making it all the more remarkable that that aspect of state building was neglected. From 1993 to 1997, the Liberian state did not improve its capacity, as reflected in indicators of economic and human development.

Humanity. International state builders interested in restoring the Liberian state's respect for human rights should have invested heavily in the Liberian justice sector and police forces, engaged with civil society and trained human rights advocates, and lent technical assistance to any transitional justice programs. There is little evidence that the international community did any of those things from 1993 to 1997. In addition, the Cotonou Agreement extended a general amnesty to all combatants in the war. The blanket amnesty, especially in the absence of judicial reform or retraining the security services, fostered a culture of impunity and allowed atrocities to continue. There was no effort in the first Liberian intervention to create a truth and reconciliation commission, investigate past abuses, or otherwise cope with the past as a way of relegitimizing the state or preventing future abuses. In the absence of a stronger international security presence or capacity-building mission, it is doubtful any of these initiatives would have independently succeeded, but their absence illustrates how comprehensively the international community's state building strategy failed to address the conditions of state failure in Liberia.

Result

International state builders implemented a strategy ill-suited to Liberia's circumstances across all dimensions of statehood. The intervention did not change the local balance of power. The NPFL understood the state-building program to be a threat to its interests, the mismatched state-building strategy enabled the NPFL to undermine the Cotonou Agreement and resist the state-building program. As a result, the Liberian intervention was a strong case of conflictual state building that led to comprehensive and total failure. The international community failed to enforce public security, compel disarmament, or back a credible process for relegitimizing the state. Thus, Liberians went to the polls in 1997 and elected the most

TABLE 7.4. Indices of Socioeconomic Development, Liberia and the World, 1993 and 1997

	1993				1997			
	Liberia	Sub-Saharan Africa	World	OECD	Liberia	Sub-Saharan Africa	World	OECD
Life expectancy at birth (years)	42.0	49.4	65.8	75.2	43.2	49.3	66.6	76.4
Infant mortality rate (per 1,000 live births)	146.1	103.4	59.8	16.0	130.7	99.2	55.6	13.1
Hospital beds (per 1,000 people)	-	-	-	6.5	-	-	-	6.1
Immunization, measles (% aged 12–23 months)	-	49.1	70.8	86.2	-	49.2	72.0	90.1
Immunization, DPT (% aged 12–23 months)	-	51.2	70.3	81.9	-	53.7	71.6	88.8
Incidence of TB (per 100,000 people)	211.0	221.0	-	-	228.0	244.0	-	-
Sanitation facilities, % pop. with access	-	25.8	49.6	95.9	11.0	26.6	53.2	96.1
Water source, % pop. with access	-	49.9	77.8	97.3	58.0	52.7	80.6	97.7
Telephone subscribers (per 100 people)	0.2	1.0	10.9	42.1	0.3	1.2	13.5	47.8
Literacy rate (% age 15+)	-	-	-	-	-	-	-	-
GDP per capita, current $USD	75.1	492.7	4,641.0	19,388.0	111.9	510.5	4,994.7	21,163.5
Government revenue, % GDP	-	-	-	-	-	-	-	-
Polity2 score	0	-	-	-	0	-	-	-
Voice and accountability, percentile	-	-	-	-	15.4	-	-	-
Political stability, percentile	-	-	-	-	6.3	-	-	-
Government effectiveness, percentile	-	-	-	-	1.5	-	-	-
Regulatory quality, percentile	-	-	-	-	2.9	-	-	-
Rule of law, percentile	-	-	-	-	1.0	-	-	-
Control of corruption, percentile	-	-	-	-	2.0	-	-	-

Note: Blank cell indicates unavailable data.
Sources: World Bank, Polity IV Project, World Health Organization.

fearsome warlord to avoid his retaliation if he lost. His administration was predictably ruthless and incompetent. Civil war re-erupted in 1999, and international military forces were back in 2003. In 2002, five years after the election and on the eve of the next international intervention, Freedom House rated Liberia "not free." Voice and accountability declined steadily over the decade, and political stability showed negligible change, according to the World Bank's governance indicators. The international community made little effort to invest in the Liberian state's capacity or reconstruct the economy. The state collected a mere 3.9 percent of revenue in GDP in 1997, and real GDP per capita fell by an average of 4.39 percent each year between 1993 and 2003. Failure is rarely so clear.

Epilogue: Liberia, 2003 — Present

Two years after Taylor's victory in the presidential election, civil war re-erupted. Liberians United for Reconciliation and Democracy (LURD) and, later, the Movement for Democracy in Liberia (MODEL) fought to overthrow Taylor's autocratic regime. Taylor resigned and fled in August 2003, and the rebels singed the Accra Comprehensive Peace Agreement. The UN authorized the United Nations Mission in Liberia (UNMIL) in September, and a national transitional government of Liberia was formed in October. The security situation was better, and the civilian situation worse, than in 1993. Liberians were poorer and worse off: real GDP per capita had fallen by more than a third from 1993 to 2003, from $1,193 to $697. Some government functions had resumed because of Taylor's autocratic rule. But most important for the armed state-building campaign, in 2003 the fighting had stopped, whereas in 1993 it had continued.

The international community deployed a much more robust security strategy in 2003. It authorized 15,000 troops, compared to 368 in 1993. In 2009, there were still 11,516 international troops in Liberia, or 37 to 10,000 civilians, close to the 42 per 10,000 in the successful Sierra Leonean operation. When Taylor threatened to return from exile in 2005, UNMIL was authorized to arrest him on charges of war crimes.[43] To that extent, UNMIL was authorized to take sides and resembled UNAMSIL in Sierra Leone. UNMIL's mandate also included a mandate to implement security-sector reform, including police training and the formation of a new military, another change from the 1993 mission, which had only been mandated to help with disarmament and demobilization.

UNMIL's civilian mandate was much more expansive than its predecessor's. In addition to monitoring the cease-fire and facilitating disarmament and demobilization, the UN force was mandated to help

43. United Nations Security Council Resolution S/RES/1638 (2005).

TABLE 7.5. Indices of Socioeconomic Development, Liberia and the World, 2010

	2010			
	Liberia	Sub-Saharan Africa	World	OECD
Life expectancy at birth (years)	56.1	54.2	69.6	79.3
Infant mortality rate (per 1,000 live births)	73.6	77.0	41.2	6.8
Hospital beds (per 1,000 people)	0.8			
Immunization, measles (% aged 12–23 months)	64.0	76.5	85.1	95.3
Immunization, DPT (% aged 12–23 months)	64.0	75.5	85.3	93.8
Incidence of TB (per 100,000 people)	293.0	271.0	-	-
Sanitation facilities, % pop. with access	18.0	30.7	62.5	97.7
Water source, % pop. with access	73.0	61.1	88.4	99.2
Telephone subscribers (per 100 people)	0.1	1.4	17.2	40.9
Literacy rate (% age 15+)	-	-	84.0	-
GDP per capita, current $USD	260.5	645.0	6,006.0	24,579.0
Government revenue, % GDP	-	-	22.9	23.0
Polity IV score	6	-	-	-
Voice and accountability, percentile	40.3	-	-	-
Political stability, percentile	29.7	-	-	-
Government effectiveness, percentile	8.1	-	-	-
Regulatory quality, percentile	16.7	-	-	-
Rule of law, percentile	17.1	-	-	-
Control of corruption, percentile	36.4	-	-	-

Note: Blank cell indicates unavailable data.

facilitate the "reestablishment of national authority throughout the country, including the establishment of a functioning administrative structure at both the national and local levels [and help] consolidate governmental institutions, including a national legal framework and judicial and correctional institutions."[44] The UN deployed 455 international civilians to implement the mandate, compared to the 105 authorized in the previous mission. Donors funded this expanded mandate with $1.5 billion from 2004 to 2007—at $120.44, nearly twice the per capita, per annum rate of

44. United Nations Security Council Resolution S/RES/1509 (2003).

the previous intervention and one of the higher recent donor rates. Finally, Liberia established a truth and reconciliation commission in 2005 to investigate and publish the truth regarding past war crimes and human rights abuses, and UNMIL was specifically mandated to assist with human rights initiatives in Liberia.

The international community's strategy was a much better match to Liberia's needs in 2003 than it was in 1993. As a result, the second intervention in Liberia appears to be an emerging success. Elections—freer and fairer than in 1997—were held in 2005 and 2011. Liberia's Polity IV score leaped from 0 in 2002 to 6 in 2006, and as of 2011 Freedom House rated it "partly free." Governance has improved across the board, showing gains in effectiveness, regulatory quality, the rule of law, and control of corruption, according to the World Bank. The economy has begun to revive. Real GDP per capita has grown by an average of 2.17 percent per year since 2004. Life expectancy rose from 42 in 1993 to 57 in 2010; the infant mortality rate fell from 146 to 73.6 per 1,000 live births in the same time frame. Most important, no additional rebel groups have emerged to challenge the government, and the peace is holding as of 2012. The dramatically different results of the 2003 intervention from the 1993 intervention illustrate the importance of designing a strategy to address the type and degree of state failure in armed state-building operations.

AFGHANISTAN, 2001–2010

Afghanistan presents a case in which the international community started with a partial match between its strategy and the type and degree of state failure on the ground. It was verging toward a mitigated failure when, in early 2007, the international community slowly began to change course and marginally improved its strategy. Although the ultimate outcome of the intervention in Afghanistan is unclear at the time of this writing—largely because it is unclear how long the intervention will last, or what the international community's long-term presence in Afghanistan might look like—this preliminary case study shows how a shift in strategies of state building in different sectors and at different time periods led to improving outcomes.[45]

Background

Al-Qaida, a multinational terrorist group headquartered in Afghanistan, murdered 2,752 people from more than ninety countries in simultaneous

45. The Afghanistan case study is reprinted with additions by permission of *Foreign Affairs*, Paul D. Miller, "Finish the Job," vol. 90, no. 1, (January/February 2011). Copyright 2011 by the Council on Foreign Relations, Inc., www.ForeignAffairs.com.

[155]

attacks in New York and Washington, D.C., on September 11, 2001. The United Nations Security Council declared the next day that "those responsible for aiding, supporting or harbouring the perpetrators, organizers and sponsors of these acts will be held accountable."[46] On September 28 it demanded that all states cooperate against terrorism, including by denying safe haven and preventing international movement for terrorists.[47] The US Congress authorized the use of military force against the perpetrators and, crucially, against anyone who harbored or aided the terrorists. After the Taliban refused to cooperate against al-Qaida, the United States assembled a coalition of the international community and allied Afghan rebels, deployed military force, and overthrew the Afghan government.

The United Nations was concerned with rebuilding the Afghan state immediately. The day after the liberation of Kabul, the Security Council outlined its vision for the next Afghan government. It should be "broad-based, multi-ethnic and fully representative," and "respect the human rights of all Afghan people." The United Nations envisioned a strong role for itself: "The United Nations should play a central role in supporting the efforts of the Afghan people to establish urgently such a new and transitional administration leading to the formation of a new government."[48] The UN, with US help, took action to make its vision a reality. It convened a conference in Bonn in late November among Afghan factions to broker an agreement on an interim administration and a process for reconstruction. The resulting Agreement on Provisional Arrangements in Afghanistan Pending the Re-establishment of Permanent Government Institutions—the Bonn Agreement—reflected the UN's program. The Bonn Agreement formed an interim administration whose goal was to establish a "broad-based, gender-sensitive, multi-ethnic and fully representative government." It also established a role for the United Nations. The Bonn Agreement requested that the UN authorize the deployment of a military force to secure Kabul and, eventually, other areas. The Afghans requested that the United Nations monitor the implementation of the agreement, advise the interim government on how to create a politically neutral environment, train a new Afghan security force, compile a voter registry, take a census, and be an honest broker throughout the process. The United Nations was given the authority to investigate human rights abuses.

The United States deferred to the UN to lead a state-building operation in Afghanistan so that the United States could focus on counterterrorism.

46. United Nations Security Council Resolution S/RES/1368 (2001).
47. United Nations Security Council Resolution S/RES/1373 (2001).
48. United Nations Security Council Resolution S/RES/1378 (2001).

President Bush told a press conference on October 11, 2001, that "my focus is on bringing al Qaeda to justice," and that "it would be a useful function for the United Nations to take over the so-called 'nation-building,'—I would call it the stabilization of a future government—after our military mission is complete." He acknowledged that state-building was necessary. He said that "we should not just simply leave after a military objective has been achieved," and that the international community should ensure "that the post-operations Afghanistan is one that is stable." He pledged that "we'll participate" in rebuilding Afghanistan, but invited the UN to "provide the framework."[49]

With US diplomatic support, the United Nations moved to implement its part of the Bonn Agreement. It endorsed the Bonn Agreement and authorized on December 20 the International Security Assistance Force (ISAF) to help provide security in the capital.[50] In March 2002, the United Nations created the United Nations Assistance Mission in Afghanistan (UNAMA) to coordinate international civilian assistance to Afghanistan.[51] Other actors in the international community took complementary action. In December donor nations met in Brussels to establish the Afghanistan Reconstruction Steering Group. By May the interim government, the UN, and the World Bank had established the Afghanistan Reconstruction Trust Fund and the Law and Order Trust Fund for Afghanistan. The creation of these institutions collectively marks the beginning of the international state-building operation in Afghanistan.

State Failure in Afghanistan

Security. In 2001 Afghanistan was the world's most failed state. The security environment was anarchic, large-scale fighting against the Taliban and al-Qaida continued until March 2002,[52] and following the fall of the Taliban, fifty to seventy thousand Northern Alliance militiamen became a poorly managed, largely unaccountable force deployed across the country.[53] There was no professional army or police force, leaving warlords to wage miniwars against each other across the country. The United Nations judged in early 2002 that "banditry continues

---

49. White House, "President Holds a Prime Time News Conference," October 11, 2001.
50. United Nations Security Council Resolution S/RES/1386 (2001).
51. United Nations Security Council Resolution S/RES/1401 (2002); Report of the Secretary-General on the Situation in Afghanistan S/2002/278.
52. Anthony H. Cordesman, "The Afghan-Pakistan War: Developments in NATO/ ISAF and US Forces."
53. Bhatia, Lanigan, and Wilkinson, Minimal Investments.

as a lingering manifestation of the war economy."[54] The drug trade, suppressed in the Taliban's last year in power, sprang back into existence as the poppy crop expanded almost tenfold—from 8,000 hectares to 74,000 hectares between 2001 and 2002.[55] The resurgence of opium production enriched a new set of elites and created a wealthy criminal class that was neither loyal to Kabul nor cooperative with international forces.

Legitimacy. The Afghan state historically rested on three sources of legitimacy: Islam, tribalism, and nationalism.[56] The Taliban government was initially successful in staking a claim to legitimacy between 1994 and 1996. It backed its claim to represent true Islam with concrete action against crime, lawlessness, and warlordism. It effectively united Pashtun tribes into a coherent movement, coming close to bridging the historic gap between Durrani and Ghilzai tribal confederations. And it appropriated and transformed symbols of Afghan nationhood by claiming to be the successors to the anti-Soviet mujahedin, enemies of the warlords responsible for the civil war, and saviors of the nation. Taliban supreme leader Mullah Omar wove together the three claims to legitimacy in one symbolic act when he took the title Commander of the Faithful and literally wrapped himself in the cloak of the Prophet Muhammad, kept in a shrine in Kandahar, the Afghan Pashtuns' spiritual metropolis. The act fused the Taliban's claim to Islamic legitimacy, tribal leadership, and national power.

However, such claims were undermined when it became increasingly evident that the Taliban's brand of Islam was extremist (not traditional) and tainted by the Taliban's increasingly brutal warfare against other Muslims and practice of ethnic cleansing against the Hazara. Their claim to tribal leadership never extended beyond Pashtun tribes, which had been weakened anyway by the Soviets' practice of targeting tribal and traditional elites for co-optation or assassination in the 1980s. And the Taliban's claim to represent and lead the nation was shown to have failed by the endurance of civil war from 1996 to 2001 against a coalition of other tribes and ethnic minorities. The Taliban government was never recognized as legitimate by all Afghans. At the time of its fall from power, it was far from clear what mechanisms were available to relegitimize the Afghan state.

Capacity. In 2001 and 2002 the Afghan state had ceased to function. The World Bank estimated that in 2000 the Afghan state was in the last

---

54. S/2002/278.
55. United Nations Office on Drugs and Crime, *Afghanistan Opium Survey* (October 2002).
56. Cramer and Goodhand, "Try Again, Fail Again," 7.

percentile in the world in all six areas of governance that it tracks: voice and accountability, the rule of law, control of corruption, government effectiveness, regulatory quality, and political stability. The Taliban government collected less than 1 percent of GDP in revenue, compared to an average of 11 percent across South Asia and 26 percent worldwide.[57] Consequently, the state had an annual budget of merely $27 million—roughly one dollar per person. The Afghan government could not hire skilled workers to run public institutions; there were only 1,417 government employees who had graduated from an institution of higher education in 2001; and most ministries and the justice sector had effectively ceased to function because they lacked the basic levels of staff, money, and equipment required to do anything. The US Institute of Peace judged in 2004 that "to a great extent, the written law in Afghanistan is not applied—or even widely known." For most practical purposes, such as education, access to clean water, or protection of property, there was no government.[58]

Prosperity. With an anarchic security situation and a nonfunctional state, the Afghan economy had collapsed by the end of the Taliban's misrule. Afghans were the world's seventh poorest people in 2001. The IMF estimated that GDP per capita in 2002 was about $176: Afghans lived on about 48 cents per day, comparable to the poorest people in sub-Saharan Africa. Lacking a national currency, different factions issued their own bills for use within their fiefdoms. What little infrastructure the country once had was in ruins: little more than a tenth of the roads were paved, less than one-third of Afghans had access to sanitation, and only a quarter had clean water. Economic collapse led to a generation of lost human capital. A third or less of Afghans could read and write, according to various estimates, and only roughly a quarter of school-aged children were enrolled in the country's nearly defunct educational system. In a country of approximately twenty-five million people, there was just one TV station, eight airplanes, sixty trained pilots, and fewer than fifty thousand passenger cars.[59]

The humanitarian situation, in short, was catastrophic. Larry Goodson, professor of Middle East Studies at the US Army War College, estimated that even before the civil war of the 1990s, 50 percent of all Afghans had been killed, wounded, or displaced by the Soviet invasion.[60] There were at least 3.8 million Afghan refugees and another 1.2 million

57. Islamic Republic of Afghanistan Central Statistics Organization, *Afghanistan Statistical Yearbook 2003*; World Bank, "World Development Indicators Database."
58. Miller and Perito, *Establishing the Rule of Law*, 5.
59. Islamic Republic of Afghanistan Central Statistics Organization, *Afghanistan Statistical Yearbook 2003*; International Monetary Fund, *Afghanistan: Selected Issues* (2005); International Monetary Fund, *Islamic Republic of Afghanistan: Fifth Review*.
60. Goodson, *Afghanistan's Endless War*, 94.

internally displaced persons in Afghanistan in 2001. Within a year, almost two million refugees and more than 750,000 IDPs had returned, overwhelming urban areas and creating massive, overcrowded slums.[61] The devastation and neglect took its toll on the Afghan population. Only a third of Afghans survived to age sixty-five. Afghans had the one of the shortest life expectancies and highest infant mortality rates in the world, according to the World Bank, at forty-six years and 104 dead infants per 1,000 live births.[62]

Humanity. The Taliban managed the remarkable feat of being both the world's weakest government and among the world's most oppressive, incapable of providing basic services while still fielding an effective Ministry for the Prevention of Vice and Promotion of Virtue. The Taliban "abandon[ed] many of the other core functions of the nation state such as welfare and representation [but] maintained effective security and military capabilities."[63] The Taliban's oppressions became infamous: they banned kite flying; compelled women to wear the burqa; disallowed women from working outside the home; banned "un-Islamic" music, art, or discussion; and recognized no check on their authority. Less well-known is the Taliban's record of massacring civilians and targeting the Hazara for ethnic cleansing—notably at Mazar-I Shari in 1998, Robatak Pass in 2000, and Yakaolang in 2001.[64] Unlike other dictatorships, they did not bother even to hold and rig elections. They took power by bribery and conquest, held power by force, and recognized no authority but Allah's. There was no transparency in government and no means of holding it accountable. Afghans enjoyed no freedom of speech, press, or worship. Freedom House ranked Afghanistan as "not free" in 2001, giving it its lowest score in both political freedoms and civil rights. The Taliban government earned a -7 Polity IV score in 2000.

The combination of oppression and weakness was extreme. Afghanistan was the only country to rank in the bottom five across all six indicators of governance in 2000, and one of only three (with Somalia and the Democratic Republic of the Congo) to rank in the bottom ten consistently. Other states that regularly show up at the bottom of world rankings are either too weak to oppress anyone very effectively (like Liberia or Haiti) or, if strong enough to oppress people, also strong enough to provide a few services to key supporters (like Iraq, Myanmar, or North Korea). The Taliban outclassed them all.

61. UNHCR, *Statistical Yearbook 2001*, 89; UNHCR, *Statistical Yearbook 2002*, 194.
62. Islamic Republic of Afghanistan Central Statistics Organization, *Afghanistan Statistical Yearbook 2003*; World Bank, "World Development Indicators Database."
63. Cramer and Goodhand, "Try Again, Fail Again," 143.
64. Human Rights Watch, *Massacre in Mazar-i Sharif*; Human Rights Watch, *Massacres of Hazaras*.

Somalia is often cited as the archetype of failed states. It is not. Despite Somalia's infamous anarchy, Somalis are still relatively free of governmental oppression and have not experienced ethnic cleansing or genocide. Afghans, by contrast, had the worst of all worlds under the Taliban. They had Somalian anarchy, Haitian poverty, Congolese institutions, Balkan fractiousness, and a North Korean–style government. In January 2001, *The Economist* awarded Afghanistan the title of the world's "worst country." Any judgments about the international community's success or failure in Afghanistan need to begin with this benchmark.

State Building in Afghanistan, 2001–2006

According to the theory I developed in the previous chapters, the depth and intensity of Afghanistan's failure as a state would have required the international community to undertake an Administrator strategy across all five dimensions of statehood. Such a strategy probably would have replicated some of the institutions and mechanisms of the missions in the Democratic Republic of the Congo (1960), Cambodia, Timor-Leste, or Kosovo with the resources of the missions in West Germany, Iraq, or at least Bosnia. In the security sector it would have involved a large military deployment with a mandate to defend Kabul and enforce the writ of the new government against spoilers, the Taliban, and organized crime. In the relegitimizing of the state it would have involved the international community proactively guiding and, when necessary, directing the process of political reconstruction. In the capacity-building sector, it would have involved, from the very beginning, embedding international civilians in Afghan government institutions as advisers, trainers, and, where necessary, decision makers *and* an aggressive effort to train Afghan government civilians. In reconstruction it would have involved a massive, well-financed reconstruction program largely drawn up, orchestrated, and implemented by international donors. And in regard to rebuilding the state's humanity, it would have involved effecting regime change followed by giving support to a system of transitional justice.

The international community largely adopted the right strategy of state building for rebuilding the Afghan state's legitimacy, prosperity, and humanity. From 2001 to 2006, the international community largely adopted the wrong strategy for rebuilding the Afghan state's security and capacity. The international community did not tailor a strategy calculated to fit Afghanistan's needs. Instead, it adopted a strategy tailored to fit the resources that were made available. The strategy involved an Observer/Trainer military strategy, and Administrator strategy for rebuilding the state's legitimacy, prosperity, and humanity, and an

[161]

Observer strategy in regard to the state's capacity. This mismatch between the strategy required and the conditions on the ground explain the international community's failure to consolidate its early gains. By 2006 the well-matched aspects of the state-building strategy resulted in robust economic growth, successful political reconstruction, and progress in human rights, while the incorrect aspects resulted in continued state weakness and incapacity and the growth of the Taliban insurgency and the drug trade.

If the international community had withdrawn from Afghanistan shortly after successfully holding elections—as it did in Cambodia, Haiti, Liberia, or as the United States did in Cuba and Nicaragua—the intervention would have been a mitigated failure. Using the same criteria by which I have measured success or failure in other state-building operations, Afghanistan in late 2006 and early 2007 had shown some political progress and economic growth, but governance had not improved and, most important, war had resumed.

Remarkably, the international community did not seize on the completion of the Bonn process as a chance to declare victory and withdraw. Reflecting a realism and resilience evident in other recent operations— Sierra Leone in 2002, Iraq in 2007—the international community recognized the emerging insurgency and endemic problems with corruption and the drug trade, and attempted a midcourse correction. Starting in 2006, the international community gradually moved to a Trainer/ Administrator military strategy and a more coherent, albeit minimal, Trainer strategy for capacity development. The greater degree of involvement and resources was better calibrated to Afghanistan's needs.

Security. After 2001, the international community's priority was to prevent the reemergence of the 1992–96 civil war between rival warlords in control of sectarian militias. UN disarmament programs coupled with the international community's forceful diplomacy successfully contained fighting between rival warlords and prevented the country from relapsing into civil war—an underrated achievement, especially considering the eruptions of violence during and after international peacebuilding missions, such as in Angola in 1992 and 1998, Liberia throughout the 1990s, Cambodia in 1997, and Iraq in 2006–7. The UN secretary-general reported in August 2005 that "factional clashes—a prominent feature of insecurity three years ago—have become a localized issue and are no longer a threat to national security."[65]

The international community's strategy toward the warlords had a flip side, however. Because the United States and the United Nations could

---

65. Report of the Secretary-General on the Situation in Afghanistan S/2005/525, 19.

not confront the warlords directly, they had to coax them into giving up their weapons by promising them a place in the new Afghan political order. The warlords thus made a successful entry into Afghan politics as governors, legislators, and cabinet ministers, without ever facing prosecution or even a truth commission for alleged war crimes. In hindsight, nearly all scholars and commentators condemn the international community for allowing the warlords to retain power. Yet these same critics often deride the reverse strategy of building up a central government at the expense of local powerbrokers. In 2002, the international community attempted to navigate between these competing imperatives—disarming the warlords without unleashing a backlash and building a government while respecting local authority. The result has been imperfect but better than permitting the warlords to retain their conventional military power, on the one hand, or risking a backlash by attempting to put them on trial, on the other.[66]

Despite success against the warlords, the international community did not meet the security challenges in Afghanistan from 2001 to 2006—by failing to train enough new Afghan security forces or to successfully contain the residual Taliban threat. Early efforts to train Afghan police and reform the security sector had not achieved notable results by 2006. Washington had spent $4.4 billion on security assistance and had trained 36,000 soldiers and a comparable number of policemen in the first five years—too few to provide effective security. The police, moreover, were widely reported to be corrupt and incompetent. Similarly, the International Security Assistance Force did not hold large swathes of territory or provide security to the vast majority of Afghans. Indeed, it did not have

---

66. Some scholars have argued that a highly invasive strategy would simply repeat the mistakes of the British Empire and the Soviet Union because history shows that Afghans are prone to resist outside interference in their decentralized tribal culture. In this view, Afghanistan has always been governed by a collection of tribes that resist central authority and outside powers. I respond that much less of Afghans' storied history stems from supposedly unique features of their history and culture than critics avow: resisting invading armies is hardly unique to Afghan history. Tribes often resisted the encroachments of the central Afghan state in Kabul—notably against the brutal autocracy of Abdur Rahman Khan (1880–1901) and the modernizing reign of Amanullah Khan (1919–29)—as critics often point out. However, the tribes rose up in those cases because, in the former case, the government was brutal and threatened tribal interests and, in the latter, because it was perceived to be un-Islamic. That tells us little about how Afghans will react to a government that attempts to be benign and govern in accord with the population's values. There is little evidence that Pashtun tribes opposed the idea of government itself. In fact, tribes welcomed and existed peacefully with the moderate Islamic government of the Musahiban Dynasty, which also coincided with Afghanistan's only prior experience with democracy, from 1964 to 1973.

[163]

the mandate or authorization to do so. ISAF was initially confined to Kabul, hampered by restrictive rules of engagement and national caveats limiting where soldiers were permitted to deploy or what kinds of operations they were allowed to engage in, and relatively small in size. (In 2003, the peacekeeping force only had 5,500 troops assigned to it.) Then, in 2005, ISAF was authorized to operate in northern and western provinces, but it still numbered fewer than 10,000 troops, or four soldiers for every 10,000 Afghans (compared, e.g., to about forty-two soldiers for 10,000 civilians in the relatively successful UN-UK operation in Sierra Leone in 2002).[67]

The net effect of the international community's light involvement in the security sector, combined with the lack of progress on governance, became evident with the rise of the Taliban insurgency, beginning in 2005. The Taliban and other insurgents initiated sporadic, uncoordinated attacks against international military forces and the Afghan government in the years following their fall from power. Yet they averaged only about four attacks per day nationwide in 2003 and five per day in 2004.[68] In May 2005, Taliban militants assassinated the head of the Kandahar Ulema Shura (cleric's council)—and then suicide bombed his funeral, the boldest terrorist attack in the country to that date. The event dramatized the Taliban's lethal reach and resilience, the Afghan government's weakness and inability to respond, and ISAF's absence. Following the sudden revelation of the militants' unexpected strength, violence grew markedly worse in the latter half of 2005, almost doubling to over eight attacks per day, killing 1,268 people. Militants began to make persistent and notable strides in the scope, scale, sophistication, and range of their attacks. The violence began to escalate dramatically each year thereafter, killing 3,154 people in 2006 and 5,818 in 2007.[69] By late 2005, what began as an incoherent and decentralized campaign of violence had gelled into a cohesive insurgency dedicated to eroding Western political will and overthrowing the Afghan government.

The Taliban was able to regroup and launch an insurgency because, effectively, nothing stood in its way. The Afghan government was still unable to offer services or resolve disputes, and there were too few international military forces to secure the whole country. The state's institutional capacity remained weak, the rule of law was nonexistent, and the security services were still embryonic. "Weak governance is a common

---

67. NATO, *Afghanistan Report 2009*, 7.
68. Government Printing Office, *Afghanistan's Security Environment*. See chart on page 4. The .pdf version only shows a chart with no numbers. The .txt version lists specific numerical values in lieu of a graphical display. The .txt version is available at http://www.gao.gov/assets/100/96714.html.
69. Sundberg, "Collective Violence 2002–2007."

precondition of insurgencies," according to RAND analyst and Afghan expert Seth Jones. "Afghan insurgent groups took advantage of this anarchic situation."[70]

Critics are right to argue that the rise of the insurgency is proof that the international state-building campaign had, as of 2006, failed to build a functioning Afghan state. But the intervention did not end in 2006. A US National Security Council review of Afghan policy in late 2006 recognized the emerging challenges and called for substantially more security and development assistance. Following the review, US funding for Afghan security forces nearly quadrupled from $1.9 billion in 2006 to $7.4 billion in 2007, and aggregate spending on security assistance increased fivefold. Starting in late 2007, entire district police units were sent to a training academy and US trainers were assigned to embed with each unit after graduation. In addition, the international community began experimenting with programs to enlist the aid of local, indigenous, and tribal security forces.

To staff the expanded training programs and provide security while the Afghan forces were coming up to speed, the United States quadrupled its military presence in Afghanistan between 2006 and 2010, from 22,100 troops to over 100,000—Washington's third-largest military deployment since Vietnam.[71] Partner nations increased their troop deployments as well, from roughly 21,500 in early 2007 to 38,400 at the end of 2009.[72] ISAF deployed nationwide in 2006, assuming responsibility for security assistance in the country's east and south for the first time. Former ISAF commander general Stanley McChrystal also began in 2009 to change how US and NATO troops were used. He sought to make the entirety of ISAF a part of the training and mentoring of the Afghan Army and police and to focus on protecting the Afghan population. The moves collectively represented a huge shift in emphasis from a light-footprint counterterrorism mission to a more robust, if still partial, counterinsurgency campaign. As a result, the United States nearly tripled the size of the Afghan Army in three years, increasing it from 36,000 soldiers to nearly 100,000 and brought the Afghan police force up to its authorized strength of 82,000, and made incremental progress improving their capabilities.

Violence continued to escalate through 2010—insurgents initiated an average of nineteen attacks per day in 2007, almost thirty per day in 2008, and sixty-seven per day in the spring of 2010[73]—a predictable effect

70. Jones, "Rise of Afghanistan's Insurgency," 8.
71. Fairfield, Quealy, and Tse, "Troop Levels."
72. Brookings Institution, *Afghanistan Index*, December 13, 2012, 5.
73. *Afghanistan's Security* Environment, 4.

of sending more troops into battle. There were more targets for insurgents to attack, and more US and NATO soldiers conducting operations. The trend, however, began to reverse in late 2011. The US Department of Defense reported that violence fell in 2011 compared to the previous year, the first time it had reported such a decline.[74] The UN secretary-general reported in March 2011 that "the number of districts under insurgent control has decreased. . . . As a result of the increased tempo of security operations in northern and western provinces, an increasing number of anti-Government elements are seeking to join local reintegration programmes. . . . In Kabul, the increasingly effective Afghan national security forces continue to limit insurgent attacks."[75] Several other observers noted improvements in security in 2010–11.[76] The trend continued in 2012, with enemy-initiated attacks in January through September declining 3 percent compared to the same timeframe in 2011 (showing a steeper decline in the spring before rising again later in the year as US troops began to withdraw), according to the US Department of Defense's reports on Afghanistan.[77] Declining violence was probably due to ISAF's improving practice of unconventional warfare while the Taliban, contrary to the tenants of successful insurgency, continued to espouse an unpopular ideology and murder fellow Pashtun Muslims, thus losing support.

Legitimacy. As previously noted, the United Nations Security Council outlined a broad, ambitious vision for the next Afghan government. It should be "broad-based, multi-ethnic and fully representative" and "respect the human rights of all Afghan people."[78] The unbrokered Bonn Agreement was the mechanism for reestablishing and legitimizing the new Afghan government. The United Nations oversaw the Bonn Agreement with help from the International Security Assistance Force and the United States, representing a deep and invasive international involvement in rebuilding the new Afghan state's legitimacy.

A principal step in the Bonn process was the drafting and ratification of a new constitution, which UN advisers helped a commission of Afghans to draft in 2003. The resulting document protects equal rights for

74. US Department of Defense, *Report on Progress toward Security and Stability in Afghanistan*, October 2011.
75. Report of the Secretary-General on the Situation in Afghanistan S/2011/120, 2.
76. Gall, "Losses in Pakistani Haven"; "Single or Quits," *Economist*, May 12, 2011, http://www.economist.com/node/18681950.
77. US Department of Defense, *Report on Progress*, December 2012.
78. United Nations Security Council Resolution S/RES/1378 (2001), 2.

men and women; individual liberty; freedom of expression and association; the right to vote and run for office; property; and religious freedom. But the document also acknowledged Afghanistan's traditional sources of legitimacy: Article 1 established Afghanistan as an "Islamic Republic." Article 2 enshrines Islam as the state religion. Article 3 states that "No law shall contravene the tenets and provisions of the holy religion of Islam in Afghanistan." And Article 62 requires that the president and two vice presidents of Afghanistan be Muslims. Although the Afghan government's efforts to balance modern law with traditional customs have not always satisfied human rights activists, it is nonetheless an unmitigated improvement over the Taliban and one of the most progressive constitutions in Central Asia or the Middle East.

After the constitution was ratified, the international community funded and administered a voter registration drive that culminated with the voting of over eight million Afghans in the nation's first-ever presidential election in October 2004. And 6.4 million elected the nation's legislature in September 2005, Afghanistan's first freely elected legislature since 1973.[79] Freedom House upgraded the country to "partly free" and 77 percent of Afghans said they were satisfied with democracy in 2006, according to the Asia Foundation.[80] The success of the Bonn process was not a foregone conclusion. Similar UN-sponsored processes in postconflict countries have collapsed and led to renewed violence, including in Angola and Liberia in the 1990s. It succeeded in Afghanistan because of strong international engagement and support at every stage of the process.

Afghans face continuing challenges in their effort to institutionalize a process of peaceful political contestation. The 2009 and 2010 elections, administered by the Afghans, were notoriously marred by fraud and low turnout, which may suggest the international community transferred leadership for political reconstruction to the Afghans too quickly or that the electoral process was not accompanied by a robust capacity-development effort. Nonetheless, the 2009 and 2010 election still happened, which is an improvement over the record of other states, like Angola, in which the first postconflict election was also the last. The fact that Afghan powerbrokers bothered to hold and participate in elections at all, even if they were fraught with corruption, is significant: powerbrokers participated in the electoral system, rather than skip elections

---

79. For the implementation of the Bonn Agreement, see Reports of the Secretary-General on the Situation in Afghanistan S/2002/278, S/2002/737, S/2002/1173, S/2003/333, S/2003/754, S/2003/1212, S/2004/230, S/2004/634, S/2004/925, S/2005/183, and S/2005/525.
80. Asia Foundation, *Survey of the Afghan People* (2006), 3, 45.

altogether, because they recognized that Afghans continue to accept the new democratic constitution as the basis for their state's legitimacy. The international community clearly needs to press the Afghan government to crack down on corruption and develop robust political parties. But it is equally clear that the Bonn process has been a transformational event in Afghan history. Compared to the Soviet and Taliban efforts to legitimize their respective governments in Afghanistan prior to 2001—admittedly a low bar—the democratic constitution has been a success.

Capacity. In one respect the effort in Afghanistan has seriously faltered. The international community has largely stuck with a failing "light footprint" approach toward Afghan governance and capacity development. Partly in reaction to recent UN missions in Kosovo and Timor-Leste, which were criticized for relying too heavily on international help, the UN secretary-general publicly and openly instructed UNAMA to try "relying on as limited an international presence and on as many Afghan staff as possible."[81] UN officials never considered whether the Afghans, whose human capital was destroyed by war and depleted by emigration, were able to do the job. Donors similarly neglected governance programs. They pledged a total of $1.2 billion for Afghan governance and rule of law programs between 2001 and 2006, or about $200 million per year, and only disbursed about half that amount.[82] A substantial amount of this was dedicated to the 2004 and 2005 elections, leaving just a few hundred million dollars to train civil servants, judges, prosecutors, and lawyers; rebuild government offices and courthouses; and pay international advisers and consultants to ministers and other government officials. Considering Afghanistan was the weakest state in the world in 2001, these funds did not come close to meeting Afghanistan's need. The international community was effectively asking Afghans with no shoes to lift themselves up by their bootstraps.

For example, the Independent Administrative Reform and Civil Service Commission was supposed to lead efforts to streamline the bureaucracy, introduce a new pay and grade system, develop merit-based hiring and promotion criteria, and establish a civil service training institute. For this ambitious agenda, the Asia Development Bank gave $2.2 million starting in 2003 and UNDP gave $528,000.[83] A review of capacity-development efforts by USAID concluded in 2007 that "capacity building has not been a primary objective of USAID projects" and that "what has

81. S/2002/278, 16.
82. Figures for donor disbursements here and elsewhere come from the Islamic Republic of Afghanistan, Ministry of Finance, "Donor Assistance Database" and reflect amounts actually disbursed, not merely pledged, committed, or obligated.
83. Lister, *Moving Forward?*, 5.

occurred has been more ad hoc and 'spotty' rather than systematic and strategic." The review could only identify four ministries out of twenty-five that "are considered reasonably competent to carry out their primary responsibilities."[84] An Afghan NGO judged in late 2006 that public administration reform "has been 'cosmetic', with superficial restructuring of ministries and an emphasis on higher pay rather than fundamental change" and that "there has not been sufficient competent technical assistance" from the international community. The Civil Service Institute did not open until January 2007, and after five years the government could boast of only 7,500 civil servants hired under the new merit-based criteria in a government of 240,000 employees.[85]

Similarly, the international community did not prioritize assistance to the justice system. The US Department of State's Bureau of International Narcotics and Law Enforcement and USAID did initiate a host of programs, but in practice they were too small to make a measurable difference in the worst justice sector in the world. The Afghans estimated that it would cost $600 million to implement their National Justice Sector Strategy, but donors had disbursed just $38 million in aid to the justice sector by the end of 2006. The UN secretary-general wrote in 2006 that "with approximately 1,500 judges and 2,000 prosecutors in the judicial system, demand for training far outstrips supply."[86]

As a result of these shortcomings, Afghanistan remained second-worst in the world for the rule of law, after Somalia, according to the World Bank's governance indicators. And without the rule of law, but with a large amount of money flowing from international aid and rapid economic growth, corruption predictably exploded. As Samuel Huntington noted long ago, modernization without strong institutions almost always yields corruption, and Afghanistan was no exception.[87]

Corruption was increasingly fueled by the drug trade. The poppy crop had soared to 408,000 acres in 2006 and 477,000 acres in 2007 and it produced 82 percent of the world's poppy and 93 percent of the world's heroin. In 2007, the drug trade was worth $4 billion, equivalent to half of Afghanistan's licit GDP.[88] Because the Afghan government lacked strong institutions and the ability to enforce the rule of law, Afghanistan was becoming a lawless and corrupt narco-state.

When the crisis in governance became apparent with the rise of the Taliban insurgency in 2005 and 2006, the international community moved

84. Blue, *Assessment of the Impact of USAID*, 8–9.
85. Lister, *Moving Forward?*, 2, 8.
86. Report of the Secretary-General on the Situation in Afghanistan S/2006/145, 7.
87. Huntington, *Political Order in Changing Societies*, chap. 1.
88. United Nations Office on Drugs and Crime, *Afghanistan Opium Survey* (October 2007).

to bolster its governance programs. In dollar terms, the international community roughly doubled its training efforts in the Afghan civil administration and justice sector to $688 million over the next three years, still a paltry figure relative to Afghanistan's needs. In 2007, USAID started the Capacity Development Program, a $219 million, five-year project to strengthen Afghan institutions such as the Ministries of Finance and Education and the Civil Service Institute.[89] The program was a big improvement but still small in absolute terms. US spending on rule-of-law programs doubled from 2006 to 2007, and nearly doubled again in 2008. The United States also doubled its much more substantial investment in counternarcotics programs—to $3.3 billion.

The increased focus on governance and the rule of law spurred some institutional innovations in the Afghan government, but they have, to date, failed to markedly improve the quality of governance. President Karzai named an entirely new slate of justices to the supreme court in late 2006. The new court established a regulation of judicial conduct, and the new justices began inspection tours of provincial courts to ensure their compliance with judicial standards. The Afghan government formed an anticorruption unit in the attorney general's office in 2009 to investigate and prosecute cases of high-level corruption, but Afghanistan fell further on Transparency International's Corruption Perceptions Index, to 179th—second from the bottom—in 2009. The percentage of Afghans who said the government was doing an excellent or good job fell from 80 percent in 2007 to 73 percent in 2011,[90] probably because Afghans' high hopes and expectations after 2001 had gone too long unfulfilled. The international community paid an enormous opportunity cost by failing to assert a greater role with sufficient resources from the start.

Prosperity. In response to the economic and humanitarian emergency in Afghanistan in 2001, the international community undertook one of the largest and most ambitious relief, reconstruction, and development efforts in the world—eventually committing a total of $22.7 billion in aid to economic reconstruction, development, and humanitarian relief between 2001 and 2011. The donors invested heavily in rebuilding the ministry of finance, the central bank, the treasury, and the customs service, and helped phase out the old Afghan currency and launch a new one.

The result was strong economic growth. Partly because of US and international aid, Afghanistan experienced a postwar economic boom. Real GDP grew by nearly 29 percent in 2002 alone—faster than West Germany in 1946–7—and averaged 15 percent annual *licit* growth from 2001 to 2006, making it one of the fastest-growing economies in the world

89. Trujillo, *Audit of USAID/Afghanistan's Capacity Development Program.*
90. Asia Foundation, *Survey of the Afghan People* (2011), 53.

(it was still averaging 13.5 percent through 2009 after a drought in 2008), according to the IMF.[91] The pace of its growth was due in part to the low base from which it started and reflected the typical boom many postwar states experience, but the rapid pace itself was an important achievement of the state-building effort. Afghanistan had not grown significantly in more than two decades: the economic boom signaled a new era in Afghan life.

Between 2001 and 2010 almost every indicator of human development showed measurable improvement. In September 2008, 80 percent of the population had access to basic health services, up from 8 percent in 2001, according to the US Department of Defense. By 2010, Afghanistan had doubled its immunization rate and nearly caught up to its regional cohort. Life expectancy inched upward. After the fall of the Taliban, school enrollment skyrocketed from 1.1 million in 2001 to 5.7 million students in 2008—a third of whom were girls—promising to double or triple Afghanistan's literacy rate in a decade.

Meanwhile, infrastructure greatly improved with international help. USAID built 1,600 miles of roads, and the international community rebuilt three-quarters of Highway 1 from Herat to Kabul. In total, almost a third of roads were paved in 2008, up from 13.3 percent in 2001. The mobile phone industry, nonexistent before 2001, had nearly eight million subscribers by the end of 2008. The construction sector tripled in size. Donors spent $312 million on water projects, and the number of Afghans' with access to water nearly doubled from 26 percent to 50 percent.[92]

The impressive growth and improvement since 2001—stronger than in any postconflict state in which the UN has deployed a peace-building mission since the end of the Cold War—demonstrates that progress is achievable with robust resources and international attention. The economy is still dependent on donor aid and not well diversified—there are weaknesses in how the substantial amount of international aid has been used—but the greatest threat is that recent gains will unravel without greater progress on security.

Result

Afghanistan was the most failed state in the world in 2001, and one of the most failed states ever, and thus required the most invasive and resource-intensive state-building effort possible. The international

91. International Monetary Fund, Islamic Republic of Afghanistan: Fifth Review.
92. World Bank, "World Development Indicators Database"; Islamic Republic of Afghanistan, Central Statistics Organization, *Statistical Yearbook 2003* and *National Risk and Vulnerability Assessment 2007/8*.

community implemented a mixed strategy from 2001 to 2006. It adopted an Administrator strategy toward rebuilding the Afghan state's legitimacy, which helped ensure the success of the Bonn process. It administered economic reconstruction, which helped Afghanistan's economy to grow quickly. In these two areas, the international community adopted a strategy appropriately tailored to Afghanistan's needs and saw corresponding success. However, the international community neglected to round out its strategy with a serious training effort, letting years pass without investing significantly in Afghan's political parties or reconstruction capacity, and thus enabled local free-riding on international efforts.

The international community had a Trainer strategy toward capacity development and the justice sector *on paper*, but the effort had so few resources that it was *in effect* a monitor-and-encourage strategy. Even a fully resourced train-and-equip effort might have been insufficient considering the state of Afghan governance in 2001. Regardless, the monitor-and-encourage effort was radically insufficient. The international community was merely monitoring continued state failure and encouraging Afghans to do things they could not do. The mismatch between strategy and circumstances led to failure. Continued state weakness allowed corruption and the drug trade to spiral out of control.

In the security sector, the international community adopted a strategy of monitoring and encouraging security reforms; initiating a small and nascent effort to train and equip new security forces, while directly providing security in only tiny areas. The security strategy was inadequate for Afghanistan's security environment. As a result, the Taliban insurgency was able to emerge.

But the international community began to change course starting in 2006. It vastly increased its involvement in the security sector, both accelerating the training of new Afghan security forces and becoming far more involved in directly providing security. Similarly, though to a lesser extent, the international community increased its train-and-equip effort for Afghan government capacity. This change of strategy brings the international state-building effort closer to Afghanistan's needs, is more likely to alter the local balance of power away from the Taliban, and is thus more likely to succeed. In particular, it seems likely that Afghan and international forces will contain and roll back the Taliban insurgency and establish a level of livable stability in Afghanistan.

However, the international state-building effort is likely to achieve only a shallow success, not a full success. The international community did not directly administer institutions of the Afghan government, missing an opportunity to jump-start the capacity-building process and

TABLE 7.6. Indices of Socioeconomic Development, Afghanistan and the World, 2001 and 2010

	2001				2010			
	Afghanistan	South Asia	World	OECD	Afghanistan	South Asia	World	OECD
Life expectancy at birth (years)	45.6	62.2	67.4	77.3	48.3	65.3	69.6	79.3
Infant mortality rate (per 1,000 live births)	103.8	64.0	50.8	10.5	103.0	51.6	41.2	6.8
Hospital beds (per 1,000 people)	0.4	0.7	2.6	5.6	0.4	-	-	5.2
Immunization, measles (% aged 12–23 months)	33.0	62.8	74.5	94.2	66.0	76.2	85.1	95.3
Immunization, DPT (% aged 12–23 months)	37.0	58.1	73.2	91.9	62.0	77.2	85.3	93.8
Incidence of TB (per 100,000 people)	189.0	215.0	-	-	189.0	192.0	-	-
Sanitation facilities, % pop. with access	32.0	30.1	56.3	96.5	37.0	38.2	62.5	97.7
Water source, % pop. with access	26.0	81.4	83.3	98.2	50.0	90.0	88.4	99.2
Telephone subscribers (per 100 people)	0.1	3.1	16.7	50.8	0.4	2.7	17.2	40.9
Literacy rate (% age 15+)	-	58.0	81.8	-	-	61.6	84.0	-
GDP per capita, current $USD	-	457.4	5,306.0	22,890.1	-	745.8	6,006.0	24,579.0
Government revenue, % GDP	0.9	11.2	25.7	27.4	10.1	11.9	22.9	23.0
Polity IV score	-	-	-	-	-	-	-	-
Voice and accountability, percentile	1.0	-	-	-	8.1	-	-	-
Political stability, percentile	0.5	-	-	-	1.4	-	-	-
Government effectiveness, percentile	0.0	-	-	-	4.8	-	-	-
Regulatory quality, percentile	1.0	-	-	-	4.8	-	-	-
Rule of law, percentile	1.4	-	-	-	0.5	-	-	-
Control of corruption, percentile	0.0	-	-	-	1.0	-	-	-

Blank cell indicates unavailable data.
Sources: World Bank; Polity IV Project; Islamic Republic of Afghanistan, Central Statistics Organization.

saddling Afghans with the double burden of weak institutions *and* the legacies of Soviet and Taliban misrule. International administration could have rapidly put in place processes of transparency, accountability, decision making, budgeting, planning, and executing, which, if backed by adequate resources and competent implementation, could have been transferred to Afghan leadership as local capacity improved. After the change in strategy, the international community began an appropriate training and capacity-building effort, but it may still be too small and inadequate for Afghanistan's needs. Additionally, ten years of aggregate frustration between Afghan and international actors have limited the international community's ability to increase its efforts in governance. Absent effective governance, Afghanistan is likely to remain weak and thus vulnerable to instability in the future. It may not face the same challenges in the future as it does today, but other challenges will rise. How it deals with those challenges will determine if Afghanistan is ultimately a shallow success or a mitigated failure. In particular, the cases of Haiti after 1934, Nicaragua after 1933, the Dominican Republic after 1924, and South Korea after 1953 suggest a common danger for weak governments with foreign-trained security forces. If the Taliban are defeated and the international community withdraws, a coup by a victorious Afghan Army, fed up with civilian corruption and incompetence, is not unthinkable. Once again, building strong civilian institutions of governance would help prevent that outcome.

[8]

Conclusion

In this chapter I summarize conclusions, sketch the scope conditions under which my conclusions hold, suggest avenues of further research, consider alternative hypotheses, offer policy recommendations, review the most recent state-building operations, and engage briefly with the discussion about the normative merits of armed state building.

SUMMARY OF CONCLUSIONS

Most contemporary definitions of international state building focus on rebuilding institutions, an overly narrow understanding of the phenomenon. Institution building is only one facet of a broader type of international behavior. In fact, international state building bears some resemblance to both imperialism and development. Different norms—liberal and Westphalian versus imperial—help distinguish international state building from imperialism, while different forms of power—military versus economic and diplomatic—distinguish state building from development. International state building is the attempt by liberal states to use military, political, and economic power to compel weak, failed, or collapsed states to govern more effectively, as understood by Westphalian and liberal norms.

This definition enables us to identify the universe of cases of armed state building with greater rigor and breadth than in other scholarship on international state building, to include cases of post–Cold War UN complex peacekeeping; all five post–World War II military governments; a selection of the US interventions in the Caribbean and Central America in the early twentieth century; the US operations in South Vietnam, Iraq, and Afghanistan; and the UN operation in the Democratic Republic of the Congo in 1960 (see appendix A).

To understand state building, we must first ask what kind of state is being built. That, in turn, begs the question: What is the state? A review of political theory suggests that the state is composed of five aspects or dimensions: security, legitimacy, capacity, prosperity, and humanity. The state is a human institution that successfully invokes a theory of justice: (a) to claim the monopoly of the legitimate use of physical force, the right to expropriate resources and perform other functions at its discretion, and sovereign authority to make and enforce rules within a given territory and over a given human population, and to serve human life; (b) by providing (professedly) public goods to at least some of the population in a contractlike exchange: goods for legitimacy (agreement to its claims). The kind of goods that the state provides are cast in terms of the theory of justice that the state embodies, and the provision of just services constitute, in part, the state's claim to legitimacy.

States can fail to varying degrees in any aspect of statehood, which yields five types of state failure: anarchic, illegitimate, incapable, unproductive, and barbaric. These failures are not mutually exclusive but can, and often do, happen in concert with each other. State builders must recognize that there are unique dynamics of power balancing in the conditions of state failure, highlighting that some groups benefit from failure and thus work to defend the status quo.

State builders must have a strategy for all five dimensions of statehood, contrary to scholars who claim that state builders can focus primarily on security or on building institutional capacity or that they must sequence efforts in a predetermined pattern. Strategies of state building can be defined by a fundamental choice in how they approach a state-building mission. They can choose to (1) observe, monitor, and encourage reform; (2) build things and train and equip people to implement reform, or (3) assume control and directly administer reform efforts. I termed these, respectively, the Observer, Trainer, and Administrator strategies of state building. State builders must match the strategic degree of invasiveness to the degree of failure *in each dimension.* State builders should use an Observer strategy for aspects of the state that are weak but still functioning; a Trainer strategy for aspects of the state that are no longer functional but when there are still local citizens willing to lead reform efforts; and an Administrator strategy for aspects of the state that have completely collapsed and when there are no locals willing or able to lead reform and reconstruction.

[176]

Conclusion

SCOPE CONDITIONS AND FURTHER RESEARCH

There is a large and growing body of research on early post–Cold War cases of armed state building. The field's principle need for further research is for more case studies. Continued case study research on more recent and ongoing operations—in Bosnia, Kosovo, Sierra Leone, Burundi, Côte d'Ivoire, Timor-Leste, Iraq, Afghanistan, Haiti, the Democratic Republic of the Congo, and Lebanon—will help test, corroborate, and refine the theory presented here, especially as the interventions in these states conclude. Additionally, further case study research is needed on older operations that have not traditionally been viewed as cases of armed state building, including the Caribbean interventions, South Korea, South Vietnam, Italy, and Austria. Finally, some classic cases—including the US occupation of Germany—are surprisingly understudied considering their importance in international relations, European history, and security studies.

There are four additional areas for further research. First, scholars should compare cases of state building to "negative cases" of failed states in which international actors did not intervene to isolate the impact interventions have in postconflict societies. Second, scholars should explore other eras of history to identify pre–twentieth century cases of state building. Third, scholars should test the distinction between state building and imperialism and explore if dynamics of imperial rule mirror those of state-building operations. Last, scholars should begin to look at the foreign policy processes of state building.

Negative Cases

The set of forty cases of armed state building should be contrasted with a set of "negative cases," that is, cases of failed states in which there was not an armed state-building intervention. There is, unfortunately, no comprehensive data set of failed states available for a rigorous comparison. The closest is the data set assembled by the Political Instability Task Force (indeed, its original name was the State Failure Task Force).[1] The PITF data set includes 103 incidences of ethnic or revolutionary war or genocide—their definition of state failure—between 1955 and 2008. There were twenty-six cases of international state building during that time frame. If the cases of international state building

1. Center for Global Policy, Political Instability Task Force, "Political Regime Characteristics Transitions, 1800–2010" dataset.

[177]

correspond to cases of state failure included in the PITF data set, that would indicate the two data sets are roughly comparable, at least for illustrative purposes, and that the remaining cases in the PITF data set could be considered negative cases—cases of state failure in which the international community did not intervene.

In fact, there is a high degree of correspondence between the two data sets. Of the twenty-six cases of international state building that occurred during the timeframe covered by the PITF data set, all but four correspond to a PITF case of state failure. (Haiti is coded a case of regime change in 1991. Namibia, the Central African Republic, and Haiti in 2004 are not coded as having experienced a state failure event during or immediately prior to the intervention.) We can infer that the remaining seventy-eight cases of state failure are the negative cases—candidates for an armed state-building mission in which international actors chose not to intervene.

The negatives cases, at least anecdotally, confirm that successful state building makes a difference. Nearly one-third (twenty-five of seventy-eight) of state failure events were recidivist; that is, there were twenty-five cases of war or genocide that were not the object of a state building operation, and which subsequently experienced another state failure event within the next few decades. That compares to one-sixth of state-building events that showed recidivism within a much longer time frame—and only one *successful* state-building operation that showed recidivism (Haiti in 1915). Twenty-one of the seventy-eight cases are ongoing incidences of failure, and they have an average duration of almost fourteen years—far longer than the duration of a typical state-building operation. Failed states do not fix themselves, it appears, but international state builders sometimes fix them.

These are only illustrative observations. Scholars could build on these suggestions by assembling a more rigorously defined data set of state failure and then carrying out more robust comparisons—for example, charting the economic and political progress of all negative cases during and following state failure—to establish a baseline of a typical failed state's performance or trajectory against which to compare cases of international state building. That would enable scholars to make stronger statements about the relative impact of armed state building compared to postconflict recovery without international assistance.

Beyond the Twentieth and Twenty-first Centuries

One of the strengths of this study's research design is that cases are drawn from throughout the twentieth century: its findings are not limited to the post–Cold War or post-9/11 environment. However, this study is limited in scope to the twentieth and twenty-first centuries, and to operations by the United States and United Nations. These cases take place within the current Westphalian international system during an age in which liberalism and nationalism have both grown increasingly influential. The growth in nationalism made military occupation and imperialism more costly, while liberalism made them less acceptable. The combination is, in all likelihood, what created the possibility of liberal armed state building itself: state builders claim to be devoted to fostering, not undermining, effective sovereignty and self-determination, and have proven responsive to nationalist and local demands that state-building operations be brief. Are there cases of liberal state building prior to 1898, led by other powers? If so, could the theory presented in this study be extended to them?

During the French Revolution, the French Revolutionary Army effected regime change and attempted to spread early liberalism across Europe. This period of history offers the greatest potential for expanding the study of liberal state building beyond the twentieth century, complicated, of course, by the collapse of the First Republic and its transformation into an empire, and because the territories of French conquest do not easily fit the category of "failed states." Regardless, revolutionary France's role in spreading liberal ideals across Europe has long been recognized by historians. Case studies on the impact of French military occupation in Spain, Italy, the Netherlands, or elsewhere, would be valuable in expanding the state-building field of research.

Imperialism and Decolonization

In this book I sharply distinguish between state building and imperialism and have excluded the latter, including European and Soviet imperialism. One of the key distinctions, and virtues, of a successful state-building strategy is that it is more likely to be consistent with local citizens' own aspirations—a key objective of liberal state builders. Imperial and illiberal interventions need not heed local preferences, opening up policies and strategies of raw coercion that are (happily) unavailable to liberal state builders.

Further research could, however, challenge this distinction. There may be some cases of European and American imperialism in which liberal norms played a large enough role that some of the findings in this study might apply, perhaps in revised form. American imperial rule in the Philippines, the League of Nations mandate system, or the system of decolonization through the UN Trusteeship Council would be good candidates for further research. Possible cases include, but are not limited to, much of the Middle East, Botswana, Sierra Leone, Tanganyika, the Philippines (after the initial

[179]

war of 1899–1902), the Marshall Islands, Micronesia, Palau, Nauru, Kiribati, Tuvalu, and others.

Foreign Policy Process

State-building operations are more likely to succeed if undertaken with an appropriate strategy. But how do individual policymakers, bureaucracies, military commanders, or intergovernmental institutions develop their strategies of intervention? Why do they choose, and often stick with, failing strategies? How are some policymakers able to shift strategy midintervention? These questions are a fruitful avenue of further research.

Part of the answer lies in domestic political considerations. Policymakers develop foreign policy, especially when it involves military deployments, partly in response to the political environment they face at home. For example, they may be pressured to keep deployments small, short, and inexpensive, when a successful intervention may require a longer, larger, and costlier military presence. Further research on the foreign policy process surrounding state-building choices will help illuminate this dynamic.

Additionally, policymakers face a cost-benefit calculation when considering whether to undertake a state-building intervention and, if they decide to do so, how to design the intervention. The benefits of an intervention—including increased stability in the target state, gaining valuable experience in multilateral complex operations, and perhaps gaining a modest domestic political benefit by appearing decisive—must be weighed against the potential risks, including the risk of failure, casualties, and rising costs. When all considerations are taken into account, some potential state-building operations may be unlikely to succeed given costs that outweigh the benefits or given the constraints that state builders must act within, creating a selection effect: the most failed states, requiring the costliest interventions, are least likely to be chosen for intervention by policymakers. This effect counters another dynamic at work in selecting cases for intervention: by definition, only states fraught with insecurity, privation, or institutional breakdown require intervention, suggesting any possible intervention will face unfavorable circumstances.

ALTERNATIVE EXPLANATIONS

In this section, I consider three alternative explanations of the outcome of state-building efforts: the presence or absence of ongoing violence, the absolute level of economic prosperity, and multilateralism.

The Security Environment

State building has failed in almost all cases in which there is ongoing violence, including in South Vietnam, Angola, the Congo in 1960 and 1999, Somalia, Rwanda, Nicaragua in 1927, and Iraq. Instead of a complicated argument about matching a state-building strategy against the degree and type of failure across five dimensions of statehood, some scholars have offered a simpler and more straightforward argument that the presence or absence of security is the independent variable with the greatest explanatory power.

For example, Edelstein developed a convincing argument about the causal mechanism linking the security environment to the outcome of an armed state-building operation. He argued that a state that faces continuing internal threats, such as from an insurgency or factional violence, is likely to present sharper dilemmas for international military forces because ongoing fighting and multiple actors will make it harder for international forces to be universally welcomed.[2] We can expand on his insight and argue that international forces will either have to attempt neutrality, and risk becoming ineffective for fear of jeopardizing their relationship with the warring parties, or pick sides and go to war. Even if international state builders can successfully remain neutral, ongoing violence raises the cost of doing business: it makes logistics, transportation, and communication slower, more difficult, and more expensive. Security costs must be added into every reconstruction and capacity-development project. Higher costs will sap international will more quickly, making a long duration less likely. The nearly perfect record of failure among states with ongoing internal security threats seems to corroborate the hypothesis that the security environment can convincingly explain the outcome of state-building operations.

The security environment appears to be an accurate explanation of how and why some state-building operations fail. However, it cannot account for the variance in outcomes among operations that did not fail. Nor can it explain why some operations fail even in permissive security environments. Relying solely on the security environment to explain or predict a state-building outcome works only for a subset of state-building cases: those in which security is contested. Several state-building operations, in which there has not been ongoing violence, have still failed, including Cuba in 1898 and 1906, Haiti in 1915 and 1993, the Dominican Republic, and Côte d'Ivoire.

Furthermore, there is an endogeneity problem with the security hypothesis when formulated simplistically. If all states in which there is

2. Edelstein, *Occupational Hazards.*

ongoing violence will result in a failed state-building operation, then ongoing violence is simply part of the definition of failure. In this view, ongoing violence is both an independent and dependent variable. This is not a mere academic quibble over methodology. It has practical consequences. If policymakers use the security environment as a shorthand to assess the likelihood of success and to determine which state-building efforts to undertake, then it becomes a self-fulfilling prophesy. State builders will either not attempt, or will preemptively end, operations in states with ongoing violence, and will only attempt state-building operations in already pacified states. This may exaggerate security challenges and underestimate economic or institutional challenges—possibly leading policymakers to underselect interventions in states with ongoing violence and overselect interventions in peaceful states.

There are a few cases—Haiti in 1915, Cambodia, and Afghanistan—that suggest success in the midst of violence is possible. Not all scholars agree these cases constituted a success—but even if they disagree with the terminology of "success," observers should recognize that the ambiguous outcomes in those three cases are clearly better than the total failures in Rwanda, Liberia in 1993, South Vietnam, or Angola. In other words, even granting that Haiti, Cambodia, and Afghanistan are far from perfect, we can still recognize that there is a spectrum of positive and negative outcomes, and that among states with internal security challenges some have slightly more positive (or less negative) outcomes than others. The security hypothesis by itself cannot account for the variance. The international strategy of state building can.

In practical terms, policymakers may overlook the way that their decisions will affect the likelihood that a potential target state will revert to war: the decision to deploy forces by itself can change the dynamic within a state to make war less likely. Armed state-building operations, even in states with internal security challenges, can still make a difference.

Prosperity

Another factor that accounts for variance among cases is the overall level of prosperity in a society. GDP per capita and a state's human development index (HDI) are reasonably accurate predictors of state-building outcomes. Once again, we might ask if scholars and policymakers would be better off relying on these variables as a simpler way of determining if a state-building operation is likely to succeed or fail.

Economic conditions by themselves cannot account for the variance within subsets of the cases—poor states that succeeded, like Sierra Leone, or comparatively more developed states that failed, like Nicaragua in 1927. A hypothesis that focuses only on indigenous economic conditions has the same endogeneity problem—HDI and GDP become both independent and dependent variables—and can occasion policy-makers' self-fulfilling prophesies.

Neither the security hypothesis nor the prosperity hypothesis is without merit, but they are too parsimonious. A theory focused on the strategy of state building and its match or mismatch with conditions in the failed state is less simple than either but seeks to combine the insights of both. The presence or absence of ongoing violence is a major factor in the outcome of a state-building operation, as is the overall level of prosperity—and both are as important as to how the international state builders account for military and economic conditions in their strategy of state building. Only by combining the effects of all significant variables can we maximize our explanatory power.

Multilateralism and US-Led versus UN-Led Operations

It may be that success or failure in state-building operations is not primarily a function of the strategy of state building, but the identity of the state builder. Under this view, unilateral interventions are less likely to succeed because the local population is likely to be more suspicious of a single outsider power's motives. Multilateral operations give more credible commitments to exit and restore the state's sovereignty. Often this view is reduced to a simplistic contrast between US-led and UN-led operations.

I reject this view for several reasons. Many UN-authorized military forces are dominated by a lead state, either in numbers or leadership. Australia led INTERFET prior to the deployment of UNTAET in Timor-Leste, and continued to play a dominant role after INTERFET redeployed. The United Kingdom played a crucial role supporting UNAMSIL in Sierra Leone in 2000 and in training Sierra Leonean military forces afterward. Indonesia contributed more than 10 percent of the troops deployed for UNTAC in Cambodia. Bangladesh contributed nearly a quarter of the troops deployed for ONUMOZ in Mozambique and for UNAMIR in Rwanda. (The Bangladeshis, in fact, were renowned in the 1990s for their disproportionately large participation in peacekeeping operations, yet scholars do not make a distinction between "Bangladeshi-led" and "UN-led" operations.)

I cite these examples to demonstrate that the supposed contrast between unilateral and UN operations is surprisingly weak. To take just the example of operations usually classified as "US-led," several such operations have involved strong US leadership at one chronological stage and a strong UN or NATO presence at another, such as in Somalia, Haiti in 1993, Bosnia, and Kosovo. We cannot classify these operations simply as

[183]

a US, UN, or NATO operations: they were all of the above, at different times. Other missions divide functionally as well as temporally. In Afghanistan the United States played a dominant role in security affairs early on. NATO then increased its role substantially starting in 2006, until the United States reasserted its leadership role starting in 2009. Meanwhile, the United Nations, donors, and other international organizations played a dominant role in reconstruction and institution building. Is Afghanistan a US-led mission or a UN-led mission? It is not clear that the question is usefully framed.

Moreover, some supposedly "unilateral" operations were not, in fact, unilateral. Even in Iraq, where the United States accounted for a large majority of the international military personnel, some thirty-nine other states deployed troops. West Germany was rebuilt by the Allies, not by the United States. Austria was occupied by the Allies and by the Soviet Union together. As previously mentioned, the United States shared its responsibilities in Bosnia, Kosovo, and Afghanistan with NATO and other partner nations. Only a few operations, such as the United States in the Caribbean and Central America in the early twentieth century and in Japan and South Korea after World War II, were fully and completely unilateral.

The view that multilateral operations operate under fundamentally different dynamics than unilateral ones must account for these realities by arguing that the difference is one of degree, not a binary either-or variable. This view must argue, in effect, that as the number of states participating in an armed state-building operation goes down, or as the proportion of an operation's force that is composed of a single actor goes up, the credibility of state builders' commitment to depart decreases. As state builders' credibility decreases, local willingness to cooperate with an intervention also decreases, leading to an overall smaller likelihood of success.

There are a number of problems with this view. It almost certainly overstates the extent to which local populations care about or even are aware of the fine details of an armed state-building operation. Locals are probably unaware of, and possibly unconcerned with, the precise proportion of troop contributions to an intervening force. They care about whether or not the state builders will help improve their lives, bring order, and facilitate reconstruction. They *may* believe that multilateral operations are more effective or credible in doing so, or they may not; but regardless, many other variables influence their perception of state builders as well, including how well armed and funded the operation is, what its mandate is, and how effective it proves in addressing key challenges on the ground. To focus on whether one or many states make up the state-building mission misses the point.

[184]

This view is also needlessly complex. To operationalize this hypothesis, we would need to posit some threshold numbers—say, operations conducted by fewer than ten states, or in which 40 percent of resources originate from one state—beyond which local cooperation begins to erode. But it is not the numbers that offend local sensibilities but local beliefs about what those numbers signify. Local perception of international intentions is the causal mechanism in this hypothesis. Once we go this route, it becomes evident that the hypothesis about multilateralism is unnecessary. Perception is indeed an important variable—so important, in fact, that claiming that perception functions primarily as an effect of the numerical status of the intervener is implausible on its face. It would be more effective and simpler to construct a theory around local perceptions than to get at perceptions through multilateralism.

Finally, the history of state-building operations does not support the belief that multilateral operations end more quickly or are more successful, or that unilateral interventions lead to neo-imperialism. Australia did not seek regional hegemony in the South Pacific through its intervention in Timor-Leste. The United Kingdom did not resurrect its African colonial rule through the operation in Sierra Leone. Even the United States' interventions in the Caribbean and Central America definitively ended. Within US cases, there is substantial variance, from the comprehensive success of Japan to the clear failures in Cuba. Similarly, there is variance within the UN cases, including successes in Namibia and Mozambique and failures in Liberia and Rwanda. The different outcomes in those cases are best explained, not by reference to which actor led the operation, but what they did and whether it effectively addressed the situation in each state.

Studying the relative roles of the United States or United Nations would be valuable in a study about how decisions about state-building operations get made. We might ask, for example, what caused state builders to adopt successful strategies in some situations and failing strategies in others. The answers might be found in domestic US politics or the ideology of the different presidential administrations, or by reference to politics within the UN security council—in which case the identity of the state builder would be clearly relevant for generating explanations—another avenue for further research.

POLICY RECOMMENDATIONS

Many of the policy recommendations in the literature about state building are straightforward and need little additional comment. For example, much attention focuses on how to improve coordination both within and between governments. That is undoubtedly a wise goal, on which I have little to say in this book—except that coordination is always easier when actors coordinate around a winning strategy. Other scholars and policymakers have offered recommendations on how best to organize and deploy military forces and civilian embassies. Still others have engaged in a much broader discussion about whether and when to undertake state-building operations in the first place. Instead of engaging these discussions, I offer recommendations to policymakers who have already chosen to undertake an armed state-building operation. The single most important policy recommendation resulting from this book is that policymakers should tailor a strategy of intervention to the conditions on the ground in the state they wish to rebuild. Several implications follow.

First, area expertise matters. Policymakers, especially at the lower levels and among the personnel who actually implement policy, need to have a deep and nuanced appreciation of the conditions on the ground in order to understand how their strategy is supposed to fit. Area expertise is especially useful for understanding how states in different cultural contexts legitimize themselves, an understanding that requires a careful and detailed study of each state's culture, history, and social mores. Jacks-of-all-trades, generalists, grand strategy theorists, and international relations scholars are unlikely to be best suited to provide this kind of knowledge and advice. Ideally, policymakers will want this kind of expertise available before choosing whether to undertake a state-building operation or not. Officials should thus be more proactive and less reactive in how they apportion resources, assign personnel, and develop experts. Specifically, officials should retain a human knowledge base on states that may appear strategically unimportant at the moment but could damage national interests if they collapsed. For example, if Marvin Weinbaum is right that the international community consistently underestimated the challenges in Afghanistan, it seems likely this kind of expertise was broadly lacking in 2001—which is not surprising considering the importance accorded to Afghanistan before the terrorist attacks.

Second, strategy matters. The plan that the international actor uses is one-half of the equation in an international intervention. Large, basic, and early choices, such as whether or not to impose direct rule over a failed state and whether or not to assume full responsibility for its security, are the most important choices that policymakers will make in the intervention. Area experts are unlikely to be best suited to make these decisions. Senior-level officials with deep and long experience in the tools of foreign policy, who have a grasp of what is and what is not practicable, are more likely to understand what goes into a coherent strategy, how long it will take, and how to implement it.

[186]

Third, as the foregoing paragraphs suggest, policymakers are likely to arrive at an optimal solution through close dialogue between area experts and foreign policy generalists. Only together are they likely to understand the situation on the ground, the tools at their government's disposal, and how to apply the latter to the former to achieve intended results. Strategists without experts can flounder and lapse into prefabricated cookie-cutter approaches. Experts without strategists can overemphasize the distinctiveness and uniqueness of the state under consideration and underestimate the complexity of policy design and implementation. The interplay between strategists and experts is probably more important in armed state-building operations than in other foreign policy challenges. For example, diplomacy and negotiations probably can rely more on area or technical experts. Large-scale conventional war can rely more heavily on strategists and military doctrine. State building—a unique blend of civilian and military action, requiring constant negotiation with local actors while employing military force and designing large reconstruction projects—requires a more intense level of back-and-forth discussion between experts, strategists, and implementers.

Fourth, if state builders intend to succeed, their decisions about troop deployments should be made with regard to the security situation, not to forces' availability or international or domestic political dynamics. This may be unrealistic for democratically elected policymakers accountable to an electorate, but one of the more common errors in state-building failures is the deployment of an inappropriately sized force, such as in Angola, Afghanistan until 2006, Liberia in 1993, Rwanda, or the Congo. In particular, the international community appears to have a hard time determining if the security environment is permissive or not. It radically misjudged some cases, including Angola, Afghanistan, and Cambodia, where fighting continued or reemerged after the intervention started. It may have overestimated the need in some a few cases, including Kosovo and Bosnia, in which tens of thousands of troops were deployed despite a permissive security environment (of course, it is possible the environment is permissive because so many troops were deployed up front). It also seems to have a hard time changing course once it becomes apparent that the security situation is more dangerous than initially thought, as the cases of Angola and Somalia show. Unilateral operations may be at an advantage, as it is easier for a single lead government to change course than for a coalition under a UN mandate to do so.

One of the key questions confronting policymakers at the outset of an armed state-building operation is whether to establish direct rule, military government, or international transitional administration, or to recognize the state's sovereignty and work through whatever institutions

[187]

remain intact. When is military government or international administration appropriate? The question is not as exceptional as it sounds: as I argued in chapter 6, it is, in fact, another form of the question about the level of resources that need to be dedicated to the effort. The resource in question is not troops or money but (to use military terms) command and control. The US Army views command and control as an essential element of combat power (FM 3–0, section 4–24), a concept that can and should be readily applied to joint, interagency, and civilian operations such as armed state building. Viewed in this light, the question is easier to answer. International command and control over a state-building operation is required when local capacity is unable to provide it. Policymakers should thus, in consultation with their area experts, evaluate the level of capacity of the institutions of government in the target state. A key part of governance capacity is the quality of leadership available to lead the institutions, and the ability of local leaders to work with one another. In postconflict settings or in states recovering from civil war, institutions may be damaged and interpersonal trust among local leaders destroyed so thoroughly—rare even in the annals of failed states—that international trusteeship is required as a temporary measure to close the governance gap until institutions can be repaired and trust restored.

A final implication of this book is that policymakers probably cannot design appropriate shelf-ready strategies in advance of a state failure because it matters *how* states fail. Rebuilding North Korea, for example, would require a different strategy if the state were to collapse peacefully from internal pressures, like the Communist regimes of Eastern Europe in 1989, than if it were destroyed through conquest and overthrow, like Iraq in 2003. Different scenarios will lead to entirely different political and military dynamics within the collapsed state, requiring a different international strategy. At best policymakers could draft several different courses of action—at least in outline or draft form—that would take effect under different scenarios. That, however, would become a labor-intensive task unlikely to draw the voluntary attention of bureaucracies already overburdened with everyday tasks. A specialized office, like the State Department's Bureau of Conflict and Stabilization Operations might attempt the task, although it would be hampered unless it had strong participation from the Department of Defense and other organizations.

OPERATIONS SINCE 2005

In my earlier case selections I omitted cases that started after 2005, which excluded the missions in Chad, Sudan, Lebanon, and South

Sudan. In this section I review the first three of these operations and suggest tentative conclusions about their current trajectory.

Sudan: UNMIS/UNAMID

Sudan has been at civil war for most of its independent existence. A Comprehensive Peace Agreement in 2005 established a roadmap for peace between the government and rebels in the south and led to the deployment of the UN Mission in Sudan (UNMIS). In addition to traditional peacekeeping tasks, such as verifying a ceasefire and facilitating demobilization, UNMIS was mandated to help train police, assist in "promoting the rule of law, including an independent judiciary, and the protection of human rights of all people of Sudan," and "to support the preparations for and conduct of elections."[3] Starting in 2003 a separate conflict with rebels in the western region of Darfur drew international notice when many observers characterized the conflict as genocide by the government against the people of Darfur. The Darfur Peace Agreement (the Abuja Agreement) in 2006 appeared to promise the end of the violence there. The UN tried to expand UNMIS to Darfur but failed because of the Sudanese government's opposition. It succeeded in creating instead the UN–African Union Hybrid Mission in Darfur. UNAMID had a broadly similar mandate, including verifying a ceasefire and promoting the rule of law, with additional responsibilities: to "assist the political process" and "contribute to a secure environment for economic reconstruction and development."[4] UNMIS terminated operations in July 2011, when South Sudan declared independence, while UNMID continues.

At their peak, UNMIS and UNAMID together comprised over thirty thousand UN and AU troops and nearly two thousand international civilians.[5] They were the UN's largest post–Cold War military deployments that did not involve the United States or NATO, but they rank near the bottom of all state-building operations for the ratio of troops to the population and the landmass because of Sudan's large size. Reconstruction assistance was not well funded from 2005 to 2010. Donors gave more than $2 billion in inflation-adjusted dollars to Sudan each year, averaging only $69.53 per person, per year.[6]

3. United Nations Security Council Resolution S/RES/1590 (2005).
4. Monthly Report of the Secretary-General on Darfur S/2007/307/Rev.1.
5. Figures for troops and civilians are available from United Nations, UNMIS and UNAMID Facts and Figures.
6. World Bank, "World Development Indicators Database."

More important, the UN and AU mandates were inappropriate for the types of state failure in Sudan. Sudan in 2005 was an anarchic security environment. Violence has slowed, but not stopped, since the signing of the peace agreements and deployment of international military personnel. Large swaths of the population did not view Khartoum as a legitimate government—and, in fact, the South seceded in a referendum in 2011. Institutions of government had not completely collapsed but were clearly faltering. The Sudanese government ranked in the bottom tenth percentile for government effectiveness. Its HDI was .53 and GDP per capita was $1,266, both slightly above average for states targeted for state-building operations but still among the worst in the world.[7] Sudan's worst failure, aside from security, was its atrocious track record on human rights. It joins only Serbia, Rwanda, and a few others in being accused of committing genocide since the end of the Cold War.

Under these circumstances, if the international community was serious about stopping the genocide, ending the perennial civil wars, improving governance, and building sustainable peace in Sudan, it should have seriously considered regime change followed by a war crimes tribunal for Sudanese leaders, coupled with at least a very large civilian capacity-development program or embedding international civilians in the Sudanese bureaucracy (as in Cambodia). Short of those drastic measures, the international community should have recognized its inability to affect governance in Sudan. Instead, UNMIS and UNAMID are largely observer missions with train-and-equip elements added to them. But the Sudanese government was not and is not a viable partner in a state-building effort because it was largely the cause and perpetrator of state failure. The ongoing presence of what I have called a "barbaric state failure" makes progress on other aspects of state building unlikely. As it is, Sudan's president has indeed been indicted by the International Criminal Court—an indictment that only highlights the absurdity of the reliance of UNMIS and UNAMID on the Sudanese government for "responsibility" in maintaining security in the areas in which it has been accused of committing genocide. The UN's unsurprising failure to expand UNMIS to Darfur because of

7. The sources for case studies in this chapter are identical for those in the previous chapter. HDI figures are derived from the UN Development Program's *Human Development Reports* for the year closest to the start of an intervention. The Human Development Reports are available at the UN Development Program's website, http://hdr.undp.org/en/reports/. GDP per capita is derived from Maddison, *Historical Statistics for the World Economy, 1–2006 AD,* dataset, accessed November 5, 2009.

Sudan's opposition to it demonstrates the naïveté that still character-izes some UN operations a decade after the Brahimi Report warned against such thinking.

The economy has grown since the end of the North-South civil war, averaging 4.66 percent real GDP per capita growth since 2005. But vio-lence in Darfur has continued. The quality of national governance has not improved, nor has there been progress toward democracy, according to the World Bank Governance Indicators, the Polity IV database, or Freedom House. The regime in Khartoum remains in power, and there are no realistic prospects for a change in the regime's basically oppres-sive character, accountability for war crimes, or truth and reconciliation. Violence in the west appeared to lull starting in 2010, and Sudan's focus shifted to the brewing conflict with the new state of South Sudan in 2011, but all indicators suggest the ingredients for conflict remain firmly rooted in place. A number of other flash points remain, such as access to oil re-sources, that could reignite conflict. Absent a significant change in the international community's strategy toward Sudan, the country is likely to continue its ongoing plight in state failure and war.

Chad: MINURCAT

Like Sudan, Chad has been at civil war for much of its independent existence. The latest round of fighting started in 2005 when rebel groups in the east of the country, apparently enjoying safe haven in the anarchy of next-door Darfur, began launching cross-border raids into Chad. Chadian government officials accused Sudan of supporting the rebels. A peace agreement in fall 2007 paved the way for a UN-mandated EU peacekeeping force in eastern Chad, which the UN took over in early 2009. (The UN also deployed troops to the Central African Republic to facilitate refugee issues.) Fighting continued after the peace agreement, including a significant rebel offensive on the capital in 2008.

It is not clear that the EU and UN deployments in Chad should be considered full-fledged state-building operations. MINURCAT's man-date contains expansive state-building language. In addition to training and working with Chadean security forces and helping resettling refu-gees, the UN mandate includes provisions to observe and promote human rights, help promote the rule of law "including through support for an independent judiciary and a strengthened legal system," and sup-port capacity-building efforts in government and civil society.[8] But

---

8. United Nations Security Council Resolutions S/RES/1778 (2007); S/RES/1861 (2009); S/RES/1923 (2010).

MINURCAT appears to be focusing on protecting and resettling refugees, and forces are primarily deployed in the east of Chad and north of the Central African Republic. If MINURCAT is counted as a state-building operation, it is one of the least well resourced in history. The EU and UN deployed two soldiers per ten thousand civilians, and donors gave $33.97 per person in 2007.

Early indicators do not bode well for the operation, whether it is considered a state-building operation or not. Fighting continued in Chad and Sudan. From 2007 to 2010, Chadian governance showed little to no improvement in government effectiveness, the rule of law, control of corruption, or regulatory quality, according to the World Bank. Real GDP per capita declined almost 1 percent per year from 2007 to 2010. MINURCAT ceased operations at the end of 2010, and there is little to suggest that the situation will change.

Lebanon: UNIFIL

The UN Interim Force in Lebanon (UNIFIL) was originally deployed in 1978 to observe the withdrawal of Israeli troops from Lebanon—which Israel had invaded to destroy the Palestine Liberation Organization (PLO) headquartered in Lebanon—and help the Lebanese government reestablish its authority. UNIFIL also provided humanitarian assistance during Israel's extended occupation of Lebanese territory. Israel eventually withdrew from Lebanon in 2000. UNIFIL's mandate changed dramatically in 2006, expanding from a traditional peacekeeping and humanitarian force to a state-building operation.[9] Two conditions enabled the UN to take a larger role in Lebanon. First, Syria's dominance of Lebanese affairs markedly declined following the "Cedar revolution" of Lebanese citizens against Syria in 2005. Second, the Israeli-Hezbollah war of 2006 highlighted the continued fragility of the Lebanese state, endemically weak since the 1975–90 civil war, and its need for greater outside assistance.

Lebanon in 2006 was one of the least-failed states ever to be targeted for a state-building operation. With a GDP per capita of $3,380 (in 1990 dollars), it was the second richest (after Croatia) of the states considered in this book. The Lebanese government demonstrated a capacity comparable to the most effective states outside Europe and North America. It had the absolute highest human development index (tied with Kosovo at .80) of any state in this study. Life expectancy and infant mortality rivaled that of the developed world. The government collected over 20 percent of GDP in taxes, comparable to the United States. It had a brief

9. United Nations Security Council Resolution S/RES/1701 (2006).

experience with democracy before the war in the 1970s—and started out in the intervention with a polity 2 score of 7, the highest in its history. The recent expulsion of Syria from Lebanese affairs had arguably bolstered the state's legitimacy to its highest point in a generation because it was no longer seen as a pawn of a neighboring state. Security was still fragile because of the recent Israeli incursion (targeting Hezbollah, not Lebanese security forces) and because of the continued presence of armed militias inside Lebanon. The government's struggle to monopolize the instruments of coercion was arguably the only sign of state failure in Lebanon. By all indicators Lebanon was a favorable environment for state building.

The international community responded with a strategy, backed by resources and a mandate, seemingly well matched to Lebanon's challenges. The United Nations expanded UNIFIL from about 2,000 troops to over 12,000, a respectable force of 31 troops per 10,000 civilians. Donors backed reconstruction with almost $4 billion from 2006 to 2010, or $196.78 per person per year—a lavish effort. UNIFIL's mandate was expanded to address Lebanon's specific security failings, including by helping Lebanese military forces deploy throughout the south to prevent the southern region from being used as a base of military operations and to help enforce the government's ban on importing weapons. The UN Security Council further mandated that all states refrain from exporting weapons to Lebanon or providing training or assistance to militias in Lebanon.

However, the most direct measure to restore the Lebanese government's monopoly on coercion—the disarmament of armed groups in Lebanon—was left to the government of Lebanon to implement without any explicit UNIFIL role. It is unclear if the government of Lebanon is any more able to implement this responsibility now than in past years when it failed to disarm militias. This appears to be a major and critical weakness to the international intervention in Lebanon. The presence of nonstate armed groups in Lebanon, and the state's lack of monopoly on the use of force in its own territory, is the signature failing of the Lebanese state; the state builders' failure to address it risks undermining whatever other progress they may be able to achieve there.

Lebanon thus presents an odd case of armed state building. By most measures it should be, and is, succeeding. The environment was favorable, and the strategy has been fairly robust. The Lebanese economy has grown dramatically since 2006, averaging a growth of 4.67 percent in real per capita GDP. Parliamentary elections were held in June 2009. Fighting has stopped, at least for the moment. But Lebanon rightly ranks near the bottom of all states on the World Bank's indictor for political stability. Hezbollah has not been disarmed. Lebanon is probably incapable of disarming the group by itself. Israel continues to feel threatened by Hezbollah's presence—and thus the Lebanese state still lacks a monopoly on coercion within its own borders. Ongoing political wrangling between Lebanese political factions, including Hezbollah's political arm, have induced political paralysis in the capital, and it may not remain within the peaceful political process for long.

NORMATIVE CRITICISMS OF STATE BUILDING

This book has addressed itself to a pragmatic question: What causes success and failure in armed state-building operations? There is, however, an implicit normative agenda behind this inquiry. This inquiry is most relevant for those who believe that state building can be a good thing and that we should therefore attempt to learn how to do it better. Not everyone shares this belief. A significant (and perhaps growing) community of scholars have expressed hesitancy about armed state building based on three related grounds. First, some critics believe state building is *too* similar to imperialism, that it is, in fact, imperialism in new garb. Second, other critics worry that state building is almost guaranteed to fail because it involves the effort to transfer Western forms of governance to non-Western societies—an effort that is ethically suspect on its face and probably doomed to fail like an organ transplant to a patient with the wrong blood type. Third, some critics evince a deeper concern to protect the norms of Westphalian sovereignty and the Wilsonian norm of self-determination.

This book is not primarily an engagement with the literature on the norms and ethics of state building, but it seems appropriate to address these criticisms after having discussed how to make state building succeed more effectively. State building is indeed an exercise of power, like imperialism, but important differences remain. Far less of the state-building project that is commonly assumed involves the transfer of Western institutions. Criticisms of state building seem to rely on a sacralization of Westphalia that is unwarranted considering the net costs and benefits of an unamended Westphalian system compared to one which allows for selective cases of intervention. In responding to these criticisms, I seek to adapt "just war" theory to develop a "just intervention" framework with which we can evaluate when interventions are justified.

State Building and Neoimperialism

Some critics oppose state building because of its similarity to imperialism, because of the seemingly inherent contradiction between the means of state building (military force and international administration) and

[194]

the end (local sovereignty), and because it appears to go against the grain of the Westphalian system of states that are sovereign within their borders. State building is felt to violate the basic principle of noninterference among states.

For example, David Chandler, a leading critic of international state building, calls state building "empire in denial" and "empire-lite." State building is best understood by him as "attempts by Western states and international institutions to deny the power which they wield and to evade accountability for its exercise." State building is the latest manifestation of the power dynamic that has always characterized relations between rich, powerful states and poor, weak ones. The change in norms that I argue defines the difference between state building and imperialism is, in fact, merely the rhetorical mechanism state builders use to deceive themselves and the world about the true nature of the state-building project. Further, the rhetoric of state building and local partnership allows them to evade responsibility for the power they continue to wield over poor states and place the onus of burden on the poor states themselves for the failures of the state-building projects. Because state building emphasizes local sovereignty in the midst of international interference, state builders are able to exercise power at will while blaming local actors for difficulties or failures. State building is "no less elitist and patronizing and, in its consequences, no less divisive, destabilizing, and restricting" than imperialism. State building is problematic because it is framed in terms of "non-political, therapeutic or purely technical, administrative and bureaucratic forms."[10]

Chandler recognizes that his argument and similar views from other scholars bring a Foucauldian approach to international politics. Echoing Michel Foucault's argument in *Discipline and Punish* about how relations of power characterize everyday institutions such as prisons, militaries, and schools, and in *The Order of Things* about how the very delineations of fields of knowledge influences how we think about human life, Chandler argues that "intervention takes forms which appear to be consensual rather than coercive, through which the technologies and practices of domination simultaneously produce or constitute the subjects being dominated through the discursive practices and frameworks of knowledge, meaning, and values."[11] I understand Chandler to be arguing that the international community subtly dominates poor states partly by enticing them with promises of liberalism and good governance while actually controlling them through capacity building and aid conditionality.

10. Chandler, *Empire in Denial*, 1, 9.
11. Ibid, 15.

[195]

Chandler is essentially correct that armed state building is an exercise of power by strong states over weak ones. Chandler is right again when he accuses state builders of cloaking their efforts in technical, bureaucratic, or administrative language. Armed state building is, at least in part, the imposition of outside powers' collective will on a weak state. Owning up to that fact will help state builders understand their own activity more clearly. However, Chandler seems to think that this by itself is grounds for viewing state building as nothing but "empire in denial" and normatively suspect. He discounts the norms invoked to justify state building and differentiate it from imperialism. The exercise of power by itself is not inherently suspect. Chandler repeats the error characteristic of much postmodernist analysis of social phenomena: he ties social relations to power dynamics and condemns the former by taint of association with the latter. But even Foucault recognized that power can be *productive* even while remaining a relation of dominance. Schools and armies rely on relations of power to produce scholars and soldiers. So too with state building. It is a relation of dominance with a productive goal in mind: the production of statehood and effective governance in areas lacking them. This is why norms matter. The invocation of norms indicates what productive goals are in mind, and they become manifest in behavior. Chandler's effort to blur the difference between the two and elide the former into the latter is unconvincing.

State Building and Cultural Imperialism

Other scholars oppose state building because they believe it is unlikely to succeed in most or any contexts because it wrongly seeks to transfer Western forms of governance to other cultures, an act of illegitimate cultural imperialism. Beate Jahn argues that state building rests on the faulty assumptions that weak states lack something that the international community can provide. State building cannot take place without a notion of what the state is and should be; Jahn argues that the international community has settled on the model of liberal free-market democracy as the pattern for all polities, but argues that that model may be inappropriate.[12]

Similarly, David Roberts argues that democratic state building fails because culture and history trump institutions: "Superimpositions of democratic practice cannot substitute for or replace, in the short-term, political behaviors derived from needs, experiences, histories and evolutions quite different from those from which Western democracy is

---

12. Jahn, "Tragedy of Liberal Diplomacy."

derived." Pushing democracy and Western norms can be counterproductive. He writes, "The transformation of such systems can often lead to volatility as the introduction of Western liberal framings of the rule of law and democracy conflict with non-Western social norms and practices." Roberts does not think state building is useless but that the goal should be redefined. State building cannot result in democratic governance, but it can result in stable "hybrid polities" that reflect a mix of international and domestic, democratic and traditional forms of governance.[13]

Those who advance this criticism typically fail to specify which exact parts of the state-building program are supposed to be Western impositions. In fact, far less of the liberal state-building project than is commonly assumed uses inherently Western notions of governance. The criticism conflates Western norms, not just with democracy, but with good governance generally and implies that cultures outside the West do not have traditions of good governance. Bureaucracies, law codes, and military forces were not invented by Europe and are not Western phenomena. Tribal societies elsewhere in the world have adapted to legal-bureaucratic mechanisms of governance. Elections, majoritarian rule, and representative decision-making bodies, which do have European roots, have been successfully adapted in countries outside of Europe and North America: one-third of democratic countries are in Africa, Asia, or Latin America. Concepts of human rights are probably the most uniquely Western element of liberal state building, but their incorporation into the UN Universal Declaration on Human Rights suggests their universal appeal (if not enforcement). Given the success of these institutions in states outside of Europe and North America, the effort to paint state-building operations as a hidden attempt at Westernization and cultural imperialism gives the West too much credit for the development of good government.

State Building and Sovereignty

Chandler, Roberts, and other critics' views seem to stem from an overemphasis on key norms that underpin the international system: sovereignty and self-determination. International norms have been defined for nearly four centuries by Westphalian sovereignty and, for almost one century, by Wilsonian self-determination. The Westphalian regime was advanced as a means of containing and limiting interstate

13. Roberts, "Hybrid Polities and Indigenous Pluralities," 64, 71.

war. Self-determination was advanced as a means of solving an alleged root of war and of promoting human flourishing. The Westphalian regime, especially after its enshrinement in the United Nations system and its global expansion through decolonization, has effectively limited interstate war. In exchange, there has been a rise in intrastate war. The concept of self-determination has, arguably, been a proactively destabilizing force in human affairs. That is not to say it is wrong, or that there is no right to self-determination. It is, however, evident that after a century we still lack the legal, diplomatic, and nonviolent tools to advance the cause of self-determination peacefully.

The two norms argue that all peoples have a right to govern themselves, and that all states are sovereign in their domain and have a right to noninterference from outside powers. While the norms have transformed the world in some indisputably positive ways, it is also increasingly clear that the combination of sovereignty and self-determination has allowed some states to murder their citizens, become embroiled in endless civil wars, neglect social and economic development, engage in wholesale theft, permit and even encourage the destruction of human beings, dissolve or dominate civil society, destabilize neighbors and regions, destroy wealth and prosperity inside and outside their borders, and generally advance the ideals of barbarism. In the face of such clear failings, the burden of proof lies with defenders of the status quo to explain why that price is an acceptable one to pay to maintain the norms of sovereignty and self-determination without revision.

Armed state building can be seen as an attempt to revise Westphalia and Wilsonianism to better answer the problems of civil war, genocide, state failure, and postconflict collapse. Armed state-building operations are not always fully consistent with the recognition of failed states' sovereignty and may involve a temporary denial of a people's right to self-determination. They may involve military government or international administration, whether it is called conservatorship,[14] "shared sovereignty,"[15] or "neo-trusteeship."[16] But critics fail to acknowledge that armed state building is not designed to overturn the Westphalian system but rather to make it work better. The long-term goal of armed state building is to improve failed states' empirical, positive, or "de facto" sovereignty, even at the short-term expense of its negative or "de jure" sovereignty.[17]

14. Helman and Ratner, "Saving Failed States."
15. Krasner, "Sharing Sovereignty."
16. Fearon and Laitin, "Neotrusteeship and the Problem of Weak States."
17. Jackson, *Quasi-States.*

Armed state-building operations clearly must be undertaken with care and even with humility. In this book I have sought to demonstrate that such operations are possible, that they can and have resulted in success, and that success has *reinforced* sovereignty and self-determination while bringing better government and economic opportunity to real human beings. If that is indeed the case, criticism of armed state-building operations on the grounds that they bear a superficial resemblance to imperialism is simply unimpressive.

State Building and Just War

Following the worldwide failure to halt genocide in Rwanda in 1994, the UN and the government of Canada established the Commission on Intervention and State Sovereignty to study when, if ever, intervention is justified. The commission recommended in 2001 that the international community intervene—violate sovereignty—to halt large-scale loss of life and ethnic cleansing (criteria that would be clarified a few years later as applying to genocide, war crimes, crimes against humanity, and ethnic cleansing). The commission rested its argument on the idea that exercising sovereignty entails a "responsibility to protect" (R2P) the people under one's care; if a state is unable or unwilling to protect its people, that responsibility passes to the international community.[18] The international community *unanimously* endorsed this norm at the UN's 2005 World Summit.[19]

R2P is explicitly rooted in "just war" thinking. The authors of the original report wrote in *Foreign Affairs* that "on the core issues there is a great deal of common ground, most of it derived from 'just war' theory." Much of their argument is structured with the familiar categories of the "just war" tradition: just cause, right authority, right intention, last resort, proportional means, and the like. A just cause for intervention is "serious and irreparable harm occurring to human beings, or imminently likely to occur," specifically, "large scale loss of life" or "large scale ethnic cleansing." Right intention is halting or averting human suffering. Right authority was the UN Security Council if possible, although other multilateral bodies or even a unilateral intervention were not ruled out.[20]

18. Responsibility to Protect, International Commission on Intervention and State Sovereignty, December 2001, http://responsibilitytoprotect.org/ICISS%20Report. pdf.
19. United Nations General Assembly Resolution, "2005 World Summit Outcome" A/RES/60/1.
20. Evans and Sahnoun, "Responsibility to Protect," 102–3.

R2P illustrates that the "just war" tradition can provide a useful normative framework for understanding intervention. The authors of R2P applied it narrowly to the problem of stopping genocide and related atrocities, and other scholars have applied "just war" thinking to humanitarian intervention more broadly, but they have often failed to recognize the great strength of the tradition: "just war" thinking, rightly understood, offers a framework both broad enough to require meaningful interventions yet narrow enough to prevent crusading.[21] The next logical step is to apply "just war" thinking to interventions in failed states generally.

First, state building must be undertaken for a just cause that, according to the earliest formulations of "just war" doctrine, goes beyond a narrow understanding of self-defense. James Turner Johnson, a leading scholar of just war theory, argues that for Saint Thomas Aquinas, "insofar as the need for defense provides just cause for public use of the sword, it comes from the responsibility of government to protect order, justice, and peace, not simply from the right to respond to an attacker in kind."[22] What is being defended is not merely territory but justice, peace, and order. States use force to uphold public order generally, whether disorder comes from international aggression (war) or domestic crime and lawlessness (police power), a natural disaster (as in the deployment of the National Guard after a hurricane or earthquake), insurgency, pandemics, terrorism, rioting, civil unrest, ecological or environmental catastrophe, or even cyber attack. This provides a more expansive and realistic writ to deploy force even when immediate self-defense is not at issue. There is an intuitive validity in this reading of "just war" theory in that it is closer to states' actual practice. It describes how states use what we might call *normal force* on a fairly regular basis in many different circumstances, as opposed to the overly restrictive reading of "just war" theory, which applies only to formal, conventional, large-scale war.

The application of this idea to international interventions is straightforward: just as any state should use force to uphold order domestically, they may also help other states that are threatened with disorder but unwilling or unable to respond on their own. In short, states may intervene in cases of state failure, using force to restore order to other states.

Does a just cause *obligate*, or merely *permit*, an intervention? In other words, may the international community decline to intervene in the face

---

21. See Elshtain, "Just War and Humanitarian Intervention"; Fixdal and Smith, "Humanitarian Intervention and Just War."
22. Johnson, "Just War, as It Was and Is," 14.

of state failure? Let me suggest three variables for judging whether the criterion of just cause makes a state-building intervention permissible or obligatory: severity, threat, and cost. The more *severe* a case of state failure, genocide, or humanitarian disaster, the more obligated the international community is to intervene. The greater a failed state presents a *threat* to another state, the more obligated that state is—ideally, in cooperation with others—to intervene to defend itself. And the greater the *cost* of an intervention, the less obligated the international community is to intervene. The balance of these competing considerations is the work of statesmanship.

But it is still begs an important question: Can one state deploy force to uphold the order of another state? This raises the second criterion, that state building should be undertaken by a right authority. R2P argues that the UN is the preferred legitimate authority for interventions, barring which another international organization or a multilateral coalition can be a right authority. I suggest that the "right authority" and "just cause" be defined by reference to the "public" that is affected by the instability and violence of a state's failure. When disorder is effectively contained within the boundaries of a single state, and that state is willing and able to address the problem, then the public affected is only the citizenry of that state, in which case right authority for deploying force is the individual sovereign state. Outside actors do not have authority to intervene. Importantly, this limits when outside powers may violate sovereignty in the name of humanitarian values and prevents crusading.

However, when a state either cannot or will not uphold order, there no longer is a locally available right authority. An intervention in these circumstances does not violate another sovereign's right authority because there is none. Right authority then passes to the only other legitimately constituted authorities for wielding just force: other sovereign states (typically in concert with local actors seeking to reconstitute local sovereign authority). This is especially true of neighboring states, who are often threatened by disorder, state failure, or anarchy on their borders and for whom intervention is a form of self-defense.

In between these two cases is a more common type: when a weak state invites and welcomes outside help. In this case the local government has the final right authority but has delegated some to other actors. In practice, the international community has almost always secured some kind of local agreement or invitation for state-building interventions since the Cold War—for example, through a UN-sponsored agreement that asks for help from international peacekeepers and technical experts. The international community's moral burden here is to respect the local government's authority by ensuring such agreements are reached fairly, not under duress, and treat the weak state as a truly independent actor.

[201]

Does right authority attach only to multilateral coalitions or intergovernmental organizations, or are unilateral operations permissible? There seems to be a trade-off: interventions by a single power have more coherent unity of effort and purpose, but multilateral interventions may enjoy greater legitimacy with the local citizens. An Augustinian appreciation for humanity's corruptibility would be at least wary of unilaterally initiated operations because of the lack of accountability inherent when a single powerful state is the judge and jury of its own righteous cause. Ideally right authority would be constituted in two stages: it would be *authorized* by a multilateral "public" such as the UN or NATO to enforce accountability, but *implemented* by a single state or a coalition with an identified leader, another way in which "just war" thinking can both authorize but limit state-building interventions.

Third, state building should be undertaken with a right intention. This is a difficult principle to apply in practice because it regards policymakers' inner thoughts and motives. In the secularized version of "just war" thinking prevalent today it amounts to little more than an exhortation that policymakers must mean well. But the earlier theologically grounded version of "just war" thinking makes this a central criterion, and Daniel Bell, a contemporary Lutheran theologian, argues that right intention shows itself in how one treats one's enemies and neutral civilians during and after a war. He writes, "If one's intent in waging war is indeed just, if one really loves one's enemies and intends to bring the benefits of peace and justice to them, then one will not abandon them when the shooting stops but will be involved in the restoration of a just peace. If one truly desires justice, then one will stay the course and see justice through to completion . . . which may include a financial commitment, devoting adequate civil affairs and police personnel, as well as perhaps coordinating with nongovernmental organizations in the work of reconstruction."[23] Even the secular "just war" theory has begun to approach these concepts through the idea of *jus post bellum*.

Right intention requires interveners to work for the ultimate goals of peace and justice, not only for themselves, but also for those whom they are intervening *against*. That does not mean state builders must be disinterested. Disinterested state builders in fact can be dangerous because they are more likely to lose political will and withdraw too early. Neighboring states should contemplate an intervention precisely *because* their interests, their public, and their order are threatened by another state's failure. "Just war" and "just state building" are, and should be, self-interested enterprises. They should also be, simultaneously, beneficial for the failed state. State building succeeds when there is a harmony of interests

23. Bell, *Just War as Christian Discipleship*, 167, 179.

between the failed state and outside powers. When policymakers assert they are rebuilding a failed state to protect their own security, that is *not* a violation of the principle of right intention.

Fourth, state building should be a last resort after other policy options—such as aid, technical assistance, or traditional peacekeeping—have failed, are likely to fail, or would be inappropriate. Even though state building is well intentioned, it is still often harsh, messy, expensive, and potentially lethal, leaving it the least-preferable way of handling state failure.

Fifth, according to the conventional criteria of just war, state building must achieve more good than evil. While normatively sound, this principle is almost impossible to apply. It asks policymakers to see into the future and discern beforehand the possible effects, intended and otherwise, beneficial and harmful; ascribe units of value to the good and the bad; and apply a cost-benefit calculation, subtracting the bad from the good. If the balance is positive, the intervention may proceed. This decision tool is of no use to human policymakers, who cannot predict the future. And it is inapplicable to complex scenarios with noncomparable aspects. How do you measure the good and bad of, for example, having stopped a genocide but, in the process, having destroyed parts of a nation's economic infrastructure? Or having provided widespread humanitarian relief after an earthquake at the expense of sidelining a weak and incapable sovereign government? Both good and bad often result from state-building interventions, but they cannot be given a dollar value and weighed against each other.

Sixth, state building must have a reasonable chance to succeed. Perhaps the most widespread popular argument for the injustice of state building today is the argument that it cannot succeed at an acceptable cost and is therefore a waste of resources. State building is hard and complex, and there is a widespread belief that international actors are not especially good at doing it. This argument depends on what "success" in state building means. If it means turning poor, violent, autocratic societies into fully rich, peaceful, democratic ones, then Germany and Japan are the only successful examples of state building in history. But there is a much humbler and more practical definition of success. State builders aim at *changing the trajectory* of poor, violent, autocratic societies so that they are on a sustainable path of economic growth, peaceful contestation for power, and political transition, which has proven possible at acceptable costs. If failed states are better off a decade after state builders leave than in the midst of failure, state builders have achieved some basic threshold of "success." Under this definition not just Germany and Japan but also much cheaper interventions such as those in Namibia, Mozambique, Nicaragua, El Salvador, Guatemala,

[203]

Bosnia, Croatia, Kosovo, Timor-Leste, and Sierra Leone can be seen as various degrees of success, despite the oft-recorded shortcomings, missed opportunities, and difficulties in each of those missions. And if success is possible, then interventions can meet this criterion for justice.

Some may criticize my argument for glossing over the avowed justice of armed state building in the first place. According to this view, whether a state-building operation is undertaken in self-defense or not is beside the point: it is simply unjust to try to use armed force to make other countries govern more effectively according to our view of "governance." State building is an act of political coercion and an exercise of power by the strong over the weak. For that reason alone, it is highly suspect. Government is simply a mechanism of control; rebuilding government is simply another means of exercising dominance over people. "Failed states" are not problems to be solved but experiments that we should watch to see what might grow and develop there.

This criticism goes to the heart of the state-building enterprise. As I acknowledged before, state building does indeed involved the exercise of power by the strong over the weak. But good governance is not merely the technical ability to control people. It is an agent of power to maintain public order. It is an effort to uphold and reflect shared norms of right and justice. It is a set of institutions for distributing goods. It is a framework for promoting commerce and trade. It is a tool for human life. Government, performed well, blesses human life. Good governance that is also liberal creates states that are stable and self-governing, which are less likely to go to war against each other.

Armed state building is an attempt to provide good governance in the places where it is most severely lacking. When it succeeds—and I have attempted in this book to demonstrate how it can—it promotes human flourishing and less frequent war. Whatever our understanding of justice, human flourishing and peace should surely be part of it. We must conclude that state building can be a just cause for concerted international efforts. It should remain a legitimate policy option for the international community, and learning to get it right should be a top priority for scholars and policymakers alike.

Appendix A

Case Selection

Without a consistent and operationalizable definition of state building, scholars have been unable to tell the history of state building consistently, identifying which interventions count as state building or offering a persuasive tally of how many state-building successes and failures there have been—an obvious obstacle to understanding how state building works. In this book I have defined state building as the attempt by liberal states to use military, political, and economic power to compel weak, failed, or collapsed states to govern more effectively and accountably, as understood by Westphalian and liberal norms. Key in this definition is (1) the deployment of international military forces, excluding cases of nonmilitary development assistance; (2) the adherence to liberal and Westphalian norms, excluding imperialism and annexation; and (3) the intent to improve a failed state's governance, excluding traditional peacekeeping.

I did not find an extant catalogue of military interventions that used these exact criteria. John Owen's list of 221 instances of "forcible regime promotion" from 1510 to the present, including 71 cases in the twentieth century, includes a few cases of liberal state building alongside many instances of imperialism, but excludes UN interventions.[1] Lists of imperial interventions, even ones that differentiate between liberal and illiberal colonialism,[2] are even less relevant for this study. The Political Instability Task Force's data set looks at failed states but not state building, while the Correlates of War data set looks at cases of armed *conflict* but not necessarily armed *interventions*.

1. Owen, *Clash of Ideas in World Politics*, chap. 1.
2. Lange, Mahoney, and Hau, "Colonialism and Development."

[205]

In response to the absence of a comprehensive data set of cases of international state building, scholars studying the subject have gone about constructing their own list of cases. The lists of cases are wildly inconsistent. *Making States Work* includes case studies that involved international military intervention, including Afghanistan and Mozambique, and those that did not, such as North Korea, Costa Rica, and Pakistan, and a case of imperialism (Britain in Singapore), an unconvincing conglomeration of cases that do not appear to be usefully grouped together.[3] *Statebuilding and Intervention* includes essays on Bosnia and Cambodia, par for the literature, and one on debt in Africa, a wholly separate phenomenon.[4] *The Dilemmas of Statebuilding* takes the set of post–Cold War UN interventions as its touchstone, but then includes essays on Afghanistan and Iraq.[5] They do not explain how or why the interventions in Afghanistan and Iraq fit in with the UN cases. There is a presumed similarity that is not spelled out explicitly.

Some scholars include cases of US interventions in Central America but do not explain what differentiates them from cases of imperialism or regional hegemony and include some doubtful cases.[6] Many scholars include the post–World War II military occupations of Germany and Japan but universally neglect the simultaneous occupations under identical circumstances of Italy, Austria, and South Korea, without identifying the criteria by which they include the former and exclude the latter.[7] Most scholars focus on post–Cold War cases of UN complex peacekeeping, starting with Namibia and Nicaragua in 1989, but even that data set is not consistent. Paris includes Guatemala in 1997, which almost no other scholars do.[8] No one, that I have found, includes the Central African Republic, despite its similarities to other post–Cold War UN operations. Most scholars include Iraq and Afghanistan, as do I, but exclude South Vietnam, despite the three cases displaying a similar overlap between state building and counterinsurgency.

UN PEACE OPERATIONS

To construct my data set, I started by examining the official list of sixty-six UN peacekeeping operations since 1948.[9] I examined their

3. Chesterman, Ignatieff, and Thakur, *Making States Work.*
4. Chandler, *Statebuilding and Intervention.*
5. Paris and Sisk, *Dilemmas of Statebuilding.*
6. Pei, Amin, and Garz, "Building Nations."
7. For example, Dobbins's *America's Role in Nation-Building: From Germany to Iraq* includes Germany and Japan but not the others.
8. Paris, *At War's End.*
9. United Nations Department of Peacekeeping, "List of Peacekeeping Operations, 1948–2012," accessed July 5, 2012, http://www.un.org/en/peacekeeping/documents/operationslist.pdf.

mandates to determine the purpose of the deployment. I coded UN missions that were limited to monitoring ceasefires or the withdrawal of troops as traditional peacekeeping and excluded them from my data set of international state-building operations. As expected, that eliminated almost all UN operations prior to 1989 (with two exceptions). It also eliminated UN missions to Iraq and Kuwait (UNIKOM, 1991–2003), Libya and Chad (UNASOG, 1994), Uganda and Rwanda (UNOMUR, 1993–94), Georgia (UNOMIG, 1993—2009), Tajikistan (UNMOT, 1994–2000), Bosnia (UNPREDEP, 1995–99), Prevlaka (UNMOP, 1996—2002), and Ethiopia and Eritrea (UNMEE, 2000–2008). I also exclude the UN Mission for the Referendum in Western Sahara (MINURSO, 1991—present). While its mandate does include a requirement to oversee a referendum, in practice MINURSO has been unable to achieve this goal and has instead acted as a traditional ceasefire monitoring and verification mission.

I coded as cases of state building UN missions that included in their mandate a requirement to promote national reconciliation, support an electoral process, reform or train security forces, report on or help protect human rights, assist with capacity development, or implement a transitional authority. While it may seem too expansive to include missions that include one *or* another of these clauses in its mandate, in practice these different mandate clauses tend to occur together; few mandates include one without some combination of the others (those that do tend to be the earliest post–Cold War missions).

These criteria eliminate earlier, more traditional phases of missions that grew, under new mandates, into state-building operations. For example, I exclude the first UN Observer Mission in Angola (UNAVEM I, 1989–1991), but include the second and third (1991–97). Similarly, I exclude the first UN Operation in Somalia (UNOSOM I, 1992–3) but include the second (1993–95). I exclude the UN Observer Mission in Sierra Leone (UNOMSIL, 1998–99) but include the UN Mission in Sierra Leone (UNAMSIL, 1999–2005). I exclude the UN Advance Mission in Cambodia (UNAMIC, 1991–92) but include the UN Transitional Authority in Cambodia (UNTAC, 1992–93). I exclude the UN Protection Force (UNPROFOR, 1992–95) but include the UN Mission in Bosnia and Herzegovina (UNMIBH, 1995—2002). I exclude the UN Confidence Restoration Operation in Croatia (UNCRO, 1995–96) but include the UN Transitional Administration for Eastern Slavonia, Baranja, and Western Sirmium (UNTAES, 1996–98). Most notably, I exclude the UN Interim Force in Lebanon (UNIFIL) from its inception in 1978 until 2006, but include UNIFIL after 2006 when its mandate was expanded. These coding choices affect how I measure the beginning and duration of the cases. In all I count six cases of what I label "pre–state-building" operations.

In addition to the above, the criteria capture widely recognized cases of state building, including UN missions in Namibia (UNTAG, 1989–90), El Salvador (ONUSAL, 1991–95), Mozambique (ONUMOZ, 1992–94), two in Haiti (UNMIH, 1993–96 and UNSMIH, 1996–97, counted as one case; and a separate case, MINUSTAH, 2004–present), Rwanda (UN-AMIR, 1993–96), two separate cases in Liberia (UNOMIL, 1993–1997 and UNMIL, 2003–present), Kosovo (UNMIK, 1999–present), Timor-Leste (UNTAET, 1999–2002 and UNMISET, 2002–5), Côte d'Ivoire (UNOCI, 2003–present), and the Democratic Republic of the Congo (1999–present). I also include several cases that are not well studied in the literature because they are recent, including Burundi (ONUB, 2004–6), Sudan (UNMIS, 2005–11, and UNAMID, 2007–present), Chad (MINURCAT, 2007–10), and South Sudan (2011–present), although the later three are too recent to code a success or failure.

Some of my coding decisions are less well accepted in the broader literature. For example, I include the UN Operation in the Congo (ONUC) from 1960 to 1964 because its mandate included a requirement for the UN "to assist the Government in maintaining law and order and to provide technical assistance."[10] The UN's execution of this mandate, as reflected in general histories of the operation, included exercising some sovereign functions of the Congolese government and set it apart from the traditional peacekeeping operations common in the Cold War era.

Similarly, I follow Paris (but not many others) in including some cases in which the UN mandate did not explicitly include expansive state-building language but overlapped with international state-building efforts by other organizations. Therefore, I include the international operation in Nicaragua that coincided with the UN Observer Group in Central America (ONUCA). ONUCA was limited to observing the border and assisting with demobilization, but it was accompanied by the UN Observer Group for the Verification of Elections in Nicaragua, a civilian organization, as well as efforts by the International Monetary Fund, the World Bank, and the US Agency for International Development to reform and improve Nicaragua's institutions of economic governance. Similarly, I include the UN Verification Mission in Guatemala (MINUGUA)—a civilian organization that helped observe and verify a wide range of activities under a peace agreement from 1994 to 2004—because of the brief phase during which it was accompanied by a UN-mandated military force in 1997.

10. United Nations Department of Peacekeeping "Republic of the Congo—ONUC: Mandate," accessed July 5, 2012, http://www.un.org/en/peacekeeping/missions/past/onucM.htm.

I include the UN Mission in the Central African Republic (MINURCA, 1998–2000), which is inexplicably absent from the literature on state building. MINURCA's mandate included requirements to "assist in co-ordination with other international efforts in a short-term police trainers programme and in other capacity-building efforts of the national police, and to provide advice on the restructuring of the national police and special police forces," and "provide advice and technical support to the national electoral bodies regarding the electoral code and plans for the conduct of the legislative elections." Later, its mandate was expanded to include the "transport of electoral materials and equipment," "ensuring the security of electoral materials and equipment," and "play[ing] a supportive role in the conduct of the presidential elections." These seem to place MINURCA well outside the bounds of traditional UN peacekeeping.[11]

In all I count twenty-seven cases of UN-led state building (in thirty-two separate UN missions).

US Interventions

I also included in my data set US military deployments that had state building as part of their purpose or operations. I consulted the Congressional Research Service's report, "Instances of Use of United States Armed Force Abroad, 1798–2010," the US State Department's list of "Armed Actions Taken by the United States without a Declaration of War, 1789–1967," Senator Barry Goldwater's "list of 199 US military hostilities abroad without a declaration of war," and John M. Collins's book, *America's Small Wars*. Collectively, these four sources list hundreds of instances of US military deployments along with a brief descriptor of their purpose.[12]

11. UN Department of Peacekeeping, "Central African Republic—MINURCA: Mandate," accessed July 5, 2012, http://www.un.org/en/peacekeeping/missions/past/minurcaM.htm.
12. Grimmett, "Instances of Use of United States Armed Forces Abroad"; "Armed Actions Taken by the United States without a Declaration of War, 1789–1967," Research Project 806A, Historical Studies Division, Bureau of Public Affairs, US Department of State; Collins, *America's Small Wars*; Senator Barry Goldwater, "War without Declaration: A Chronological List of 199 US Military Hostilities Abroad without a Declaration of War. 1789–1972," 93rd Congress, Congressional Record, vol. 119, S14174–S14183 (July 20, 1973).

Table A.1. Cases of UN State Building

Mission	Name	Start	End	Mandate	Source
ONUC	United Nations Operation in the Congo	July 1960	June 1964	To maintain the territorial integrity and the political independence of the Republic of the Congo. To assist the central government of the Congo in the restoration and maintenance of law and order.	S/RES/169 (1961)
UNTAG	United Nations Transition Assistance Group	April 1989	March 1990	To ensure conditions in Namibia that will allow the Namibian people to participate freely and without intimidation in the electoral process under the supervision and control of the United Nations leading to early independence of the territory.	S/RES/632 (1989)
ONUCA	United Nations Observer Group in Central America	November 1989	January 1992	To play a part in the voluntary demobilization of the members of the Nicaraguan resistance.	S/RES/650 (1990)
UNAVEM II, UNAVEM III	United Nations Angola Verification Mission II and III	June 1991	June 1997	To assist in restoring peace and achieving national reconciliation on the basis of the Peace Accords for Angola. To monitor and verify the extension of state administration throughout the country.	S/RES/976 (1995) S/1995/97
ONUSAL	United Nations Observer Mission in El Salvador	July 1991	April 1995	To monitor all agreements of the peace accords. To verify general elections.	S/RES/693 (1991), S/RES/832 (1993)
UNTAC	United Nations Transitional Authority in Cambodia	March 1992	September 1993	To exercise the powers necessary to ensure the implementation of [the 1991 Paris] peace agreement, including those relating to the organization and conduct of free and fair elections and the relevant aspects of the administration of Cambodia.	S/RES/745 (1992)

ONUMOZ	United Nations Operation in Mozambique	December 1992	December 1994	To facilitate impartially the implementation of the peace agreement. To provide technical assistance and monitor the entire electoral process. To coordinate and monitor humanitarian assistance operations.	S/RES/797 (1992), S/1992/24892
UNOSOM II	United Nations Operation in Somalia II	March 1993	March 1995	To assist the people of Somalia to promote and advance political reconciliation, through the reestablishment of national and regional institutions and civil administration in the entire country.	S/RES/814 (1993)
UNMIH, UNSMIH	United Nations Mission in Haiti, United Nations Support Mission in Haiti	September 1993	July 1997	To establish and maintain a secure and stable environment conducive to the organization of free and fair legislative elections. To promote institution building, national reconciliation, and economic rehabilitation in Haiti.	S/RES/940 (1994), S/RES/1063 (1996)
UNOMIL	United Nations Observer Mission in Liberia	September 1993	September 1997	To support humanitarian assistance activities. To investigate and report on violations of human rights. To observe and verify the election process.	S/RES/1020 (1995)
UNAMIR	United Nations Assistance Mission for Rwanda	October 1993	March 1996	To monitor the security situation leading up to the elections. To assist in the coordination of humanitarian assistance. To help achieve national reconciliation. To support the government of Rwanda in its ongoing efforts to promote a climate of confidence and trust.	S/RES/872 (1993), S/RES/997 (1995)

[211]

(Continued)

TABLE A.1. *Continued*

Mission	Name	Start	End	Mandate	Source
UNMIBH	United Nations Mission in Bosnia and Herzegovina	December 1995	December 2002	To establish lasting security. To promote a permanent reconciliation between all parties. To facilitate the achievement of all political arrangements agreed to.	S/RES/1035 (1995), S/1995/999
UNTAES	United Nations Transitional Administration for Eastern Slavonia, Baranja and Western Sirmium	January 1996	January 1998	To establish a temporary police force. To undertake tasks relating to civil administration. To undertake tasks relating to the functioning of public services. To organize elections.	S/RES/1037 (1996), S/1995/951, S/1995/1031
MINUGUA	United Nations Verification Mission in Guatemala	January 1997	May 1997	To verify all agreements, in both their substantive and their operational aspects.	S/RES/1094 (1997), S/1994/53
MINURCA	United Nations Mission in the Central African Republic	April 1998	February 2000	To support the conduct of legislative and presidential elections.	S/RES/1230 (1999)
UNMIK	United Nations Interim Administration Mission in Kosovo	June 1999	Present	Performing basic civilian administrative functions. Organizing and overseeing the development of provisional institutions for democratic and autonomous self-government. Facilitating a political process designed to determine Kosovo's future status. Supporting the reconstruction of key infrastructure and other economic reconstruction. Maintaining civil law and order.	S/RES/1244 (1999)

UNTAET, UNMISET	United Nations Transitional Administration in East Timor, United Nations Mission of Support in East Timor	October 1999	May 2005	To provide security and maintain law and order throughout the territory of East Timor. To establish an effective administration. To assist in the development of civil and social services. To ensure the coordination and delivery of humanitarian assistance, rehabilitation, and development assistance. To support capacity building for self-government.	S/RES/1272 (1999)
UNAMSIL	United Nations Mission in Sierra Leone	October 1999	December 2005	To assist the efforts of the government of Sierra Leone to extend its authority, restore law and order, and stabilize the situation progressively throughout the entire country, and to assist in the promotion of a political process.	S/RES/1346 (2001), S/2001/228
MONUC, MONUSCO	United Nations Organization Mission in the Democratic Republic of the Congo	November 1999	Present	[2003] To provide assistance for the reestablishment of a state based on the rule of law and the preparation and holding of elections throughout the territory of the Democratic Republic of the Congo [2010]. To facilitate the consolidation of state authority throughout the territory, through the deployment of Congolese civil administration, in particular the police, territorial administration, and rule of law institutions.	S/RES/1493 (2003), S/RES/1925 (2010)

[213]

(Continued)

TABLE A.1. *Continued*

Mission	Name	Start	End	Mandate	Source
ONUB	United Nations Operation in Burundi	June 2004	December 2006	To assist the transitional government in extending state authority and utilities throughout the territory, including police and judicial institutions. To carry out institutional reforms. To proceed with electoral activities.	S/RES/1545 (2004)
MINUSTAH	United Nations Stabilization Mission in Haiti	June 2004	Present	To assist the transitional government in extending state authority throughout Haiti and to support good governance at local levels. To ensure a secure and stable environment. To assist with the restoration and maintenance of the rule of law, public safety, and public order in Haiti. To foster principles and democratic governance and institutional development. To assist the transitional government in its efforts to bring about a process of national dialogue and reconciliation.	S/RES/1542 (2004)
UNMIS, UNAMID	United Nations Mission in the Sudan, African Union–United Nations Hybrid Operation in Darfur	March 2005	Present	To assist in promoting the rule of law, including an independent judiciary, and the protection of human rights of all people of Sudan with the aim of contributing to long-term peace and stability. To assist the parties to develop and consolidate the national legal framework.	S/RES/1590 (2005)

[214]

UNIFIL	United Nations Interim Force in Lebanon	June 2006	Present	To assist the government of Lebanon to exercise its authority throughout the territory.	S/RES/1701 (2006)
MINURCAT	United Nations Mission in the Central African Republic and Chad	September 2007	December 2010	To assist the governments of Chad in the promotion of the rule of law, including through support for an independent judiciary and a strengthened legal system.	S/RES/1778 (2007)
UNMISS	United Nations Mission in the Republic of South Sudan	July 2011	Present	To support to the government of the Republic of South Sudan on political transition, governance, and establishment of state authority.	S/RES/1996 (2011)

I disregarded scores of brief military operations described as "punitive" (usually in Latin America), counterpiracy expeditions, gunboat diplomacy, and those undertaken for the purpose of protecting or evacuating US citizens or property. I also excluded cases of covert action, US-sponsored coups, or support for individual leaders without accompanying investments in governance and broader reform, which excludes, for example, coups in Iran (1953), Guatemala (1954), the Dominican Republic (1961), and leadership changes in Grenada (1983) and Panama (1989), among others. I also exclude cases of US peacekeeping—brief deployments of troops to halt or deter political violence in another state—such as interventions in Lebanon (1958), Thailand (1962), and the Dominican Republic (1966).

From the remainder, I composed a preliminary list of US military interventions that might qualify as state-building operations (but *not* including US contributions to UN operations listed above) based on the description of them in the aforementioned sources, or based on their inclusion as cases of state building by other scholars. I then conducted brief historical research. I examined presidential rhetoric and military directives to determine if US policymakers described the operations in state-building terms; I also examined US behavior to determine if official pronouncements were supported by military deployments, aid expenditures, the occurrence of elections, and the departure of US forces. Similarly to the UN interventions, I coded as "state building" operations those that included efforts to promote national reconciliation, support elections, assist with capacity development, or build a new government while respecting sovereignty and giving credible assurances of leaving.

I follow the scholarly consensus in including as cases of state building the military occupations of Germany and Japan, which are conventionally treated in the literature as cases of armed state building. But I also include the military governments in Italy, Austria, and South Korea. Their omission from the literature is curious, as they occurred under similar conditions as the other Allied post–World War II cases.

I include some, but not all, US interventions in the Caribbean and Central America in the early twentieth century. These cases are not widely treated as cases of state building in most of the literature, and scholars who do include them are not always clear about how they selected some cases and not others. The cases resemble state-building operations insofar as the United States did not annex territory, continued to recognize the de jure sovereignty of the states (and in the case of Cuba in 1898, the intervention was officially for the purpose of transferring sovereignty to Cuba), and invested resources in improving the security and economic environment of the target states. The interventions were relatively ephemeral and tended to be far shorter than cases of imperialism and

[216]

(with the exception of Haiti from 1915–34) and fell well within the range of the duration of state-building operations. Because of the shorter durations and continued recognition of sovereignty, the dynamic between international and local actors more closely resembles that of state-building operations than imperialism.

I include the interventions in Iraq and Afghanistan as cases of armed state building. The recent sharp growth in the literature on state building is due partly to these operations, which have heightened the urgency for good scholarship on the issue. Uniquely in the literature, I have also included the US intervention in South Vietnam. Critics might argue that the primary dynamic at work in the South Vietnam intervention was that of inter- or intrastate war, not state building. State building, in this view, was peripheral to the main effort, which was to defeat North Vietnam. This view misunderstands the nature of counterinsurgency. The United States waged a counterinsurgency campaign in South Vietnam for over a decade, which involved investing in state institutions and economic reconstruction as a major element of war strategy. State building was a means to an end—to win the war—but that is nearly always the case. State building serves a broad array of possible ends, including economic development, successful military occupation, peace building, and, in the case of South Vietnam, Iraq, and Afghanistan, counterinsurgency. The intervention in South Vietnam was a war, but that does not mean it was not also a case of state building. There is no clear reason to exclude South Vietnam while including Afghanistan and Iraq, which have a similar overlap of counterinsurgency war and state building. Excluding South Vietnam would argue for excluding Iraq and Afghanistan as well.

In all, I count thirteen cases of US-led state building (again, not counting US participation in UN operations, discussed above). Table A.2 summarizes the cases of state building with illustrative notes on each intervention's "mandate," drawn from primary sources. Below, I explain my decisions to exclude borderline cases.

Philippines, 1898–1946. The hardest case to decide is the US administration of the Philippines, which I narrowly code as imperialism. President McKinley described the United States' purpose in the Philippines in language similar to that regarding Cuba. America's purpose is, he said, "to facilitate the most humane and effective extension of authority throughout the islands, and to secure with the least possible delay the benefits of a wise and generous protection of life and property to the inhabitants." The United States was committed to the Filipino's development and prosperity. He continued, "No effort will be spared to build up the waste places desolated by war and by long years of misgovernment. . . . We shall continue, as we have begun, to open the schools and the churches, to set the courts in operation, to foster industry and trade and agriculture, and in

[217]

TABLE A.2. Cases of US State Building

Location	Start	End	Mandate	Source
Cuba	1898	1902	To give aid and direction to Cuba's people to form a government for themselves. To build up the waste places of the island, encourage the industry of the people, and assist them to form a government which shall be free and independent.	McKinley, FRUS 1898, 66–67
Cuba	1906	1909	To restore order and protect life and property in the island of Cuba. To establish therein a provisional government.	Taft, FRUS 1906, 491.
Haiti	1915	1934	To afford the inhabitants of Haiti the privileges of government, exercising all the functions necessary for the establishment and maintenance of the fundamental rights of man.	Adm. Caperton, FRUS, 1915, 484.
Dominican Republic	1916	1924	To give aid to that country in returning to a condition of internal order that will enable it to observe the obligations resting upon it as one of the family of nations.	Cpt. Knapp, FRUS, 1916, 247
Nicaragua	1926	1933	To terminate the Nicaraguan civil war. To secure a free, fair, and impartial election. To train and command a nonpartisan national constabulary.	Stimson, FRUS, 1927, 345
Italy	1945	1946	To work for the relief of hunger and sickness and fear and the reconstruction of an Italian economy, the restoration of power systems, railways, motor transport, roads and other communications. To speed the day when the last vestiges of Fascism in Italy will have been wiped out and the day when free elections can be held throughout Italy.	Hyde Park Declaration, FRUS, 1944 (Conf. at Quebec), 498
Austria	1945	1955	To ensure the reconstruction of Austria as a free, independent, and democratic state. To facilitate the development of a sound Austrian economy. To foster the restoration of local self-government and the establishment of an Austrian central government freely elected by the Austrian people.	FRUS, 1945 (Potsdam I), 339.

Germany	1945	1955	To prevent Germany from ever again becoming a threat to the peace of the world through the eventual reconstruction of German political life on a democratic basis.	JCS Directive 1067, April 1945
Japan	1945	1952	To ensure that Japan's war-making power is destroyed. To remove all obstacles to the revival and strengthening of democratic tendencies among the Japanese people. To establish freedom of speech, or religion, and of thought, as well as respect for fundamental human rights.	Potsdam Declaration
South Korea	1945	1948	To work toward the assumption by the Koreans themselves of the responsibilities and functions of a free and independent nation and the elimination of all vestiges of Japanese control over Korean economic and political life.	Truman, FRUS, 1945, vol. 6, 1048.
South Vietnam	1962	1973	To assist South Vietnam in preserving its freedom and independence.	Johnson, FRUS, 1964–68, vol. 1, 623
Afghanistan	2001	2012	[2002 Donor's conference] To establish peace, representative governance, and stability in Afghanistan, and eliminating terrorism and narcotics production and trafficking. [2004 NATO Summit] To assist in the emergence of a secure and stable Afghanistan, with a broad-based, gender sensitive, multiethnic, and fully representative government, integrated into the international community and cooperating with its neighbors.	2002 Tokyo Conference, NATO 2004 Summit Declaration
Iraq	2003	2011	To provide for the effective administration of Iraq during the period of transitional administration. To restore conditions of security and stability. To create conditions in which the Iraqi people can freely determine their own political future, including by advancing efforts to restore and establish national and local institutions for representative governance and facilitating economic recovery and sustainable reconstruction and development.	CPA Regulation 1

[219]

Note on sources: FRUS is the Foreign Relations of the United States series published by the US State Department. "JSC" is the Joint Chiefs of Staff. "CPA" is the Coalition Provisional Authority.

every way in our power to make these people whom Providence has brought within our jurisdiction feel that it is their liberty and not our power, their welfare and not our gain, we are seeking to enhance."

However, McKinley pointedly did not use the words "sovereign" or "independent" in describing the Philippine government. He went on to explain that "the claim of the rebel leader that he was promised independence by any officer of the United States in return for his assistance has no foundation in fact." In fact, a presidentially appointed commission believed it was impossible "to withdraw our forces from the islands either with honor to ourselves or with safety to the inhabitants," because the Filipino insurgents had started a war. In fact, McKinley knew that "the suggestion has been made that we could renounce our authority over the islands and, giving them independence, could retain a protectorate over them." He dismissed the idea: "This proposition will not be found, I am sure, worthy of your serious attention. Such an arrangement would involve at the outset a cruel breach of faith." McKinley asserted the Philippine islands "are ours by every title of law and equity. They cannot be abandoned. If we desert them we leave them at once to anarchy and finally to barbarism."[13] In line with McKinley's arguments, the United States defeated Filipino insurgents in a brutal fourteen-year counterinsurgency campaign and exercised sovereignty over the Philippines for forty-eight years, placing it far closer to the typical case of imperialism than to international state building.

Panama (1903–14; 1918–20). I follow Pei in including several US interventions in Central America and the Caribbean. However, unlike Pei, I exclude the US interventions in Panama, which he characterizes as a single intervention stretching from 1903 to 1936. I exclude the Panamanian interventions because they did not involve the investment of resources into improving Panamanian governance. President Roosevelt told Congress that "the cities of Panama and Colon are not embraced in the canal zone," in which the US exercised sovereignty, "but the United States assumes their sanitation and, in case of need, the maintenance of order therein."[14] Far from laying the groundwork for a far-reaching state-building effort, this clause was, essentially, payment for the cession to the United States of the Canal Zone. Since the US military and commercial resources present in Panama for the construction of the canal far exceeded those of the embryonic Panamanian state, the United States agreed to let some of its resources be used for Panamanian purposes on occasion. Under this clause US military personnel observed elections in 1908 and 1912, and withdrew in 1914 after completion of the canal. They

13. President McKinley, "Message of the President," December 5, 1899, xlv–vi.
14. President Roosevelt, "Message of the President," December 7, 1903, xli.

returned briefly in 1918–20 to promote order and oversee elections, and in 1925 (for eleven days) to maintain order during strikes and riots— always to protect the Canal Zone from civil unrest, not to invest in Panamanian governance. The Congressional Research Service and the State Department both claim the 1903–14 mission was only to guard or protect US interests. The later interventions were brief and disconnected. Pei's construction of a single thirty-one-year intervention, and his characterization of it as a state-building mission, are unjustified.

Nicaragua (1912–25). Pei includes an earlier phase of the US intervention in Nicaragua, from 1912 to 1925. I code this phase of the US intervention as the protection of American lives and property, consistent with its description by Presidents Taft and Coolidge and by the Congressional Research Service and State Department reports. Taft informed Congress that he deployed two thousand Marines to Nicaragua in 1912 "to protect American life and property against acts of sheer lawlessness," and that they were withdrawn a short time later. President Coolidge, speaking to Congress in 1927, gave a consistent description of the earlier operation: "It is well known that in 1912 the United States intervened in Nicaragua with a large force and put down a revolution, and that from that time to 1925 a legation guard of American marines was, with the consent of the Nicaraguan Government, kept in Managua to protect American lives and property."[15] It was not until 1927, when US Marines returned to Nicaragua, that the United States undertook a broader mission "to terminate [the Nicaraguan civil] war; to secure . . . a free, fair, and impartial election; to train and command a non-partisan national constabulary," as described by Henry Stimson, who, as the president's Personal Representative in Nicaragua, brokered a deal that year with Nicaraguan factions to sanction the US presence.[16] I therefore code the US state-building operation in Nicaragua as beginning in 1927, not 1912.

Cuba (1917–22). Pei counts the Cuban intervention of 1917–1922 as a state-building operation. However, the Congressional Research Service and State Department record that the intervention aimed narrowly at protecting American lives and property during unrest, not at administering or rebuilding Cuban governance; Collins and Goldwater do not even mention the intervention, nor do other scholars who wrote on the prior, wide-ranging occupations of Cuba.[17]

15. President Taft, "Message of the President," December 3, 1912, xii–xiii; President Coolidge, "Message of the President," January 10, 1927, 288.
16. Henry Stimson, "The Personal Representative of the President of the United States in Nicaragua (Stimson) to General Moncada," May 11, 1927, 345.
17. For example, Langley, *Banana Wars,* and Lenz, *Power and Policy,* cover the prior occupations of Cuba but do not even mention the 1917–22 intervention.

Russia (1918–20). As the Bolshevik Revolution was unfolding, the United States deployed up to fourteen thousand troops to Russia to reestablish an Eastern Front in World War I, aid the anti-Bolshevik forces, guard against Japanese expansionist plans in Siberia, and provide moral support to a legion of Czech soldiers stranded in Russia after the latter's exit from the war.[18] The Allies temporarily occupied Vladivostok to keep the trans-Siberian railway open and ensure the secure flow of military supplies—"to prevent danger from Austro-German agencies and influence which are known to be at work in the city," according to the Allied proclamation announcing the occupation[19]—but they did not attempt to occupy Russia's main centers of political power. The Allied attempt to fight the Bolsheviks and support the White Russian forces does not qualify it as a state-building operation: the US intervention in Russia was akin to its interventions in Grenada (1983) or Panama (1989) in that the goal was to support a specific set of leaders not the broad reconstruction of a state.

Laos, 1956–75. Foreign forces were prohibited in Laos by the Geneva Accords of 1954. The United States aided the Laotian government's counterinsurgency campaign against Communist insurgents with several hundred million dollars of economic and military assistance per year in the 1950s and 1960s, but the tiny US military presence from 1956 to 1975 rarely comprised more than two dozen troops, hardly more than a normal defense attaché contingent. (They briefly spiked to almost three hundred in 1962 before abruptly dropping again; the United States also gave air support in 1964–5.) It is also unclear if the United States was concerned with the capacity or democratic credentials of the Laotian government, so long as it was not Communist. US efforts in Laos were closer to conventional security assistance, culminating in over $1 billion per year in military aid in 1972 and 1973, than to a state-building effort.[20]

El Salvador (1979–92). US efforts in El Salvador were similar to those in Laos (although more successful). US involvement in El Salvador from 1979 to 1992 consisted of several hundred million dollars of economic

---

18. See note 12. See also Boot, *Savage Wars of Peace*, chap. 9.
19. Knight, et al. "Proclamation by the Commanders of Allied and Associated Forces at Vladivostok," 271.
20. See Collins, *America's Small Wars* for a short description of the conflict. Figures for US economic and military assistance are derived from US Agency for International Development (USAID), US Overseas Loans and Grants: Obligations and Loan Authorizations, July 1, 1945–September 30, 2010. Figures for deployments of US troops are derived from Tim Kane, "Global US Troop Deployment, 1950–2005," Heritage Foundation Center for Data Analysis, May 2006 and its accompanying online database, accessed July 11, 2012, http://www.heritage.org/research/reports/2006/05/global-us-troop-deployment-1950–2005.

and military assistance, peaking at just over $1 billion in 1985, and tens of millions of dollars of weapons sales. But, because of pressure and restrictions by Congress, only a few dozen US troops were in El Salvador. As with Laos, US commitment to the quality of governance or democracy was doubtful. I code the US intervention in El Salvador one of security assistance, not state building.[21]

Lebanon (1983). Responding to a call by Lebanese factions for an outside peacekeeping force, several thousand US, British, French, and Italian troops deployed to Lebanon from late 1982 to early 1984, initially to assist the Lebanese Army verify the withdrawal of the Palestine Liberation Organization from Lebanon. But in 1983 Congress declared that the purpose of US participation in the Multinational Force was "to restore full control by the Government of Lebanon over its own territory."[22] The mission appears to have been gravitating toward a broad peace-building effort in response to requests by the Lebanese government—a pattern that would be repeated in the 1990s—but was abruptly aborted after attacks on US installations in 1983–4. As a result, there was no broad effort by donors or international institutions to follow through on their rhetoric about rebuilding the Lebanese state for two more decades.[23]

Grenada (1983). The 1983 US mission in Grenada involved "evacuating US citizens, disarming hostile forces, and restoring orderly government to Grenada." Within two days of the invasion, however, Assistant Secretary of State Langhorn Motley and the Caribbean Peacekeeping Force—drawn from other Caribbean island nations, not US forces—were "fully in charge of efforts to reconstruct a viable government on the island." The CPF, not US troops, were given the responsibility for providing "peace and order in the capital and its vicinity." US troops were withdrawn a month and a half after deploying and did not play a significant role in fostering the new Grenadian government and were not present to oversee or observe elections a year later.[24] The United States did increase its aid to Grenada from nothing to $110 million in economic support over the following two years, but it promptly dropped again. I code the US intervention in Grenada as one of regime change, not state building.

21. Ibid.
22. Public Law 98–119, "Multinational Force in Lebanon Resolution," October 12, 1983.
23. Kelly, *US and Russian Policymaking*, "Lebanon, 1982–1984," chap. 6. See also Global Security, "US Multinational Force (USMNF) Lebanon," accessed July 17, 2012, http://www.globalsecurity.org/military/ops/usmnf.htm; US Foreign Policy in Perspective, "Lebanon, 1982–83," accessed July 17, 2012, http://www.us-foreign-policy-perspective.org/index.php?id=311.
24. Cole, *Operation Urgent Fury*, 26, 57.

Panama (1989). Some twenty-six thousand US troops intervened in Panama in December 1989 "to safeguard the lives of Americans, to defend democracy in Panama, to combat drug trafficking, and to protect the integrity of the Panama Canal treaty." In practice, this meant the overthrow of General Manuel Noriega, the nation's dictator and an indicted drug trafficker. Combat operations ceased after a few days; some US troops remained for a few weeks "patrolling city streets, collecting a wide assortment of small arms, and assisting the civilian population" by improving "roads, electricity, and clean water."[25] These efforts, however, were small, unsystematic, and brief—the operation was officially over within a month—and characteristic of combat relief operations, not state building.

Other. I do not include Puerto Rico or Guam, which the United States annexed after the War of 1898 and has governed now for over a century, or the Northern Mariana Islands, which has remained a territory of the United States since World War II. Some similar dynamics were at work: the United States deployed military force and spread norms of liberal governance. However, the polities never claimed sovereignty or independence. The cases are closer to colonial administration or domestic political development. US governance of American Samoa, annexed after an agreement with Germany in 1899, and the Virgin Islands, purchased from Denmark in 1917, are similarly excluded. And, as I discuss, I code as cases of imperialism the US administration of the Pacific Trust territories.

LEAGUE OF NATIONS MANDATE SYSTEM AND UN TRUSTEESHIP COUNCIL

Of the 193 sovereign states in the world today, 19 were previously mandates under the League of Nations, trusteeships under the United Nations, or both. The mandates were created to give the former colonies of Germany and the Ottoman Empire, which were defeated in World War I, to the victors, Britain and France. (In addition, Belgium took two mandates in Africa; Australia and New Zealand aided in the administration of some Pacific islands; and South Africa took Southwest Africa, today's Namibia). The former Ottoman colonies were granted independence before or immediately after World War II; the remaining mandates were turned into trusteeships under the new UN Trusteeship Council. The same state served as trustee that previously served as the mandatory power, with the exception of the South Pacific mandate, which passed from Japan to the United States.

25. Phillips, *Operation Just Cause*, 3, 9, 42, 44.

The administration of the mandates and trusts involved the deployment of military force and was purportedly for the purpose of helping weak polities become capable of independent governance, and thus bears some similarity to today's international state-building projects. The professed aim of the mandatory power and trustee was to help prepare the dependencies for independence. According to Article 22 of the League of Nations Covenant, "the tutelage of such peoples [of former colonies] should be entrusted to advanced nations who by reason of their resources, their experience or their geographical position can best undertake this responsibility, and who are willing to accept it." Similarly, the UN Trusteeship System was created "to promote the political, economic, social, and educational advancement of the inhabitants of the trust territories, and their progressive development towards self-government or independence," according to Chapter 12 of the UN Charter.

However, I code the mandates and trusts and cases of imperialism and decolonization, not international state building. While the mandatory powers and trustees employed broadly similar rhetoric as today's international state builders and claimed to be working for the independence of the dependent territories, their claims were not credible. In most cases (except the United States, Australia, and New Zealand in the South Pacific), the mandatory powers and trustees were overtly self-described empires that held other territories as dependencies. They had decades, sometimes centuries, of history acting as imperial powers. Little in the controlling states' behavior suggested they intended to work toward the independence of the mandates or trust territories. The mandates and trusts lasted an average of forty years—forty-seven years for those territories not granted independence before or immediately after World War II, and ended in large part because the European powers were bankrupted during and after the war and were thus compelled to abandon their empires, likely a more pressing reason than any change in norms they may have experienced. The territories were imperial possessions previous to their absorption into the League and UN systems; little likely changed from one way of organizing imperial rule to the next.

Five cases may be an exception: Nauru, Papa New Guinea, the Marshall Islands, Micronesia, and Palau. Their governance by relatively less imperialistic powers—the United States, Australia, and New Zealand—suggest their experience may be qualitatively different than, for example, Iraq under the British, although the duration of their dependency (seventy-five years in the case of Palau) suggests their experience may also differ from cases of international state building. Exploring these cases may be a fruitful avenue for further research.

[225]

Objections and Reply

Having defined armed state building and established my universe of cases, I anticipate an objection that my data set suffers from a lack of unit homogeneity. A critic may argue that I have defined armed state building too broadly or too loosely, and the resulting set of forty cases contains too much internal variance. For example, a critic may argue that the Allied military administration of West Germany, which involved millions of people, billions of dollars, and a decade of work cannot be usefully compared to the brief UN foray into Guatemala in 1997. In this view, it is unlikely that any theory can adequately explain the outcomes of such a diverse range of phenomena. If I were to generate and defend an explanation, it would be methodologically flawed because I would be attempting to generalize across unlike cases. Essentially, according to this criticism, my research design is comparing apples to oranges and any theory purporting to cover both will either be too vague or simply inaccurate. My research design should be refined to make the definition of armed state building tighter, and to narrow the universe of cases.

I respond that my data set appears broader than others' precisely because I am attempting to improve on prior scholars' methodology. Mine is the first attempt to offer a definition of armed state building that is both more accurate—including the role of military power and norm propagation as well as institution building—and operationalizable, able to be turned into a rigorous research design with consistent criteria for case selection. I reviewed some of prior scholars' inconsistencies. I am not the first to include cases of US intervention in the Caribbean and Central America, but I am the first to apply a consistent set of criteria to identify which are cases of state building (as opposed to imperialism, regional hegemony, development assistance, or peacekeeping). Nor am I the first to include cases of post–World War II military occupation, but scholars almost universally focus exclusively on Germany and Japan, to the exclusion of Italy, Austria, and South Korea, without identifying the criteria by which they include the former and exclude the latter. Most scholars focus on post–Cold War cases of UN complex peacekeeping, starting with Namibia and Nicaragua in 1989, but even that data set is not consistent. Most scholars include Iraq and Afghanistan, as do I, but exclude South Vietnam, despite that the three cases display a similar overlap between state building and counterinsurgency. My research design follows the literature in including both US and UN cases, cases from before, during, and after the Cold War, and cases with a diverse set of historical pathways leading up to a state-building intervention—and, in fact, my research design improves on the literature by making the field's implicit case criteria explicit and applying it more consistently and rigorously. Far from being a weakness, the breadth of my data set is one of this book's unique contributions to the research program.

This may not be sufficient. A critic may claim that the flaw is not with my research design so much as with the field of study generally. According to this criticism, I have succeeded in simply illustrating a broad and irreparable methodological flaw in the research program on armed state building. By applying the field's implicit criteria more rigorously and making it explicit, I have made clear that the literature has been attempting to lump diverse phenomena into a single category and apply generalizations across unlike units. The category of "armed state building" as I have defined it is essentially flawed. Any theory built on it is bound to be simplistic and neglectful of important nuances between cases.

In one sense, this is precisely the criticism I level against the conventional hypotheses of armed state building. Current theories are too simplistic and fail to account for variance across the cases, which is why they lack explanatory power. However, I do not believe the effort is irredeemably flawed or violates unit homogeneity; rather, I argue that current hypotheses fail because they do not account for various *subtypes* of armed state building, and thus fail to explain the full range of phenomena. The cases are indeed all apples, but some are Fuji and some are Golden Delicious. I do not assume that the same logic applies to all cases: rather, I seek to develop a theory in this book that accounts for different dynamics at work in the different subtypes of state failure and state building.

Appendix B

Measuring Success and Failure

I measured success and failure across the five dimensions of statehood described in chapters 3 and 4, and aggregated them to develop a fourfold ranking of success and failure. A "success" is one in which the state-building effort showed progress across four or five dimensions of statehood, including at least security, legitimacy, and humanity, and sustained the success for at least ten years after the end of the intervention. A "shallow success" is a case in which the state showed progress on security, legitimacy, and humanity, but not on capacity or prosperity. A "mitigated failure" is a case in which there was a failure of security, legitimacy, or humanity, but showed success on capacity or prosperity. A "failure" is a case in which there was a failure of security, legitimacy, or humanity, and no progress on prosperity or capacity.

I use a cutoff of ten years as a proxy to represent that at some point after the end of an intervention, the responsibility for a state's continued political development rests more with local actors within the state than with the international community's actions during the intervention. Ten years is arbitrary, but it also works well with the cases in this study: in all but one case (Haiti after 1934), states that maintained a positive political and economic trajectory for ten years went on to maintain it for much longer; those that failed, failed within ten years. (There was a coup in Haiti twelve years after the end of the US intervention.)

MEASURING SECURITY

I measure security as the absence of political violence that caused at least one thousand deaths in any one year, according to the Correlates of War and Uppsala Conflict Data Program data sets.[26] I measure every year for ten years *after* the intervention. Any case in which political violence occurred in any year up to ten years postintervention is coded either a failure or a mitigated failure.

I do not automatically count violence *during* an intervention as a failure, which would overcount failures. Often the outbreak of violence is the reason why state builders choose to intervene in a state in the first place, making violence during interventions fairly common; the mere fact that violence is ongoing during an intervention does not tell us whether the intervention is effective or not. Rather, I examine how the international actors respond to the violence. For example, the United States dealt effectively with small uprisings in Haiti from 1918 to 1920 and the Dominican Republic from 1916 to 1924. The United Nations fought a war in the Congo from 1960 to 1964, and the ongoing conflicts in Iraq and Afghanistan are cases of simultaneous conflict and state

---

26. The COW data is available at http://www.correlatesofwar.org, accessed July 17, 2012. It is described in Sarkees, Reid, and Wayman, *Resort to War: 1816–2007*. I consulted the inter-, intra-, non-, and extrastate war lists in the COW data. For the Uppsala conflict data, see Uppsala University, Uppsala Conflict Data Program, "UCDP Battle-Related Deaths Dataset v.5–2011," accessed July 17, 2012, http://www.pcr.uu.se/digitalAssets/63/63680_UCDP_Battle-related_deaths_dataset_v5-2011.xls.

building. I consider some of these cases failures—not because of midintervention violence, but because either the international actor simply lost the war it was fighting, as in South Vietnam, or because security continued to deteriorate after the intervention, as in the Congo. The ultimate outcome in Afghanistan is still uncertain.

Sharply distinguishing between violence during an intervention and violence after an intervention is how I avoid a potential endogeneity problem. If I counted violence during an intervention as an automatic failure, then the data used in describing the case (violence during an intervention) would be part of the definition of failure. The theory that poor security causes state-building operations to fail, then, would be a self-proving theory.

MEASURING LEGITIMACY

I measured legitimacy as the continuity of constitutional, liberal government for ten years after an intervention, as related in general histories of each case and cross-checked with each state's Polity IV score during and after an intervention.[27] A coup, regime collapse, or dictatorship in any year up to ten years after an intervention is coded as either a failure or mitigated failure. (Interestingly, the growth of authoritarianism in Cambodia that many scholars have noted is not reflected in its Polity IV score, which is therefore coded as retaining legitimacy.)

Some critics may disagree with counting coups and dictatorships as a failure of state building. Coups and dictatorships depend on individual personalities and circumstances, are unpredictable, and cannot be blamed on the international community. In this view, including coups and dictatorships as failures artificially lowers the success rate of state-building operations by as many as four of the thirty-six cases (the Dominican Republic, Nicaragua in 1927, South Korea, and the Democratic Republic of the Congo in 1960). But in every case over the last century examined here, building *democratic* governance was at least a professed goal of the state-building operation. Coups are a clear failure of that objective. Further, state builders can make coups less likely. Coups are more likely in states with weak civilian institutions of government. The occurrence of a successful coup indicates that the state-building operation did not successfully strengthen the institutions of governance.

27. Marshall, "Polity IV Project."

MEASURING HUMANITY

I measured humanity as the absence of genocide or ethnic cleansing *during and ten years after* an intervention, as reflected in general histories of each case. I code genocide or ethnic cleansing *during* an intervention as a failure (which I do not do for nongenocidal political violence) because I take the prevention of genocide and ethnic cleansing to be a basic purpose of liberal interventions. If the international community fails to prevent the worst from happening while it is already on the ground with armed force, as it arguably did in Rwanda, Iraq, and the Democratic Republic of the Congo, it cannot be said to be successful, regardless of whatever other outcomes result from the intervention. The occurrence of genocide or ethnic cleansing in any year during or up to ten years after an intervention is coded as either a failure or mitigated failure.

MEASURING CAPACITY

I measure capacity in two ways. For cases prior to 1989, I measure the trend line in the government's revenue as a percentage of GDP, as recorded in B. R. Mitchell's *International Historical Statistics* series.[28] If revenue grew by more than 2 percent between the start of the intervention and ten years after its conclusion, I coded that as an improvement in governance; if it fell by more than 2 percent, I coded that as a decline in governance. If it stayed within 2 percent, I coded it as neutral. For cases after 1989, I measure the trend line across four variables tracked by the World Bank's Governance Indicators: governance capacity, regulatory quality, the rule of law, and control of corruption, starting with the year nearest the beginning of the intervention and ending with ten years after the end, the beginning of a new intervention, or the last year for which data was available.[29] If the state showed clear improvement (greater than 0.1 on the raw score) on three or four variables, or on two variables while holding steady on the other two, I coded it as an improvement in governance. If it showed a clear decline on three or four variables, or on two variables while holding steady on the other two, I coded it as a decline in governance. If it showed little movement, or a mix of improvement and decline, I coded it as neutral.

---

28. Mitchell, *International Historical Statistics*.
29. Kaufman, Kraay, and Mastruzzi, Worldwide Governance Indicators.

MEASURING PROSPERITY

I measure prosperity by the change in real GDP per capita, as measured by the IMF's World Economic Outlook database for cases after 1978 and Maddison's *Historical Statistics for the World Economy* for cases before.[30] I measure the change starting with the year nearest the beginning of the intervention and ending with ten years after the end, the beginning of a new intervention, or the last year for which data was available. I measure the percentage change rather than its absolute value because I am measuring a state's trajectory of progress or regress rather than a snapshot of its socioeconomic status at one moment (its vector, not position). GDP per capita is a better measure than simple GDP because it comes closer to measuring the impact of economic growth on the population.

Virtually all postwar societies experience a postwar economic boom; every case studied here shows a positive average GDP growth rate during and after the state-building operation, and almost all show a positive GDP per capita growth rate as well. However, some sustained high rates of growth while others saw growth slow, or experienced wide fluctuations in economic activity—especially if fighting renewed. If a state averaged less than 1 percent real GDP growth during and for ten years after an intervention, I coded it as a failure of prosperity. If it grew by more than 1 percent, I coded it as progress.

ONGOING CASES

Fifteen of the forty cases are either ongoing or ended less than ten years ago. For most of them, I estimate their likely outcome based on their track record so far, but I acknowledge these are tentative judgments subject to change. For cases that started after 2005, there is not enough of a track record on which to base even a preliminary judgment. Finally, I judge the outcome in Afghanistan to be uncertain. As I argue in chapter 7, its early trajectory was broadly negative, but at least some aspects of the mission have improved since 2007, and even more so since 2009. However, I judge its ultimate outcome depends on choices by US policymakers—for example, about the size and mission of the post-2014 stay-behind force—that have yet to be made.

---

30. International Monetary Fund, "World Economic Outlook Database," April 2012; Maddison, "Historical Statistics of the World Economy, 1–2006 AD."

TABLE B.1. Measuring Success and Failure

State	Security	Humanity	Legitimacy	Capacity	Prosperity	Outcome
	Political violence within 10 years after intervention	Genocide, ethnic cleansing, war crimes during or after intervention?	Coup, collapse, or regime breakdown within 10 years?	Governance direction during intervention and decade after	Average real GDP per capita growth during intervention and decade after	
Cuba 1898			X	↔	NA	Failure
Cuba 1906	X			→	NA	Failure
Haiti 1915				NA	NA	Shallow success
Dominican Republic			X	NA	NA	Failure
Nicaragua 1927			X	NA	1.96	Mitigated failure
Italy				←	3.47	Success
Austria				←	7.93	Success
West Germany				←	7.86	Success
Japan				↔	4.59	Success
South Korea			X	NA	4.48	Mitigated failure
Congo 1960			X	←	0.85	Mitigated failure
South Vietnam			X	NA	0.43	Failure
Namibia				→	0.77	Shallow success
Nicaragua 1989				↔	-0.10	Shallow success
Angola	X		X	↔←→	3.76	Failure
El Salvador				→	3.15	Success
Cambodia					3.54	Shallow success
Mozambique	X		X	↔	6.03	Shallow success
Somalia	X		X	→	NA	Failure
Haiti 1993			X	→	-1.37	Failure

[232]

Liberia 1993	X		NA	←	Failure
Rwanda	X	X	2.44	←	Failure
Bosnia			3.38	←	Likely success
Croatia			4.01	←	Success
Guatemala			0.75	↕	Shallow success
Central African Republic		X	-0.55	↕	Failure
Sierra Leone			6.25	←	Likely success
Timor–Leste			5.53	→	Likely shallow success
Congo 1999		X	0.99	←	Likely mitigated failure
Kosovo			2.78	←	Likely success
Afghanistan			4.98	←	Uncertain
Côte d'Ivoire			-1.39	→	Likely shallow success
Iraq		X	3.40	←	Likely mitigated failure
Liberia 2003			2.23	←	Likely success
Burundi			2.35	←	Likely success
Haiti 2004			0.00	←	Likely shallow success

[233]

COMMON SENSE

The basic determination about whether to code an intervention either a degree of success or a degree of failure was fairly straightforward. (Cambodia is the only ambiguous case.) Determining the degree of success or failure required more judgment; the line between a "shallow success" and a "mitigated failure" is thin and depends on the details of each individual case. I consulted the case study narratives and used common sense. For example, the Democratic Republic of the Congo showed strong improvements in governance after the 1960–64 UN intervention, which might argue for coding it a "mitigated failure." However, the improvement in governance was almost certainly due to the rise of the Mobutu dictatorship, not to any lingering effects of the UN intervention. Upgrading the Congolese intervention to a mitigated failure would overstate the success of the intervention. A similar dynamic is true of other cases that saw the rise of postintervention dictators or strongmen, such as Liberia (1993) and Rwanda.

Bibliography

Aboagye, F. B., and A. M. S. Bah. *Liberia at a Crossroads: A Preliminary Look at the United Nations Mission In Liberia (UNMIL) and the Protection of Civilians*. Pretoria: Institute for Security Studies, 2004.

Afghanistan: Where Things Stand. 2009 National Poll of Afghanistan. ABC News/ BBC/ARD.

Alao, A. *The Burden of Collective Goodwill: The International Involvement in the Liberian Civil War*. Brookfield, VT: Ashgate, 1998.

Alao, A., J. Mackinlay, and F. Olonisakin. *Peacekeepers, Politicians, and Warlords: The Liberian Peace Process*. New York: United Nations University Press, 1999.

Anderson, J. L. "The Man in the Palace." *New Yorker*, June 6, 2005.

Aristotle. *Nicomachean Ethics*, translated by M. Ostwald. Indianapolis: Bobbs-Merrill, 1962.

———. *The Politics of Aristotle*, edited and translated by E. Barker. Oxford: Oxford University Press, 1958.

Asia Foundation. *Surveys of the Afghan People*. 2004–2009. Washington, DC: Asia Foundation, http://asiafoundation.org/country/afghanistan/2011-poll.php.

Baker, P. "Biden No Longer a Lone Voice on Afghanistan." *New York Times*, October 13, 2009. http://www.nytimes.com/2009/10/14/world/14biden.html?

Barnett, M. "Building a Republican Peace: Stabilizing States after War." *International Security* 30, no. 4 (2006): 87–112.

Barnett, M., and C. Zurcher. "The Peacebuilder's Contract: How External Statebuilding Reinforces Weak Statehood." In *The Dilemmas of Statebuilding: Confronting the Contradictions of Postwar Peace Operations*, edited by R. Paris and T. D. Sisk, 23–52. New York: Routledge, 2009.

Beblawi, H. "The Rentier State in the Arab World." In *The Arab State*, edited by G. Luciani, 85–98. Berkeley: University of California Press, 1990.

Beblawi, H., and G. Luciani, eds. *The Rentier State*. London: Routledge and Kegan Paul, 1987.

Bell, D. *Just War as Christian Discipleship*. Grand Rapids, MI: Brazos Press, 2009.

Berdal, M. R., and S. Economides. *United Nations Interventionism, 1991–2004*, rev. and updated ed. New York: Cambridge University Press, 2007.

Bhatia, M., K. Lanigan, and P. Wilkinson. *Minimal Investments, Minimal Results: The Failure of Security Policy in Afghanistan.* Kabul: Afghan Research and Evaluation Unit, 2004.

Binder, L. *Crises and Sequences in Political Development.* Princeton: Princeton University Press, 1971.

Blue, R.N. *Assessment of the Impact of USAID Funded Technical Assistance-Capacity Building: Final Report.* Washington, DC: USAID, 2007.

Boas, M., and K.M. Jennings. " 'Failed States' and 'State Failure': Threats or Opportunities." *Globalizations* 4, no. 4 (2007): 475–85.

Boix, C. *Democracy and Redistribution.* New York: Cambridge University Press, 2003.

Boot, M. *The Savage Wars of Peace: Small Wars and the Rise of American Power.* New York: Basic Books, 2002.

Burke, E. *The Political Philosophy of Edmund Burke,* edited by I. Hampsher-Monk. London: Longman, 1987.

Call, C. "Beyond the 'Failed State': Toward Conceptual Alternatives." *European Journal of International Relations* 17, no. 2 (2011): 303–26.

——. "Ending Wars, Building States." In *Building States to Build Peace,* edited by C. Call and V. Wyeth, 1–24. Boulder, CO: Lynne Rienner, 2008.

——. "The Fallacy of the 'Failed State.' " *Third World Quarterly* 29, no. 8 (2008): 1491–1507.

Cardoso, F.H., and E. Faletto. *Dependency and Development in Latin America.* Berkeley: University of California Press, 1979.

Carment, D., S. Yiagadeesen, and S. Prest. "State Fragility and Implications for Aid Allocation: An Empirical Analysis." *Conflict Management and Peace Science* 25 (2008): 349–73.

Carnahan, M., and C. Lockhart. "Peacebuilding and Public Finance." In *Building States to Build Peace,* edited by C. Call and V. Wyeth, 73–102. Boulder, CO: Lynne Rienner, 2008.

Carothers, T. *Aiding Democracy Abroad: The Learning Curve.* Washington, DC: Carnegie Endowment for International Peace, 1999.

——. "The End of the Transition Paradigm." *Journal of Democracy* 13, no.1 (2002): 5–21.

Chandler, D. *Empire in Denial: The Politics of State-Building.* London: Pluto Press, 2006.

——. Introduction to *Statebuilding and Intervention: Policies, Practices and Paradigms,* edited by D. Chandler, 1–14. London: Routledge, 2009.

——, ed. *Statebuilding and Intervention.* London: Routledge, 2009.

Chappuis, F., and H. Hänggi. "The Interplay between Security and Legitimacy: Security Sector Reform and State-Building." In *Facets and Practices of State-Building,* edited by J. Raue and P. Sutter, 31–58. Leiden, Neth.: Martinus Nijhoff, 2009.

Charney, C., R. Nanda, and N. Yakatan. *Voter Education Planning Survey: Afghanistan 2004 National Elections.* N.p.: Asia Foundation, 2004.

Chesterman, S. *You, the People: The United Nations, Transitional Administration, and State-Building.* Oxford: Oxford University Press, 2004.

Chesterman, S., M. Ignatieff, and R.C. Thakur, eds., *Making States Work: State Failure and the Crisis of Governance.* New York: United Nations University Press, 2005.

Chopra, J. "Building State Failure in East Timor." In *State Failure, Collapse and Reconstruction,* edited by J. Milliken, 223–43. Malden, MA: Blackwell, 2003.

Cliffe, S., and N. Manning, "Practical Approaches to Building State Institutions." In *Building States to Build Peace,* edited by C. Call and V. Wyeth, 163–84. Boulder, CO: Lynne Rienner, 2008.

Cole, R.H. *Operation Urgent Fury: The Planning and Execution of Joint Operations in Grenada, 12 October–2 November 1983.* Washington, DC: Joint History Office, Office of the Chairman of the Joint Chiefs of Staff, 1997. Accessed July 10, 2012. http://www.dtic.mil/doctrine/doctrine/history/urgfury.pdf.

Coles, H. L., and A. K. Weinberg, *Civil Affairs: Soldiers Become Governors*. Washington, DC: US Army Center of Military History, 1992.

Collins, J. M. *America's Small Wars*. Washington, DC: Brassey's, 1990.

Constable, P. "For Afghans, Allies, a Clash of Values: Case against Christian Convert Puts Pressure on Karzai—and on Bush." *Washington Post*. March 23, 2006, A01.

Coolidge, President Calvin. "Message of the President." In United States Department of State, *Papers Relating to the Foreign Relations of the United States,1927*. Washington, DC: US Government Printing Office, 1927.

Cooper, H. "Man in the News: Zalmay Mamozy Khalilzad; On to a New Trouble Spot." *New York Times*. January 6, 2007.

Cordesman, A. H. "The Afghan-Pakistan War: Developments in NATO/ISAF and US Force." PowerPoint slides. Washington, DC: Center for Strategic and International Studies, 2009.

Cramer, C. "Trajectories of Accumulation through War and Peace." In *The Dilemmas of Statebuilding: Confronting the Contradictions of Postwar Peace Operations*, edited by R. Paris and T. D. Sisk, 129–48. London: Routledge, 2009.

Cramer, C., and, J. Goodhand. "Try Again, Fail Again, Fail Better?: War, the State, and the 'Post-Conflict' Challenge in Afghanistan." In *State Failure, Collapse, and Reconstruction*, edited by J. Milliken, 131–56. Malden, MA: Blackwell, 2003.

Dahl, R. A. *Polyarchy: Participation and Opposition*. New Haven: Yale University Press, 1971.

Deane, H. A. *The Political and Social Ideas of St. Augustine*. New York: Columbia University Press, 1963. Deutsch, K. W. "Social Mobilization and Political Development." *American Political Science Review* 55, no. 3 (1961): 493–514.

Diamond, L. "Promoting Democracy." *Foreign Policy* 87 (Summer 1992): 25–46.

Dobbins, J. *After the Taliban: Nation-Building in Afghanistan*. Washington, DC: Potomac Books, 2008.

——, et al. *America's Role in Nation-Building: From Germany to Iraq*. Santa Monica, CA: RAND, 2003.

——. *The Beginner's Guide to Nation Building*. Santa Monica, CA: RAND, 2007.

——. *The UN's Role in Nation-Building*. Santa Monica, CA: RAND, 2005.

Donnelly, J. "Human Rights: A New Standard of Civilization?" *International Affairs* (Royal Institute of International Affairs 1944–) 71, no. 1 (1998): 1–23.

Dower, J. W. *Embracing Defeat: Japan in the Wake of World War I*. New York: W. W. Norton, 1999.

Doyle, M. W. "Liberalism and World Politics." *American Political Science Review* 80, no. 4 (1986): 1151–69.

Doyle, M. W., I. Johnstone, and R. C. Orr, eds. *Keeping the Peace: Multidimensional UN Operations in Cambodia and El Salvador*. New York: Cambridge University Press, 1997.

Doyle, M. W., and N. Sambanis. *Making War and Building Peace: United Nations Peace Operations*. Princeton: Princeton University Press, 2006.

Durch, W. J., ed. *The Evolution of UN Peacekeeping: Case Studies and Comparative Analysis*. New York: Palgrave Macmillan, 1993.

Durch, W. J., and J. A. Schear. "Faultlines: UN Operations in the Former Yugoslavia." In *UN Peacekeeping, American Politics, and the Uncivil Wars of the 1990s*, edited by W. J. Durch, 193–274. New York: St. Martin's Press, 1996.

Edelstein, D. M. "Foreign Militaries, Sustainable Institutions, and Postwar Statebuilding." In *The Dilemmas of Statebuilding: Confronting the Contradictions of*

Postwar Peace Operations, edited by R. Paris and T. D. Sisk, 81–103. London: Routledge, 2009.

———. *Occupational Hazards: Success and Failure in Military Occupation*. Ithaca: Cornell University Press, 2008.

———. "Occupational Hazards: Why Military Occupations Succeed or Fail" *International Security* 29, no.1 (2004): 49–91.

Einsiedel, Sebastian Von. "Policy Responses to State Failure." In *Making States Work: State Failure and the Crisis of Governance*, edited by Simon Chesterman, Michael Ignatieff, and Ramesh Chandra Thakur, 13–35. New York: United Nations University, 2005.

Elshtain, J. B. "Third Annual Grotius Lecture: Just War and Humanitarian Intervention." *American University International Law Review* 17, no. 1 (2001): 1–25.

Etzioni, A. *Security First: For a Muscular, Moral Foreign Policy*. New Haven: Yale University Press, 2007.

Evans, G., and M. Sahnoun. "The Responsibility to Protect." *Foreign Affairs* 81, no. 6 (2002): 99–110.

Evans, P. B., D. Rueschemeyer, and T. Skocpol. *Bringing the State Back In*. Cambridge: Cambridge University Press, 1985.

Ewans, M. *Afghanistan: A Short History of Its People and Politics*. New York: Perennial, 2002.

Fairfield, H., K. Quealy, and A. Tse. "Troop Levels in Afghanistan since 2001." *New York Times*, October 1, 2009. Accessed January 2, 2013. http://www.nytimes.com/interactive/2009/10/01/world/middleeast/afghanistan-policy.html.

Fazal, T. M. "State Death in the International System." *International Organization* 58 no. 2 (2004): 311–44.

Fearon, J. D. "Primary Commodity Exports and Civil War." *Journal of Conflict Resolution* 49, no. 4 (2005): 483–507.

———. "Why Do Some Civil Wars Last So Much Longer Than Others?" *Journal of Peace Research* 41, no. 3 (2004): 275–301.

Fearon, J. D., and D. D. Laitin. "Neotrusteeship and the Problem of Weak States." *International Security* 28, no. 4 (2004): 5–43.

Fixdal, M., and D. Smith. "Humanitarian Intervention and Just War." *Mershon International Studies Review* 42, no. 2 (1998): 283–312.

Fleitz, F. H. *Peacekeeping Fiascoes of the 1990s: Causes, Solutions, and US Interests*. Westport, CT: Praeger, 2002.

Fortna, V. P. *Does Peacekeeping Work? Shaping Belligerents' Choices after Civil War*. Princeton: Princeton University Press, 2008.

Freedom House. *Freedom in the World*. New York: Freedom House, 2002–8. Fukuyama, F. *Nation-Building: Beyond Afghanistan and Iraq*. Baltimore: Johns Hopkins University Press, 2006.

———. *State-Building: Governance and World Order in the 21st Century*. Ithaca: Cornell University Press, 2004.

Fuller, S. M., and G. A. Cosmas. *Marines in the Dominican Republic, 1916–1924*. Washington, DC: US Marine Corps, History and Museums Division, 1974.

Gall, C. "Losses in Pakistani Haven Strain Afghan Taliban," *New York Times*. March 31, 2011.

Gates, R. "Helping Others Defend Themselves," *Foreign Affairs* 89, no. 3 (2010): 2–6.

———. R. "The Challenges Facing the Department of Defense," Congressional Testimony, January 27, 2009, 111th Congress, 1st Sess. Accessed January 2, 2013. http://www.gpo.gov/fdsys/pkg/CHRG-111shrg53123/html/CHRG-111shrg53123.htm.

Geertz, C. *The Interpretation of Cultures: Selected Essays.* New York: Basic Books, 1973.

Ghani, A., and C. Lockhart. *Fixing Failed States: A Framework for Rebuilding a Fractured World.* Oxford: Oxford University Press, 2008.

Gilman, N. *Mandarins of the Future: Modernization Theory in Cold War America.* Baltimore: Johns Hopkins University Press, 2003.

Glanz, J., and R.A. Oppel. "UN Officials Say American Offered Plan to Replace Karzai." *New York Times,* December 17, 2009, A1. http://www.nytimes.com/2009/12/17/world/asia/17galbraith.html.

Gong, G.W. *The Standard of "Civilization" in International Society.* Gloucestershire, UK: Clarendon Press, 1984.

Goodson, L.P. *Afghanistan's Endless War: State Failure, Regional Politics, and the Rise of the Taliban.* Seattle: University of Washington Press, 2001.

——. "The Lessons of Nation-Building in Afghanistan." In *Nation-Building: Beyond Afghanistan and Iraq,* edited by F. Fukuyama, 145–72. Baltimore: Johns Hopkins University Press, 2006.

Gowan, R. "UN Peace Operations: Operational Expansion and Political Fragmentation?" In *Strategies for Peace: Contributions of International Organizations, States, and Non-State Actors,* edited by V. Rittberger and M. Fischer, 109–30. Opladen, Ger.: Barbara Budrich Publishers, 2008.

Grimmett, R. F. "Instances of Use of United States Armed Forces Abroad, 1798–2010." Library of Congress, Congressional Research Service report no. R41677. March 10, 2011.

Gros, J.-G. "Towards a Taxonomy of Failed States in the New World Order: Decaying Somalia, Liberia, Rwanda, and Haiti." *Third World Quarterly* 17, no. 3 (1996): 455–71.

Harris, D. "From 'Warlord' to 'Democratic' President: How Charles Taylor Won the 1997 Liberian Elections." *Journal of Modern African Studies* 37, no. 3 (1999): 431–55.

Hegel, G. W. F. *The Philosophy of History,* edited and translated by J. Sibree. New York: Dover, 1956.

Helman, G.B., and S.R. Ratner. "Saving Failed States." *Foreign Policy* 89 (Winter 1992): 3–20.

Heupel, M. "State-Building and the Transformation of Warfare." In *Facets and Practices of State-Building,* edited by J.R. a. P. Sutter, 59–74. Leiden, Neth.: Martinus Nijhoff, 2009.

Hilderbrand, M.E., and M.S. Grindle. "Building Sustainable Capacity in the Public Sector." In *Getting Good Government: Capacity Building in the Public Sectors of Developing Countries,* edited by M.S. Grindle, 31–61. Cambridge: Harvard Institute for International Development, Harvard University Press, 1997.

Hobbes, T. *Leviathan,* edited by E. M. Curley. Indianapolis: Hackett, 1994.

Howe, H. "Lessons of Liberia: ECOMOG and Regional Peacekeeping." *International Security* 21, no. 3 (1996): 145–76.

Human Rights Watch. *Getting Away with Murder, Mutilation, Rape: New Testimony from Sierra Leone.* New York: Human Rights Watch, 1999.

——. *Liberia: Flight from Terror; Testimony of Abuses in Nimba County, 1 May 1990.* New York: Human Rights Watch, 1990.

——. *The Massacre in Mazar-i Sharif.* New York: Human Rights Watch, 1998.

——. *Massacres of Hazaras in Afghanistan.* New York: Human Rights Watch, 2001.

Huntington, S.P. *Political Order in Changing Societies.* New Haven: Yale University Press, 1968.

——. *The Third Wave: Democratization in the Late Twentieth Century.* Norman: University of Oklahoma Press, 1991.

Inglehart, R., and C. Welzel. *Modernization, Cultural Change, and Democracy: The Human Development Sequence.* Cambridge: Cambridge University Press, 2005.

International Crisis Group. *The Afghan Transitional Administration: Prospects and Perils.* Asia Briefing no. 19. Kabul/Brussels: International Crisis Group, 2002.

——. *Afghanistan: The Constitutional Loya Jirga.* Asia Briefing no. 29. Kabul/Brussels: International Crisis Group, 2003.

——. *Afghanistan Elections: Endgame or New Beginning?* Asia Report no. 101. Kabul/Brussels: International Crisis Group, 2005.

——. *Afghanistan: From Presidential to Parliamentary Elections.* Asia Report no. 88. Kabul/Brussels: International Crisis Group, 2004.

——. *Afghanistan: Judicial Reform and Transitional Justice.* Asia Briefing no. 45. Kabul/Brussels: International Crisis Group, 2003.

——. *Afghanistan's New Legislature: Making Democracy Work.* Asia Report no. 116. Kabul/Brussels: International Crisis Group, 2006.

——. *The Loya Jirga: One Small Step Forward?* Asia Briefing no. 17. Kabul/Brussels: International Crisis Group, 2002.

——. *Political Parties in Afghanistan.* Asia Briefing no. 39. Kabul/Brussels: International Crisis Group, 2005b.

——. *Reforming Afghanistan's Police* Asia Report no. 138. Kabul/Brussels: International Crisis Group, 2007.

International Monetary Fund. *Afghanistan: Selected Issues and Statistical Appendix* (No. 05/34). Washington, DC: International Monetary Fund, 2005.

——. *Islamic Republic of Afghanistan: Fifth Review under the Three-Year Arrangement under the Poverty Reduction and Growth Facility* (No. 09/135). Washington, DC: International Monetary Fund, 2009.

——. *Islamic Republic of Afghanistan: Selected Issues and Statistical Appendix* (No. 06/114). Washington, DC: International Monetary Fund, 2006.

——. *Islamic Republic of Afghanistan: Selected Issues and Statistical Appendix* (No. 08/72). Washington, DC: International Monetary Fund, 2008.

——. "World Economic Outlook Database" (April 2012). Accessed July 17, 2012. http://www.imf.org/external/ns/cs.aspx?id=28.

——. "World Economic Outlook Database" (October 2009). Accessed November 4, 2009. http://www.imf.org/external/pubs/ft/weo/2009/02/weodata/index.aspx.

Islamic Republic of Afghanistan. Central Statistics Organization. *Afghanistan Statistical Yearbook 2003.* Kabul: Central Statistics Organization, Islamic Republic of Afghanistan, 2003.

——. *National Risk Vulnerability Assessment, 2007/8.* Kabul: Central Statistics Organization, Islamic Republic of Afghanistan, 2009.

Islamic Republic of Afghanistan, Electoral Complaints Commission (ECC) *Fact Sheet.* 2009. Accessed January 2, 2013. http://www.ecc.org.af/images/stories/pdf/ECC2009GeneralFactsheet20090609Eng.pdf.

Islamic Republic of Afghanistan. Ministry of Finance. "Donor Assistance Database." Accessed December 17, 2009. http://dadafghanistan.gov.af/.

Jackson, R.H. *Quasi-States: Sovereignty, International Relations, and the Third World.* Cambridge: Cambridge University Press, 1990.

Jahn, B. "The Tragedy of Liberal Diplomacy." In *Statebuilding and Intervention: Policies, Practices and Paradigms,* edited by D. Chandler, 210–30. London: Routledge, 2009.

Jalali, A.A. "The Future of Afghanistan." *Parameters* 36, no. 1 (2006): 4.

Jarstad, A. "Dilemmas of War-to-Democracy Transitions: Theories and Concepts." In *From War to Democracy: Dilemmas of Peacebuilding,* edited by A. Jarstad and T.D. Sisk, 17–36. Cambridge: New York: Cambridge University Press, 2008.

Johnson, J. T. "Just War, as It Was and Is." *First Things* 149 (January 2005): 14–24.

Johnson, T. H., and M. C. Mason. "No Sign until the Burst of Fire: Understanding the Pakistan-Afghanistan Frontier." *International Security* 32, no.4 (2008): 41–77.

Jones, B. G. The Global Political Economy of Social Crisis: Towards a Critique of the 'Failed State' Ideology. *Review of International Political Economy* 1 no., 2 (2008): 180–205.

Jones, S. G. *In the Graveyard Of Empires: America's War in Afghanistan.* New York: W. W. Norton, 2009.

——. "The Rise of Afghanistan's Insurgency: State Failure and Jihad." *International Security* 32, no.4 (2008): 7–40.

Kant, I. *Political Writings*, edited by H. S. Reiss. Cambridge: Cambridge University Press, 1991.

Kaufman, D., Kraay A., and Mastruzzi M. "Governance Matters VIII: Aggregate and Individual Governance Indicators, 1996–2008." World Bank Policy Research Working Paper no. 4978, June 29, 2009. http://ssrn.com/paper=1424591.

——. Worldwide Governance Indicators. World Bank. Accessed July 17, 2012. http://info.worldbank.org/governance/wgi/index.asp.

Kelly, J. H. "Lebanon: 1982-1984," In *US and Russian Policymaking with Respect to the Use of Force*, edited by J. Azrael, J. and E. Payin. Santa Monica, CA: RAND, 1996.

Keohane, R. O. *After Hegemony: Cooperation and Discord in the World Political Economy.* Princeton: Princeton University Press, 2005.

Knight, A. M., et al. "Proclamation by the Commanders of Allied and Associated Forces at Vladivostok," July 6, 1918. In United States Department of State, *Papers relating to the Foreign Relations of the United States (1918).* Vol. 2, *Russia.* Washington, DC: US Government Printing Office, 1918.

Krasner, S. D. "Sharing Sovereignty: New Institutions for Collapsed and Failing States." *International Security* 29, no. 2 (2004): 85–120.

Lake, D. A. "The Practice and Theory of US Statebuilding." *Journal of Intervention and Statebuilding* 4, no. 3 (September 2010): 257–84.

Lange M., Mahoney J., and Hau, M. v. "Colonialism and Development: A Comparative Analysis of Spanish and British Colonies." *American Journal of Sociology* 111, no. 5 (2006): 1412–62.

Langley, L. D. *The Banana Wars: United States Intervention in the Caribbean, 1898–1934.* Chicago: Dorsey Press, 1988.

Lenz, L. *Power and Policy: America's First Steps to Superpower, 1889–1922.* New York: Algora, 2008.

Leonardo, E. "Analysis of USAID'S Capacity Development Program (CDP)." Report by the Checchi and Company Consulting and the Louis Berger Group for USAID. 2008. Accessed January 3, 2013. http://pdf.usaid.gov/pdf_docs/PDACM814.pdf.

Lerner, D. *The Passing of Traditional Society: Modernizing the Middle East.* Glencoe, IL: Free Press, 1958.

Lijphart, A. *Democracy in Plural Societies: A Comparative Exploration.* New Haven: Yale University Press, 1977.

Linz, J. J., and A. C. Stepan. *Problems of Democratic Transition and Consolidation: Southern Europe, South America, and Post-Communist Europe.* Baltimore: Johns Hopkins University Press, 1996.

Lipset, S. M. *Political Man: The Social Bases of Politics.* Garden City, NY: Doubleday, 1960.

——. "Some Social Requisites of Democracy: Economic Development and Political Legitimacy." *American Political Science Review* 53, no.1 (1959): 69–105.

Lister, S. *Moving Forward? Assessing Public Administration Reform in Afghanistan.* Kabul: Afghan Research and Evaluation Unit, 2006.

[241]

Livingston, I.S., H.L. Messera, and M. O'Hanlon. *Afghanistan Index: Tracking Variables of Reconstruction and Security in Post-9/11 Afghanistan*. Washington, DC: Brookings Institution, 2009.

Locke, J. *Second Treatise on Government*, edited by C. B. Macpherson. Indianapolis: Hackett, 1980.

Lowenkopf, M. "Liberia: Putting the State Back Together." In *Collapsed States: The Disintegration and Restoration of Legitimate Authority*, edited by I.W. Zartman, 91–108. Boulder, CO: Lynne Rienner, 1995.

Lujala, P., N.P. Gleditsch, and E. Gilmore. "A Diamond Curse? Civil War and a Lootable Resource." *Journal of Conflict Resolution* 49, no. 4 (2005): 538.

Maddison, A. "Historical Statistics for the World Economy, 1–2006 AD." Groningen, Neth.: Groningen Growth and Development Center, University of Groningen, 2009. Accessed November 5, 2009. http://www.ggdc.net/maddison/Historical_Statistics/horizontal-file_03–2009.xls.

Mansfield, E.D., and J.L. Snyder. *Electing to Fight: Why Emerging Democracies Go to War*. Cambridge: MIT Press, 2005.

March, J.G., and J.P. Olsen. "The New Institutionalism: Organizational Factors in Political Life." *American Political Science Review* 78, no. 3 (1984): 734–49.

Marshall, M.G. "Polity IV Project: Political Regime Characteristics and Transitions, 1800–2010." Center for Systemic Peace. Accessed July 17, 2012. http://www.systemicpeace.org/polity/polity4.htm.

Marshall, M.G., T.R. Gurr, and B. Harff. "Political Instability Task Force State Failure Problem Set: Internal Wars and Failures of Governance, 1955–2008." Fairfax, VA: Center for Global Policy, George Mason University 2009. http://globalpolicy.gmu.edu/pitf/pitfpset.htm.

Marten, K. *Enforcing the Peace: Learning from the Imperial Past*. New York: Columbia University Press, 2004.

——. "Statebuilding and Force: The Proper Role of Foreign Militaries." In *Statebuilding and Intervention: Policies, Practices and Paradigms*, edited by D. Chandler, 122–39. London: Routledge, 2009.

McKinley, President William. "Message to the Congress." In United States Department of State, *Papers relating to the Foreign Relations of the United States, with the Annual Message of the President Transmitted to Congress December 5, 1898*. Washington, DC: US Government Printing Office, 1899.

McMahon, P. C., and J. Western. "Introduction: The Supply Side of Statebuilding," In *The International Community and Statebuilding*, edited by Patrice C. McMahon and Jon Western,1–24. New York: Routledge, 2012.

Mearsheimer, J.J. "Hans Morgenthau and the Iraq War: Realism versus Neoconservatism." Open Security. May 19, 2005. http://www.opendemocracy.net/democracy-americanpower/morgenthau_2522.jsp.

Meierhenrich, J. "Forming States after Failure." In *When States Fail: Causes and Consequences*, edited by R.I. Rotberg, 153–69. Princeton: Princeton University Press, 2004.

Mesquita, B.B. d., J.D. Morrow, R.M. Siverson, and A. Smith, "An Institutional Explanation of the Democratic Peace." *American Political Science Review* 93, no. 4 (1999): 791–807.

Miller, L., and R. Perito. *Establishing the Rule of Law in Afghanistan*. Special report no. 117. Washington, DC: US Institute of Peace, 2004.

Milliken, J., and K. Krause. "State Failure, State Collapse, and State Reconstruction: Concepts, Lessons, and Strategies." In *State Failure, Collapse, and Reconstruction*, edited by J. Milliken, 1–2. Malden, MA: Blackwell, 2003.

Mitchell, B. R. *International Historical Statistics: 1750–2005*. 3 vols. New York: Palgrave Macmillan, 2007.

Morgenthau, H. J., K. W. Thompson, and W. D. Clinton. *Politics among Nations: The Struggle for Power and Peace*, 7th ed. Boston: McGraw-Hill, 2006.

Morton, A. D. "The 'Failed State' of International Relations." *New Political Economy* 10, no. 3 (2005): 371–79.

Muehlmann, T. "Police Restructuring in Bosnia-Herzegovina: Problems of Internationally Led Security Sector Reform." In *Statebuilding and Intervention: Policies, Practices and Paradigms*, edited by D. Chandler, 140–62. London: Routledge, 2009.

Musicant, I. *The Banana Wars: A History of United States Military Intervention in Latin America from the Spanish-American War to the Invasion of Grenada*. New York: Macmillan, 1990.

National Democratic Institute. *NDI Final Report on Sierra Leone's 2007 Elections*. Washington, DC: National Democratic Institute, 2007.

NATO. *Afghanistan Report 2009*. Brussels: NATO, 2009. Accessed January 3, 2013. http://www.isaf.nato.int/pdf/20090331_090331_afghanistan_report_2009.pdf.

——. "ISAF's Strategic Vision: Declaration by the Heads of State and Government of the Nations Contributing to the UN-mandated NATO-led International Security Assistance Force (ISAF) in Afghanistan." Bucharest NATO Summit: NATO, April 4, 2008.

——. *ISAF Troops in Numbers (Placemat)*. Brussels: NATO, 2007–9. The index of archived placemats showing ISAF troop numbers at different moments is not available, but individual placemats can be found, for example, at http://www.nato.int/isaf/docu/epub/pdf/placemat_archive/isaf_placemat_070129.pdf (January 29, 2007), http://www.nato.int/isaf/docu/epub/pdf/placemat_archive/isaf_placemat_071205.pdf (December 6, 2007), and http://www.nato.int/isaf/docu/epub/pdf/placemat_archive/isaf_placemat_081201.pdf (December 1, 2008).

Nelson, D. J., *A History of US Military Forces in Germany*. Boulder, CO: Westview 1987.

Nordlinger, E. A. *On the Autonomy of the Democratic State*. Cambridge: Harvard University Press, 1981. Nussbaum, M. C. "Human Functioning and Social Justice: In Defense of Aristotelian Essentialism," *Political Theory* 20, no. 2, (1992): 202–46.

Nye, J. *Soft Power: The Means to Success in World Politics*. New York: Public Affairs, 2004.

O'Donnell, G. A. *Modernization and Bureaucratic-Authoritarianism: Studies in South American Politics*. Berkeley, CA: Institute of International Studies, 1973.

Olonisakin, F. *Peacekeeping in Sierra Leone: The Story of UNAMSIL*. Boulder, CO: Lynne Rienner, 2008.

Olson, M. "Rapid Growth as a Destabilizing Force." *Journal of Economic History* 23, no. 4 (1963): 529–52.

Ottaway, M., and A. Lieven, "Rebuilding Afghanistan: Fantasy versus Reality." Carnegie Endowment for International Peace Policy Brief 12, (January 2002). Accessed January 3, 2013. http://www.carnegieendowment.org/files/Policybrief12.pdf.

Owen, J. M. *The Clash of Ideas in World Politics*. Princeton: Princeton University Press, 2010.

——. "The Foreign Imposition of Domestic Institutions." *International Organization* 56, no. 2 (2002): 375–409.

——. *Liberal Peace, Liberal War: American Politics and International Security*. Ithaca: Cornell University Press, 1997.

Oye, K. A. *Cooperation under Anarchy*. Princeton: Princeton University Press, 1986.

Packenham, R. A. *Liberal America and the Third World: Political Development Ideas in Foreign Aid and Social Science*. Princeton: Princeton University Press, 1973.

Paris, R. *At War's End: Building Peace after Civil Conflict*. Cambridge: Cambridge University Press, 2004.

——. "Does Liberal Peacebuilding Have a Future?" In *New Perspectives on Liberal Peacebuilding*, edited by E. Newman, R. Paris, and O. P. Richmond, 97–111. New York: United Nations University Press, 2009.

——. "International Peacebuilding and the 'Mission Civilisatrice.'" *Review of International Studies* 28, no.4 (2002): 637–56.

Paris, R., and Sisk, T. D. "Introduction: Understanding the Contradictions of Postwar Statebuilding." In *The Dilemmas of Statebuilding: Confronting the Contradictions of Postwar Peace Operation*, edited by R. Paris and T. D. Sisk, 1–20. London: Routledge, 2009.

Pei, M., S. Amin, and S. Garz. "Building Nations: The American Experience." In *Nation-Building: Beyond Afghanistan and Iraq*, edited by F. Fukuyama, 64–85. Baltimore: Johns Hopkins University Press, 2006.

Perito, R. M. *Afghanistan's Police*. Special Report no. 227. Washington, DC: US Institute of Peace, 2009.

Phillips, R. C. *Operation Just Cause: The Incursion into Panama*, US Army Center of Military History, pub no. 70–85–1. Ft. McNair. Accessed January 3, 2013. http://www.history.army.mil/brochures/Just%20Cause/JustCause.pdf.

Przeworski, A. *Democracy and the Market: Political and Economic Reforms in Eastern Europe and Latin America*. Cambridge: Cambridge University Press, 1991.

——. "Some Problems in the Study of the Transition to Democracy." In *Transitions from Authoritarian Rule: Comparative Perspectives*, edited by G. A. O'Donnell, P. C. Schmitter, and L. Whitehead, 47–63. Baltimore: Johns Hopkins University Press, 1986.

Przeworski, A., M. Alvarez, J. A. Cheibub, and F. Limongi. *Democracy and Development: Political Institutions and Well-Being in the World, 1950–1990*. Cambridge: Cambridge University Press, 2000.

Putnam, R. D., R. Leonardi, and R. Nanetti. *Making Democracy Work: Civic Traditions in Modern Italy*. Princeton: Princeton University Press, 1993.

Rashid, A. *Descent into Chaos: The United States and the Failure of Nation Building in Pakistan, Afghanistan, and Central Asia*. New York: Viking, 2008.

——. *Taliban: Militant Islam, Oil, and Fundamentalism in Central Asia*. New Haven: Yale University Press, 2001.

Rawls, J. *Political Liberalism*. New York: Columbia University Press, 1993.

——. *A Theory of Justice*. Cambridge: Harvard University Press, 1971.Roberts, D. W. "Hybrid Polities and Indigenous Pluralities: Advanced Lessons in Statebuilding from Cambodia." *Journal of Intervention and Statebuilding* 2, no. 1 (2008): 63–86.

Roeder, P. G. "Power Dividing as an Alternative to Ethnic Power Sharing." In *Sustainable Peace: Power and Democracy after Civil Wars*, edited by P. G. Roeder and D. S. Rothchild, 51–82. Ithaca: Cornell University Press, 2005.

Roeder, P. G., and D. S. Rothchild. "Dilemmas of State-Building in Divided Societies." In *Sustainable Peace: Power and Democracy after Civil Wars*, edited by P. G. Roeder and D. S. Rothchild, 1–26. Ithaca: Cornell University Press, 2005.

Roosevelt, President Theodore. "Message of the President." In United States Department of State, *Papers Relating to the Foreign Relations of the United States, with the Annual Message of the President Transmitted to Congress December 7, 1903*. Washington, DC: US Government Printing Office, 1903.

Ross, M. "The Natural Resource Curse: How Wealth Can Make You Poor." In *Natural Resources and Violent Conflict: Options and Actions*, edited by I. Bannon and P. Collier, 17–42. Washington, DC: World Bank, 2003.

[244]

——. "The Political Economy of the Resource Curse." *World Politics* 51, no. 2 (1999): 297–322.

Rostow, W. W. "The Stages of Economic Growth." *Economic History Review* 12, no. 1 (1959): 1–16.

Rotberg, R. I. "The Failure and Collapse of Nation-States: Breakdown, Prevention, and Repair." In *When States Fail: Causes and Consequences*, edited by R. I. Rotberg, 1–50. Princeton: Princeton University Press, 2004.

Rubin, B. R. "The Fragmentation of Afghanistan." *Foreign Affairs* 68, no. 5 (1989): 150–68.

——. "The Politics of Security in Postconflict Statebuilding." In *Building States to Build Peace*, edited by C. Call and V. Wyeth, 25–47. Boulder, CO: Lynne Rienner, 2008.

——. "Saving Afghanistan." *Foreign Affairs* 86, no. 1 (2007): 57–78.

——. "The Transformation of the Afghan State." In *The Future of Afghanistan*, edited by J. A. Their, 13–22. Washington, DC: US Institute of Peace, 2009.

Rueschemeyer, D., E. Huber, and J. D. Stephens. *Capitalist Development and Democracy*. Chicago: University of Chicago Press, 1992.

Ruggie, J. G. *Constructing the World Polity: Essays on International Institutionalization*. London: Routledge, 1998.

Rustow, D. A. "Transitions to Democracy: Toward a Dynamic Model." *Comparative Politics* 2, no. 3 (1970): 337–63.

Said, E. W. *Orientalism*. New York: Vintage, 1979.

Saikal, A. "Afghanistan's Weak State and Strong Society." In *Making States Work: State Failure and the Crisis of Governance*, edited by S. Chesterman, M. Ignatieff, and R. C. Thakur, 193–210. Tokyo: United Nations University Press, 2005.

Sandel, M. J. *Democracy's Discontent: America in Search of a Public Philosophy*. Cambridge: Belknap Press of Harvard University Press, 1996.

——. *Liberalism and the Limits of Justice*. Cambridge: Cambridge University Press, 1982.

Sarkees, M. R., and F. Wayman. *Resort to War: 1816—2007*. Washington, DC: CQ Press, 2010.

Schneckener, U. "Addressing Fragile Statehood: Dilemmas and Strategies of International Statebuilding." In *Strategies for Peace: Contributions of International Organizations, States and Non-state Actors*, edited by M. Fischer and V. Rittberger, 193–220. Opladen, Ger.: Barbara Budrich Publisher, 2008.

——. "International Statebuilding: Dilemmas, Strategies and Challenges for German Foreign Policy." SWP Research Paper 9. Berlin: Stiftung Wissenschaft und Politik German Institute for International and Security Affairs, October 2007. Accessed January 3, 2013. http://www.swp-berlin.org/fileadmin/contents/products/research_papers/2007RP09_skr_ks.pdf.

Schroeder, P. "Historical Reality vs. Neo-realist Theory." *International Security* 19, no. 1 (1994): 108–48.

Schultz, K. A. *Democracy and Coercive Diplomacy*. Cambridge: Cambridge University Press, 2001.

Schweller, R. L. "Bandwagoning for Profit: Bringing the Revisionist State Back In." *International Security* 19, no. 1 (1994): 72–107.

Shah, S. M. *Afghanistan National Development Strategy (ANDS) Formulation Process: Influencing Factors and Challenges*. Kabul: Afghan Research and Evaluation Unit, 2009.Skocpol, T. "Bringing the State Back In: A Report on Current Comparative Research on the Relationship between States and Social Structures." *Items* 36, no. 1/2 (1982): 1–8.

Special Inspector General for Afghanistan Reconstruction. *Quarterly Reports to the United States Congress*, 2008–11. Washington, DC. http://www.sigar.mil/quarterlyreports/.

[245]

Starr, S. F. "Sovereignty and Legitimacy in Afghan Nation-Building." In *Nation-Building: Beyond Afghanistan and Iraq*, edited by F. Fukuyama, 107–24. Baltimore: Johns Hopkins University Press, 2006.

Stewart, P. "Weak States and Global Threats: Assessing Evidence of 'Spillovers.'" Working Paper 73. Washington, DC: Center for Global Development, 2006.

Stimson, Henry. "The Personal Representative of the President of the United States in Nicaragua (Stimson) to General Moncada, May 11, 1927." In United States Department of State, *Papers Relating to the Foreign Relations of the United States, 1927.* Washington, DC: US Government Printing Office, 1927.

Stockman, F. "Afghanistan Wary of US Plan to Send More Advisers." *Boston Globe*, November 12, 2009. http://www.boston.com/news/world/asia/articles/2009/11/12/afghanistan_wary_of_us_plan_to_send_more_advisers/.

Suhrke, A. "The Dangers of a Tight Embrace: Externally Assisted Statebuilding in Afghanistan." In *The Dilemmas of Statebuilding*, edited by R. Paris and T. D. Sisk, 227–51. London: Routledge, 2009.

——. "Reconstruction as Modernisation: The 'Post-Conflict' Project in Afghanistan." *Third World Quarterly* 28 no. 7 (2007): 1291–1308.

Sundberg, R. "Collective Violence 2002–2007: Global and Regional Trends." In *States in Armed Conflict 2007*, edited by L. Harbom and R. Sundberg. Uppsala, Swed.: Universitetstryckeriet, 2008. Cited in http://www.pcr.uu.se/research/ucdp/datasets/ucdp_battle-related_deaths_dataset. This is the citation for the Uppsala Conflict Data Program.

Taft, President William. "Message of the President," In United States Department of State, *Papers Relating to the Foreign Relations of the United States, with the Annual Message of the President Transmitted to Congress December 3, 1912.* Washington, DC: US Government Printing Office, 1912.

Tilly, C. *Coercion, Capital, and European States, AD 990–1990.* Hoboken, NJ: Wiley-Blackwell, 1992.

——. "War Making and State Making as Organized Crime." In *Bringing the State Back In*, edited by P. Evans, D. Rueschemeyer, and T. Skocpol, 169–91. Cambridge: Cambridge University Press, 1985.

Tilly, C., G. Ardant, and D. H. Bayley. *The Formation of National States in Western Europe.* Princeton: Princeton University Press Princeton, 1975.

Toft, M. *Securing the Peace: The Durable Settlement of Civil Wars.* Princeton: Princeton University Press, 2009.

Transparency International. *Corruption Perceptions Index.* Berlin: Transparency International, 2005–9.

Trujillo, C. M. *Audit of USAID/Afghanistan's Capacity Development Program.* No. 5-306-08-012-P. Manila: USAID Office of Inspector General, 2008.

Tucker, R. C., ed. *The Marx-Engels Reader.* 2nd ed. New York: W. W. Norton, 1972.

Tyson, A. S. "A Sober Assessment of Afghanistan." *Washington Post*, June 15, 2008, A16. http://www.washingtonpost.com/wp-dyn/content/story/2008/06/15/ST2008061500237.html?sid=ST2008061500237.

United Nations. "Agreement on Provisional Arrangements in Afghanistan Pending the Re-Establishment of Permanent Government Institutions." Bonn: United Nations, 2001.

——. General Assembly Resolution 55/2 "Millennium Declaration." September 8, 2009. http://www.un.org/millennium/declaration/ares552e.htm

——. Liberia—UNMIL: Facts and Figures. Accessed October 28, 2009. http://www.un.org/Depts/dpko/missions/unmil/facts.html.

——. Liberia—UNOMIL: Facts and Figures. Accessed October 28, 2009. http://www.un.org/Depts/dpko/dpko/co_mission/unomilF.html.

——. "UNAMID Background."Accessed July 25, 2012. http://www.un.org/en/peacekeeping/missions/unamid/background.shtml.

——. UNAMID: Facts and Figures. Accessed July 25, 2012. http://www.un.org/en/peacekeeping/missions/unamid/facts.shtml.

——.UNMIS: Facts and Figures. Accessed July 25, 2012. http://www.un.org/en/peacekeeping/missions/unmis/facts.shtml.

——. "United Nations Peacekeeping Operations: Principles and Guidelines" 2008. 18. http://www.peacekeepingbestpractices.unlb.org/PBPS/Library/Capstone_Doctrine_ENG.pdf.

United Nations Development Program. *Afghanistan: National Human Development Report 2004; Security with a Human Face: Challenges and Responsibilities*. Kabul/New York: UNDP, 2004.

——. "Afghanistan's New Beginnings Program." Accessed December 26, 2008. http://www.undpanbp.org/.

United Nations High Commissioner for Refugees. *Statistical Yearbook 2001*. New York: UNHCR, 2002.

——. *Statistical Yearbook 2002*. New York: UNHCR, 2003.

United Nations Office on Drugs and Crime. *Afghanistan Opium Surveys*, 2002–11. http://www.unodc.org/unodc/en/crop-monitoring/index.html?tag=Afghanistan.

United States Department of the Army. *Field Manual 3–0: Operations*. Washington, DC: Headquarters, Department of the Army, 2001.

United States Department of the Army and United States Marine Corps. *The US Army/Marine Corps Counterinsurgency Field Manual: US Army Field Manual No. 3–24: Marine Corps Warfighting Publication No. 3–33.5*.Chicago: University of Chicago Press, 2007.

United States Department of Defense. *Joint Publication 1–02: Dictionary of Military and Associated Terms*. Washington, DC: Department of Defense, 2009.

——. *Report on Progress toward Security and Stability in Afghanistan*. Washington, DC: Department of Defense, 2008–11. http://www.defense.gov/pubs/pdfs/October_2011_Section_1230_Report.pdf.

United States Department of State. Foreign Relations of the United States (FRUS). *Conference at Malta and Yalta*. Washington, DC: Government Printing Office, 1945.

United States Government Accountability Office, *Afghanistan's Security Environment*. No. GAO-10–178R. Washington, DC: US Government Accountability Office, 2009.

Uppsala University. Uppsala Conflict Data Program. *UCDP Battle-Related Deaths Dataset v. 5–2011*. www.ucdp.uu.se.

USAID. "Providing More Afghan Ownership in Aid: $30m Agreement between US and Afghanistan Gives Afghan Government Control for Hiring Advisors." Press Release. October 18, 2009. http://afghanistan.usaid.gov/en/Article.850.aspx.

——. *US Overseas Loans and Grants: Obligations and Loan Authorizations, July 1, 1945–September 30, 2010*. Accessed January 3, 2013. http://gbk.eads.usaidallnet.gov/.

Vaishnav, M. "Afghanistan: The Chimera of the 'Light Footprint.'" Significant Issues Series. *Center for Strategic and International Studies* 26 (2004):244–62.

Von Lipsey, Roderick K. *Breaking the Cycle: A Framework for Conflict Intervention*. New York: St. Martin's Press, 1997.

Walt, S. M. *The Origins of Alliances*. Ithaca: Cornell University Press, 1987.

Waltz, K. N. *Theory of International Politics*. Reading, MA: Addison-Wesley, 1979.

Weinbaum, M. G. "Rebuilding Afghanistan: Impediments, Lessons, and Prospects." In *Nation-Building: Beyond Afghanistan and Iraq*, edited by F. Fukuyama, 125–44. Baltimore: Johns Hopkins University Press, 2006.

Wendt, A. "The Agent-Structure Problem in International Relations Theory." *International Organization* 41, no. 3 (1987): 335–70.

——. "Anarchy Is What States Make of It: The Social Construction of Power Politics." *International Organization* 46 no. 2 (1992): 391–425.

——. *Social Theory of International Politics*. Cambridge: Cambridge University Press, 1999.

White House. *National Security Strategy: May 2010*. Accessed July 12, 2012. http://www.whitehouse.gov/sites/default/files/rss_viewer/national_security_strategy.pdf.

——. "President Holds a Prime Time News Conference." October 11, 2001. Accessed July 18, 2012. http://georgewbush-whitehouse.archives.gov/news/releases/2001/10/20011011-7.html.

Witte, G. "US Cedes Duties in Rebuilding Afghanistan." *Washington Post*, January 3, 2006. http://www.washingtonpost.com/wp-dyn/content/article/2006/01/02/AR2006010201942.html.

Wolfe, R. *Americans as Proconsuls: United States Military Government in Germany and Japan, 1944–1952*. Carbondale: Southern Illinois University Press, 1984.

Wood, L. J., and T. R. Reese. *Military Interventions in Sierra Leone: Lessons from a Failed State*. Fort Leavenworth, KS: Combat Studies Institute Press, US Army Combined Arms Center, 2008.

World Bank. *Doing Business*. Washington, DC: World Bank, 2005–10.

——. "In Liberia, World Bank Support for Governance Helps a Nation Rebuild." *Journal*. Accessed February 18, 2010. http://web.worldbank.org/WBSITE/EXTERNAL/COUNTRIES/AFRICAEXT/LIBERIAEXTN/0,,contentMDK:22472709~pagePK:141137~piPK:141127~theSitePK:356194,00.html.

——. *Sierra Leone: Institutional Reform and Capacity Building Project*. Washington, DC: World Bank, 2011. http://documents.worldbank.org/curated/en/2011/10/15564379/sierra-leone-institutional-reform-capacity-building-project.

——. "World Development Indicators Database." Accessed July 18, 2012. www.worldbank.org/data.

World Health Organization. "WHO Statistical Information System." Accessed December 21, 2009. http://apps.who.int/whosis/data/Search.jsp.

Zartman, I. W., ed. *Collapsed States: The Disintegration and Restoration of Legitimate Authority*. Boulder, CO: Lynne Rienner, 1995.

——. "Introduction: Posing the Problem of State Collapse." In *Collapsed States: The Disintegration and Restoration of Legitimate Authority*, edited by I. W. Zartman. Boulder, CO: Lynne Rienner, 1995.

Ziemke, E. "Improvising in Postwar Germany." In *Americans as Proconsuls: United States Military Government in Germany and Japan, 1944–1952*, edited by R. Wolfe, 52–66. Carbondale: Southern Illinois University Press, 1984.

——. *The US Army in the Occupation of Germany, 1944–1946*. Washington, DC: US Army Center of Military History, 1990.

Zink, H. *The United States in Germany, 1944–1955*. Princeton, NJ: Van Nostrand, 1957.

Index

Note: Italic page numbers refer to tables.

Administrator strategy: and anarchic state failure, 85–89, 105, 161; and barbaric state failure, 114–16, 161; and degree of invasiveness, 78–80, *81*, 83, 176; description of, 10; and illegitimate state failure, 100–102, 161, 172; and incapable state failure, 104–9, 112, 161

Afghanistan: and Administrator strategy, 87–88, 112, 115, 161, 172; and anarchic state failure, 157–58, 161–62, 164; background on, 155–57; and barbaric state failure, 158, 160–61; and capacity, 108, 163–65, 163n66, 168–70, 172, 174; and case selection, 206; and incapable state failure, 158–59, 161–65, 163n66; and legitimacy, 33–34, 97, 158, 161, 166–68, 172; and multilateralism, 184; Pakistan as external influence in, 81n21; and prosperity, 170–72; and public goods, 62–63; results, 171–72, 174; and revisionist power groups, 69; and security, 162–66, 163n66, 172, 182, 187; and shallow success, 148n37, 172, 174; socioeconomic development indices, *173*; and state-building strategies, 20, 28, 118, 157, 161–71, 186–87; and state failure, 56, 58–59, 61, 64, 157–61, 171–72; and Trainer strategy, 85, 111, 161, 165, 172; and unproductive state failure, 159–61; and US armed state building, 2, 13–14, 123, 165–66, 176, 184

anarchic state failure: and Administrator strategy, 85–89, 105, 161; and

Afghanistan, 157–58, 161–62, 164; and capacity, 87, 164–65; and interstate war, 59–60, 59n18, 86; and legitimacy, 33, 85, 87; and Liberia, 145–48, 148n37, 151; and ongoing civil war, 59, 83, 85–86; and post–civil war, 59, 83–84; and recurring armed conflict, 60–61; and Sierra Leone, 136–37; and state-building strategies, 58–61, 77, *77*, 83–89, *88*; and Sudan, 190; as type of state failure, 9, 19, 57, 176

Angola: and Administrator strategy, 86–88; and capacity, 108–9; and legitimacy, 167; and security, 162, 181–82, 187; and sequencing, 32; and state-building strategies, 131, 139, 187; and state failure, 2, 59, 61, 64, 109, 148n37; and Trainer strategy, 111

Aristotle, 47–48, 50

armed state building: constructivist state building, 75–76, *77*; definitions of, 3–9, 175, 205, 227; and dynamics of state failure, 67–69; first hypothesis, 76–77; goals of, 71, 76, 80–82; history of, 11–14; imperialism distinguished from, 4–7, *7*, 12, 175, 177, 179, 194–96, 205, 226; institutionalist state building, 73, 76, *77*; and institution building, 3–5, 9–10; "just intervention" framework, 194; and "just war" theory, 194, 199–204; liberal state building, 73–74, 76, *77*; and local actors' dispositions, 18–19, 67–69; as military operation, 4, 7, 8–9; and